THE WORLD'S GREATEST GAMBLING SCAMS

RICHARD MARCUS

under cover publishing

First published in 2007 by Undercover Publishing

British Library Cataloguing-in-Publication Data
A catalogue record for this book is available from the British Library.

ISBN 978-0-955169-71-7

All sales enquiries should be directed to:
Undercover Publishing, PO Box 18, Hassocks,
West Sussex BN6 9WR, UK
Tel: +44 (0)1273 834680, Fax: +44 (0)1273 831629,

www.richardmarcusbooks.com
www.undercover-books.co.uk

Cover design by Horatio Monteverde.
Production by Navigator Guides.
Printed and bound in the US by Versa Press.

THE WORLD'S GREATEST GAMBLING SCAMS

Contents

For Rich Cooper, whose struggles I know first hand.

Some of the names in this book have been changed

Also by Richard Marcus:

American Roulette

Great Casino Heist

Dirty Poker

Identity Theft, Inc.

Foreword

Recently there have been several TV series based on the world's greatest gambling scams. This book takes a closer look at the ten gambling scams that I consider the best of the best. I have included some that have never aired on television, those whose colorful characters were not available to participate in filming. I felt that their stories were terrific and had to be told.

Prologue

Back in the early 1980s, on the south end of the Las Vegas Strip, where today's mega-luxurious Bellagio displays its dancing waterfalls on the surface of its manmade Lake Como, sat another Vegas centerpiece casino that occupied the southwest corner of what was then known as the "Four Corners" of Las Vegas, the prime intersection of the World's Gaming Capital that included Caesars Palace, the Barbary Coast and the original MGM Grand.

The fourth hotel on that corner was the Dunes, a longtime mainstay of the Strip's history until it got imploded in 1993 to make way for Steve Wynn's Bellagio. The Dunes had been a favorite of mine during my long casino-cheating career. For two decades I regularly peppered its gaming tables with an assortment of cheating moves. I also had my share of run-ins with their security and surveillance people, and it was there that I suffered the only indignity of my entire casino life.

Early on in my adventures, not yet the seasoned casino grifter that would make me one of the world's greatest gambling scammers, I screwed up both a pastposting move and my escape when they came running after me. I found myself handcuffed to a chair in the Dunes' security chief's office. His name was Gerald Small, and despite that he was built like a brick shithouse. After reading me the riot act, which basically was a lifetime barring from the premises, Small decided to make it as difficult as possible for me to venture back inside the Dunes without someone spotting me. He paraded me through the entire casino, up and down each pit, and presented me to all the pit bosses, announcing without the slightest discretion, "See this guy here! He's Richard Marcus, a goddamn casino cheater. If you ever see him in here again, call my office and I'll have him arrested for trespassing."

He didn't even give me the satisfaction of saying "he's a goddamn good casino cheater." But in spite of that, you can believe that I entered the Dunes and got off moves at least a hundred times after that. So you can see that I was sorry when the place caved in to six hundred pounds of dynamite.

But to me and hundreds of other casino scammers over the years, the Dunes was not the biggest loss to the construction of the Bellagio. Also knocked down to make room for the new megaresort was a Denny's restaurant, one of more than a hundred in Las Vegas belonging to the popular chain. But this particular Denny's, located a hundred yards from the Dunes' south entrance, was special. That's because many of the world's greatest gambling scams were conceived there. The Dunes Denny's, as it was referred to by those who habitually frequented it, had been a favorite gathering place for casino grifters since at least the first time I walked inside it in 1976. In its booths and across its tables, people who made their illicit living off casinos, or died or got incarcerated trying, spent many a breakfast, lunch, dinner, and late-night snack tossing around ideas how they were going to cheat, scam, steal, and hustle their way to riches in casinos from Las Vegas to London and then some. Like cops had their hangouts, so did crooks, if you really want to consider casino scammers as crooks.

The cops hung out there, too, especially the boys from the Enforcement Division of the Nevada Gaming Control Board and the private dicks from Griffin Investigations, who were hired by casinos to weed out cheaters and scammers and turn them over to casino security. Many of Denny's scamming faithful suspected that gaming agents routinely bugged the booths, hoping to garner intelligence about what scams were going down and when.

On April 12, 1983, I was sitting alone in one of those revered Denny's booths. On the table was a plate soaked in powdered sugar and globs of maple syrup. The four thick slices of golden brown French toast that had been under all that was now just a sweet memory, though my third cup of fresh-brewed coffee still steamed in the direction of my nostrils.

It was three o'clock in the afternoon on a rare cloudy day. There were just a handful of diners there and, to my recollection, none of them were scammers. At least I didn't recognize anyone. Besides, mid-afternoon was not prime grifter time at Denny's. In all, it was a very peaceful way to enjoy a late lunch while gazing out on the Strip.

By three-thirty and my fourth cup of coffee, the scene had gone from one of pure tranquility to one of the most hilarious Las Vegas had ever seen. It started with a short, pudgy guy running full-speed across the front parking lot of the restaurant. He looked to be in his twenties, had wavy brown hair and wore a suit with sneakers, a combination that even in Vegas should automatically breed suspicion. Without breaking stride, the guy's right arm drew back over his head and then came forward in a heaving motion toward the restaurant, as if he were throwing something onto the roof. Then in the next flash he was gone.

In the flash after that, a herd of blue-uniformed security men from the Dunes came tearing after him. Through the glass of the bay window above my booth I could hear a cacophony of shouts, the words not decipherable but their collective meaning would be a synonym for the word "stop." Whatever this chubby guy had done surely pissed off somebody over at the Dunes. Judging by the intensity of the chase, my guess was that the guards would catch him or shots would be fired.

I took a sip of coffee and waited anxiously for the denouement.

A minute later it came. From the other direction, the guy in the jeans marched back toward the Dunes. Two burly security hulks had him fastened from either side, their thick arms corralling his shoulders. Behind them and off to the sides were the rest of the blue platoon. When they passed directly in front of my window, something strange took place. The guy being dragged to the periphery of my viewpoint craned his head toward my booth and seemed to see me through the glass. He even shrugged and half-smiled, as if to say, "Well, I gave it my best shot. Better luck next time."

I smiled back at the guy, wondering if he could really see me, and then watched him as he disappeared with the security contingent heading back to the Dunes. I got back to finishing my fourth cup of coffee, with no intention of ordering a fifth – until what happened next.

The Dunes blue-clad security men were back. At least two dozen of them. They milled in front of the restaurant as if waiting for something. Then a white pickup truck with the Dunes insignia pulled into the Denny's parking lot from the Strip. Although the distance from the edge of the casino's property to Denny's was only fifty feet, you couldn't navigate a motor vehicle from one to the other without driving on the street – unless you had a very good reason.

Two more uniformed officers got out of the pickup truck and went around to the tailgate. They popped it open and pulled a long metal ladder off its bed. They carried it to the building and propped it up against the facade, just feet from my window. I watched in utter amazement as all but a few of the Dunes' officers began climbing up the ladder one by one. Before the second half got to the roof, I heard the first half's heavy thumping footsteps pounding the ceiling above. I tried exchanging a glance with my fellow diners or the waitress – anyone – but everyone was either looking toward the ceiling or out the window. Finally I made eye contact with an older gentleman eating a French dip with his wife. After a second of wondrous staring at each other, I said, "What the hell's going on?" Probably more to myself than to him. He shrugged anyway and got back to eating his French dip.

Well, this I had to see. Travelling around the world for twenty-five years cheating casinos, I'd seen a lot, both in casinos and out. But never anything quite like this. So I left a twenty on the table and went outside. I walked thirty feet to a freebie sex-ads leaflet dispenser on the sidewalk and sat on it, not paying the slightest attention to the starlets shining underneath my butt. From where I positioned myself I could the entirety of Denny's sloping roof. And what I saw was beyond a doubt one of the most comical things I would ever witness in Las Vegas or anywhere else.

The two dozen officers atop Denny's were crawling on their hands and knees, their faces so close to the surface of the roof that they seemed plastered to it. The first thought that came to my mind was of a massive search for a lost contact lens. The way they were creeping around like that had to mean they were looking for something very small and hard to distinguish. What could be both more than a contact lens?

I could hear the security men asking one another in harried voices, "Do you see it? Did you find it…?" I heard the answers as well. They were a mixture of negatives and expletives, as if in summation of a hopeless situation. Behind me, a symphony of automobile horns began blaring. But I couldn't tell if they were irritated or fanfare. Only that motorists were also noticing the peculiar spectacle at Denny's. Surely the commotion on the roof had nothing to do with advertising a new Denny's "Grand slam" breakfast.

Traffic along Las Vegas Boulevard had come to a standstill as drivers and passengers alike gawked at the strange happening. Some people stuck in the bottleneck were yelling but more were laughing. Then everyone on the street seemed to join forces and directed their shouts at the men in blue on the rooftop. Most of the comments were disparaging, though I did hear one woman yell from an RV to be careful of holes in the roof, the kind you could fall through.

The Denny's rooftop search went on for over an hour. They must have covered every square inch of it. Then finally the troopers began filing back down the ladder, but their search wasn't finished yet. They spent another twenty minutes rummaging in and around the bushes lined up against the base of the building and even resorted to a go-over of the parking lot, though none of the officers got on their hands and knees on the blacktop. With a bunch of shrugs and gestures of futility, the brigade of Dunes security men tossed the ladder back on the bed of the pickup and retired back to the Dunes.

I sat on the dispenser for fifteen minutes after they were gone, wondering what the hell it was all about. What were they looking for? Then I thought of something I'd noticed when the guy with the wavy hair ran by my booth window. He'd made a throwing motion. That was it! The squad from the Dunes was searching for something he'd thrown. Or something they thought he'd thrown.

I would not learn what happened that April afternoon in 1983 until twenty-three and a half years later, in October 2005. That was when I was in Las Vegas with a TV crew from a UK production company. We were there to film a TV series based on the world's greatest gambling scams. One of the notorious scammers to be featured was the guy I'd seen dash across the Denny's that day. His name was John Roy, and with his partner Gunther Rintz he perpetuated the daring "Bet and Run" scam.

When John told me what had happened that day at Denny's, I knew at once that it was the greatest story I had ever heard. And believe me, I'd heard a lot of them.

Chapter 1

The Bet and Run Scam

When looking at the world's greatest gambling scams, you see that some of them are truly ingenious, that others are even more ingenious only because of their simplicity, and still others are so plain dumb that you wonder how in God's name they ever worked.

Then those that required nothing more than sheer balls. No high-tech equipment, no computer-programmed cellphones, no gadgets of any kind, not even photographic memories. Just big monster balls. The ballsiest of these was the bet-and-run scam.

John Roy and Gunther Rintz met at the Dunes Denny's in the summer of 1980. John was a gift of gab wonder who drifted away from his New York home before his sixteenth birthday. He was half Italian-American but his French Canadian half was more dominant, as evidenced by his rotting front teeth, the result of endless bouts with the pure maple syrup Québec was so proud of. The thing that made John so likeable was that he was even more engaging. In his New York City street days John may have set panhandling records. Records were not officially kept, but if there had been a panhandlers hall of fame, John would have gone in first ballot. Those jaded New Yorkers prone to give spare change to street hustlers somehow parted with paper money for John. He didn't have to ask for it. He would just approach strangers on the street and ask for some help to get something to eat. Those willing to help out and who with their handouts admonished John not to use the money for alcohol or drugs would be quite surprised to hear John say, "Don't worry, my only vice is maple syrup." In fact, John did keep himself energized during cold New York winters with the thick, warm French Canadian syrup he bought in Manhattan gourmet shops with his panhandling earnings.

But John's true calling in life was to be an actor. No doubt the natural talent was there. When he smiled at you, you knew his smile could light up a screen. When he spoke to you, you got interested in what he was saying only because it was John saying it. The subject didn't matter. He spoke sports, politics, music, movies, everything. He was a verifiable babbling brook of bullshit. Sometimes his panhandling customers found themselves late for work because they'd been hard pressed to get away from John – *after* giving him their donations. They actually enjoyed conversation with him and forgot he was a beggar.

When not panhandling, John could be found driving a Manhattan cab, mainly in winter because panhandling could be a real pain in the ass when it was freezing outside and there were fewer pedestrians. His fares were occasional famous people, sometimes movie stars. One of those was Dustin Hoffman, whom, funnily, John resembled greatly. Most celebrities were not interested in engaging in small talk with cabdrivers, but even they gravitated toward John's chattering charms. Hoffman was surprised that John was not an actor. When he asked how come John had never auditioned, the cabbie replied that he didn't know but someday would take that plunge.

John migrated to Las Vegas in the spring of 1980. He was not drawn there by gambling. His whole life he'd never even bought a lottery ticket. What attracted him to Sin City was the prospect of either driving a cab or panhandling. He'd read about the town's incipient explosion and figured his opportunities out there would be abundant. And he wouldn't have to deal with the cold winters, which meant he'd have his choice between the two occupations, no matter what the season.

But by the time summer rolled around, John didn't want to do either. In the Mojave Desert it was just plain hot. John had dealt with the heat and humidity of summertime in New York, but the desert heat, dry as it may be, was stifling. And he wasn't so keen about air-conditioning. So before long he started thinking about returning to the streets of New York.

But then one early summer morning, when it was still relatively cool outside, he walked into the Dunes Denny's. He'd already been in there fifty times, speaking with at least one stranger on every occasion. That morning, the guy he sat next to at the counter was as bald as an egg and wore black leather that sheathed his matching tattoos. They started talking. To a bystander listening, the contrast of their accents would sound funny. The bald, biker guy spoke in a soft German accent. John, despite the fact he spoke French, spoke English with a distinct New York brogue. The two, different as night and day, hit it off immediately.

Gunther Rintz immigrated with his family to Las Vegas in 1965, when he was ten years old. His early childhood was spent in Kempten, Germany, around eighty miles outside of Munich. It was a pretty Bavarian village. But the German economy was sluggish at the time and Gunther's parents were both unemployed. His father, Wolfgang, was a chef and had a brother who was also a chef who lived in California. The brother had told Wolfgang about Las Vegas and that a new opulent casino resort called Caesars Palace was opening the following year. They were looking for all kinds of hotel and casino help and good chefs were always in demand.

His mother, Ulrike, was a multilingual schoolteacher. In an expanding tourist town like Las Vegas, foreign language skills were always sought after, especially in the hotels. Ulrike figured she could find employment as a hostess at Caesars Palace or in one of the dozen other major casinos that lined the Vegas Strip in the mid-1960s. If not, she could always find work teaching French or German in the growing Las Vegas school system.

So the Rintzes made the big move. Gunther and his seven-year-old sister, Heidi, did not yet speak English, so they received immediate tutoring from their mother and the television set in the family's new apartment on Flamingo Road. School was difficult at first, but at their young ages, fluency in English came easily and within six months Gunther was well adjusted in a Las Vegas middle school.

Things were looking rather rosy for the Rintzes, especially when Wolfgang got hired as a line chef at the Bacchanal in Caesars Palace. It became the town's number-one gourmet restaurant the day it opened. The pay was great and Wolfgang's culinary imagination was much appreciated. At the same time, Ulrike began working as a hostess at the Sands, which drew a large European clientele, the biggest part of which were German.

But then disaster struck.

One day while preparing a Bavarian delight that was to be part of the Bacchanal's famed seven-course dinner, Wolfgang dropped dead in the kitchen of a heart attack. Soon after that Ulrike took to drinking and within a year had become an alcoholic. Young Gunther went wayward in school and developed two adolescent interests: gambling and motorcycles. His game of choice was blackjack. His bike of choice was a Harley Davidson 1200. By the time he met up with John at Denny's, he'd spent a decade playing one, chasing the cash to buy the other. Up till then he had not succeeded.

"Then what kind of motorcycle do you have?" John asked him over their Grand Slam breakfast plates at the counter.

"Well, it's not even a motorcycle," Gunther confessed. "It's a Vespa 125."

"What's that?" John was capable of shooting the shit on many subjects, but he didn't know jack shit about motorcycles.

"It's a scooter."

"Is it fast?"

"Gets me around town quick enough but it's not much on the highway."

The two became fast friends and saw each other nearly every morning at Denny's. Gunther was working part-time as a mechanic while John alternated between panhandling and thinking of hitching a ride back to New York. Contrary to what John had thought, Vegas street hustling was nowhere near as lucrative as in Manhattan, and at the moment he didn't have enough cash for a plane ticket.

Every so often John and Gunther had a beer together somewhere away from Denny's, usually in one the 50-cent-beer bars in the little shithouse casinos squeezed between the big daddies on the Strip. Sometimes they went downtown to the Horseshoe. They took turns buying; usually only one of them had enough pocket money to splurge.

One afternoon at the Denny's counter, Gunther, who was between jobs, asked John if he wanted to tag along while he played a little blackjack.

"Sure, why not?" John replied.

Outside in the midday heat, John hopped on the back of Gunther's Vespa. Gunther piloted it north down the Strip, turned into the entrance of a lower tier casino called Bob Stupak's Vegas World, which a decade and a half later was demolished to clear the way for the sky-scraping Stratosphere casino that occupies the property today. Stupak was a casino maverick known for promoting gaming gimmicks such as "double exposure 21" and "crapless craps." In double exposure 21, both dealer cards were dealt faceup, which drastically changed a player's strategy for the game. Unknown to Gunther at the time, Stupak was also a diehard motorcycle enthusiast who years later came close to that when he drove his Harley into a pole.

They parked the Vespa in the self-parking garage and headed into the casino.

"Why do you play here?" John asked.

"I like this blackjack game they got here. They let you see both the dealer's cards."

"Does that increase your chances of winning?"

"No, but it makes losing interesting." Though Gunther was much less given to words than John, he could be quite sarcastic at times.

While walking through the casino, they noticed a crowd of people assembled behind a blackjack table watching a high roller with a big Stetson hat and cowboy boots play heads-up against the dealer. There was an armed security guard behind the gambler, occupying an appointed no-man's land that kept the crowd at bay. John moved in for a closer look and saw the reason for all the hoopla. The high-rolling cowboy had a small mountain of stacked $100 bills on the layout in front of him. Though John had experience in only one or two bills at a time, usually of the $1 variety, he was quite capable of estimating the amount of large chunks of hundreds. He figured the bricks of cash on the table were around a hundred grand. There were also stacks of purple chips that resembled small castles, $500 chips, though at the time John didn't know which color chips were how much, nor did he care. He was only impressed by the cash.

The cowboy was playing all seven spots on the layout. Somehow, despite his heretofore disinterest in blackjack, John was intrigued by that. For the moment he forgot he'd accompanied

nied Gunther to watch him play double exposure blackjack. Which is what drew Gunther up to his side among the crowd. Gunther's being a head taller than John allowed him to see the layout above most of the heads without straining. John had to settle for looking through cracks in the crunched together bodies in front of him. First thing Gunther noticed was that the gambler attracting all this attention was playing regular blackjack without the benefit of seeing the dealer's hole card.

"How much are those purple chips?" John asked, suddenly interested for some reason he was not yet sure of.

"They're five-hundreds."

"Dollars?" John was joking. After all, a guy with a hundred grand on the layout wasn't going to be playing with 500-cent chips.

Gunther managed a small laugh without turning his bald head from the action. The cowboy was reaching to his pillars of purple chips and placing four of them in each of the table's seven betting circles. That was $2,000 a pop, the table maximum. The guy was wagering fourteen grand on a single deal of blackjack! While John questioned the sanity of that, Gunther wondered why the heavy-hitting cowboy wasn't up at the other end of the Strip playing blackjack on the regal tables of Caesars Palace or the MGM. What was he doing at a craphouse like Vegas World? At Caesars he would be afforded a lavish penthouse suite with that kind of action. Well, maybe he'd play uptown later. High rollers often bounced around and spread out their action.

When John watched the dealer make a blackjack and sweep $14,000 of the cowboy's purple chips into her table rack, he didn't know which he resented more: the cowboy for losing it or the casino for taking it. Ten hands and ten minutes later, when the dealer swept the last of the cowboy's purple chips into her rack, John looked up at Gunther to see his reaction. His new

German friend wasn't watching anymore. His eyes had drifted toward the far end of the pit where a dealer was standing behind a dead double-exposure blackjack game. He probably would have taken off in that table's direction had there been at least one gambler playing on the game. Gunther for some superstitious reason didn't like to gamble alone, and he knew that John was not a gambler. So he hung out next to the squatty New Yorker, shifting his shiny pate between the cowboy and two double exposure tables in the casino. Together they looked comical, such was the contrast of a loose hanging shirt draped over a potbelly and a tight leather west hugging a lean torso. In fact, in tribute to both their difference in physical appearance and Dustin Hoffman, you would say that John was as incongruous next to Gunther as Hoffman's Ratzo Rizzo character was with John Voight's Joe Buck in *Midnight Cowboy*.

The gambling cowboy sounded like a real Texan with his outbursts of "goddamn" at each losing hand. When they watched him tear the money wrappers off several packets of $100 bills, peeling off twenty at a time that he slapped over each betting circle, John suddenly leaned into Gunther and said in a conspiratorial whisper, "If only you were sitting on your Vespa outside that door in the parking lot right now."

Gunther looked down at John without the faintest idea of what he meant by that.

"You said it was quick enough to get you around Vegas." John had been on the back of it and noticed that Gunther had no trouble maintaining the flow of traffic.

"So?"

"So take a look at the cash on that table."

Gunther took a look, then looked down at John. He shrugged.

"Now take a look at that side door over there." He pointed to a door in an empty corner of the casino. It was half-hidden behind a bank of slot machines and led directly outside to the valet parking lot.

Gunther looked. This time when he looked back at John, there was a vague expression of comprehension on his face. He certainly had an inking of what John was thinking but still wasn't sure. However, John's next question erased any doubt.

"Gunther, you ever heard of grab-and-dash?"

Gunther laughed. "No, but it sounds like dine and dash."

John had never called it that, but on some lousy panhandling days had done exactly that when he didn't have money to pay for his meals. He indicated the bricks of cash on the layout with a head jerk. "It would be so easy," he said with enough excitement that Gunther had to shush him.

"Are you fucking serious?" Gunther asked, a little too loud himself.

John took another gander at the cowboy's money, then looked toward the side door. He gauged the distance to the door and then to the street beyond, which he couldn't see from inside the casino but remembered from their entry on Gunther's Vespa.

"You know what, man," he whispered, "I could probably grab a few stacks of his cash and get out the door and off this property on foot. Better than 50-50 I'd make it."

"You are crazy!"

"If only I had a sack or something."

This time Gunther was right with him. He understood that John was thinking of waltzing up to the table, grabbing as many of the cowboy's stacks of cash as he could, dropping them into an open sack and running out the door.

"Only problem, John, is that the Texan might not just sit there peacefully while you're cleaning the table of his money. Let alone the security guard."

"You right," John admitted. "But one thing I'm sure of, I

could walk up to that table, swipe one stack of cash and then book out that door."

Gunther looked straight at the door. He had to admit, it was goddamn close. No more than thirty feet from the table. Even if the security guard reacted fast enough and his brain processed the impulse to shoot John in the back, he'd never get the gun out of his bulky holster before John was out the door. Suddenly, he too was sorry that he wasn't sitting outside that door on his Vespa.

They watched for another twenty minutes during which the cowboy's horse went downhill in a hurry. Both were thinking how it was a shame that his money was going through the cash slot built into the blackjack table rather than in their pockets, or sack. Then one of the double exposure tables caught a live one and drew Gunther over to it. John reluctantly gave up his surveillance of the cowboy. He watched Gunther play against the dealer with the dealer's hole card exposed. On the first hand, Gunther was dealt fifteen and the dealer had twenty. Gunther naturally took a hit. He got a 7 and busted over twenty-one. On the next hand, Gunther was dealt twenty and the dealer had fifteen. Gunther naturally stood pat. The dealer hit and drew a 6 for twenty-one.

Watching Gunther's chips get swept away again, John said, "Maybe you should find a game called triple exposure 21."

"What would that be?"

"See not only the dealer's hole card but also the next card coming out of the shoe. *Then* you might have a chance."

Gunther and the cowboy went broke at around the same time.

That night, they sat at a bar inside O'Shea's, a small grind joint next to the Holiday Casino on the Strip. They were drinking 50-cent-beers and John was buying. Gunther was both broke and pissed. He'd blown all his money gambling and was that much further from having the cash to buy his dream Harley Davidson. The last thing on his mind was that cowboy blowing off fourteen grand a hand at Vegas World. But John couldn't get it out of his head.

"Gunther," he said when they were on their fourth beer. "How bad do you want that Harley Davidson?"

"Bad," Gunther said.

"Well, I think I know a way you can get it."

Gunther grunted. "I hope you're not thinking of breaking into a motorcycle shop and stealing one."

John laughed. "Are you kidding? I would never think of such a thing. But maybe we can do the next best thing."

Gunther took a gulp on his beer and waited.

"Maybe my idea of grabbing that Texan's money and running was a little brash and risky, but if we had planned something like that in advance, it would have worked?"

"Maybe," Gunther acquiesced, "but how do you plan something like that in advance? We can't scope out the town looking for high rollers with stacks of cash on the table, then hurry up and get me on the scooter outside the casino, so you can grab the cash, hit the door and hop on the back."

"No we can't, but who said anything about scoping out high rollers?"

Gunther put the empty glass on the bar and stared blankly at John.

"We don't need high rollers. *We'll* be the high rollers."

"I don't get it, John," Gunther said with a chuckle. "What are we gonna do, rip our own cash off the table and run?"

"You're close but no cigar."

"Okay, I'm all ears, but first get me another beer."

John laid a $1 bill on the bar for another round. "It's simple," he said. "What we do is have me go to a table with two thousand bucks in chips. I bet it on a hand of blackjack. If I win, I just stand there and get paid two thousand. If I lose, I just grab the chips off the table before the dealer can pick them up and get out of Dodge. Whaddaya think?"

Gunther looked at John long and hard. John thought Gunther was about to dismiss both him and his idea with permanence, but then he noticed a spark in Gunther's eye that gleamed like sun rays bouncing off the shiny chrome fenders of a Harley Davidson motorcycle.

"If we set it up with you waiting for me outside on the Vespa, we'd be gone before they knew what hit 'em."

"The only risk would be you making it out of the casino." That was Gunther's first conscious contribution to the embryonic scam. Once John heard it, he knew that his leather-clad German friend was game.

"Are you kidding me!" John enthused. "There's no risk. Didn't you see how close that door was to the blackjack table at Vegas World? There's got to be hundreds of layouts like that in Las Vegas. And you know what? It doesn't even have to be a blackjack table. Suppose it's a roulette wheel. I could just put the chips on red or black. If the wrong one comes in, I just swoop up the chips and boogie. If it wins I get paid. Then I just cash out and we're two grand ahead of the game." Before Gunther could reply, John's brain had already gotten another step ahead. "Wait a minute! Why cash out? Why not just take the two grand in profits and let it ride. Then if I win again, I get paid again. If I lose, I grab and go. But we still got the two grand in profit. I just keep playing and getting paid till I lose. Imagine if we get lucky and I win ten in a row!"

"I bet the casino would really get pissed off once it hit 'em that you were planning on bolting after the first losing bet."

"Tough titty on them," John said and slugged his beer.

"How would we cash out?" Gunther asked intelligently.

Something John hadn't thought of. "What you mean? Just go

to the casino cage and cash out."

"Yeah, but after you won ten hands in a row for two grand and then ran off after losing the eleventh, don't you think they might balk at giving you the cash?"

John put the glass on the bar and thought for a moment. "You're right. That would be a problem. But don't worry about it. We'll figure it out."

"Then there's another problem."

"Something wrong with the Vespa?"

"No. Something's wrong with my bank account. There's nothing in it."

"That could be a problem," John agreed with amusement.

"Do you have any ideas where we could get two grand for that first bet?"

"Well, I guess I can start hustling. Can you get a temporary job?"

Gunther was currently collecting unemployment, which paid him about as much as his last mechanic's salary did. "I guess I could work somewhere off the books, but the pay would be shit and it might take a while to accumulate any worthwhile money."

"What about your sister?"

"My sister is married and doesn't wanna know about my needing money to gamble."

"It's not gambling. It's a sure thing."

Gunther frowned. "How am I supposed to tell her that? 'Heidi, can you lend me two-thousand dollars so I can have my friend John bet it. But don't worry because if he loses it, he's gonna grab his chips off the layout and come running out the door, and I'll pick him up on my Vespa and we'll make our getaway.' I'm sure she'll run to crack open her piggy bank for that."

John nodded fatefully. "I guess if I had a sister, she wouldn't go for that either."

The next morning, John hit the streets panhandling and Gunther perused the classifieds for "mechanics wanted." John hustled his ass off and earned two hundred bucks, by far his biggest payday since he'd been in Vegas. Gunther couldn't find work as a mechanic, but he did get industrious and drove his Vespa to the Country Club Estates, at the time Vegas's chicest neighborhood, where he went door to door offering to simonize residents' luxury cars for thirty-five bucks. He got lucky and hit on two cars, made a hundred bucks with tips.

By sundown they were in the living room of Gunther's modest apartment near the university. Gunther was stretched out on the sofa drinking a longneck. John sat on an adjacent easy chair munching potato chips. On the coffee table lay all the cash to their names, slightly more than $300. John lived downtown in one of the weekly budget motels populated by transients, low-level criminals and hookers. It was located a block off Fremont Street, the main downtown drag that for three blocks was filled on both sides by arcade-like casinos. There were normally crowds of people up and down the sidewalks in front of these casinos. This got John thinking that they could try a few moves down there to build up their bankroll.

"We wouldn't even need the Vespa to do Fremont Street," he said. "The casinos are all like arcades; they remind me of Coney Island..."

"Coney Island?"

"Oh, I forgot, you've never been to New York. You ever hear of Nathan's famous hot dogs?"

"They're delicious."

"Well, Coney Island is a beach in Brooklyn with amusement parks and arcades and all that. Kinda like an old Atlantic City without the casinos. Anyway, this guy named Nathan Handwerker – I think he was a German – started a nickel-a-hot-dog stand maybe ninety, hundred years ago. Like you said, they're delicious and they're all over the place now, 'specially New York..."

"There's at least one in Vegas."

"No shit! Gotta go there sometime. So you've noticed those Fremont Street casinos, right? They're just like the open-air arcades in Coney Island. They got tables literally two feet from the sidewalk. Don't even have to worry about doors. What I'm thinking is I go up to one of those tables by the sidewalk and bet the three hundred bucks. If I lose, I grab up the chips and turn around and I'm gone. Disappear in the throng. Shit, I wouldn't even have to run. It would be a walkaway. And you can run interference. You could be standing on the sidewalk. If anyone tries to be a hero and chase me, you just get in their way. Bump into them or something."

Gunther glanced at the cash lying on the coffee table. "I don't like it. It's too dangerous on foot. Plus there're plenty of motorcycle cops down there. If one of them spots you running outta the casino, he'd be on your ass in seconds flat."

"We'd only have to risk it a few times. Each time we win, we double up the bet. After three wins, we'd have more than the two grand needed for the maximum bet."

"Why not just do it for the smaller amount on the Strip with the Vespa?"

"Because we might take some serious heat with this stuff. I don't know how many times we'll be able to do it before the word gets out. Don't want to burn a Strip casino for a few hundred bucks when we could've done the same move for two grand."

Gunther shook his head. "I don't think downtown is a good idea. Not unless we use the Vespa."

They discussed it until Gunther fell asleep on the couch. John passed out a few minutes later on the chair. The next morning, still in limbo about their plans for the first runaway, as John coined the term, they each returned to their occupations. John scrounged up another hundred and fifty begging while Gunther beautified four cars for around the same amount.

Back in Denny's for dinner, they decided to forgo the idea of betting and running for less than the table maximum. They would each tend to business until they had $2,000, which was the highest bet allowed in most Vegas casinos.

Over the next few days, they scouted out the Strip casinos. With military attentiveness, they noted each salient detail. It wasn't only about how close gaming tables were to doors. Not by a longshot. There was much to concern themselves outside a casino. Firstly, what kind of traffic was just outside the door? Though it might be a cakewalk to get out of the casino with the chips, once outside a world of things could go wrong. Which hotel employees were out there? Who among them posed a potential problem? In addition to security patrols, there were valet parkers, bellmen, landscapers, carpenters, maintenance men, delivery people, any of whom might decide to play hero or just plain get in the way.

Then there were the different kinds of security patrols. Casinos routinely had uniformed security guards patrolling the grounds not only on foot but also driving a variety of vehicles, motorized and non-motorized. Bicycle patrols were very common. So were golf carts. About the only thing you could count on not encountering on casino grounds was a security officer mounted on a horse.

Inside as well there were problems, even with a table just feet from the door. You had the constant flow of foot traffic in and out of casinos. Many had revolving doors, inside of which you could get stuck. John hitting a revolving door slot too hard or one that already had too many occupants could cause that exact problem. By that time in Vegas, most casino revolving door entrances were wide and could house several people, but there could always be unforeseen problems with these, including electrical ones that might get stuck on their own. Then, of course, you could never lose sight of the possibility that an unsuspecting patron would turn into a would-be hero trying to make a diving tackle on someone fleeing a casino.

Security forces habitually stationed guards near doors, whether they roved or just anchored there. Naturally any crime committed inside a casino, be it a purse-snatching or armed robbery of the cashier cage, ended with the perpetrators exiting the casino, more often than not through the front doors. Thus casino exits were never left totally unguarded or unattended to. Casinos also had plainclothes officers patrolling inside. Add to that armed gaming agents from the Nevada Gaming Control Board Enforcement Division, who in Nevada had the same powers of crime prevention and arrest that regular Las Vegas cops had.

So there was a plethora of potential problems to contend with.

They decided that the Tropicana casino, located on the Strip at its southeast intersection with Tropicana Avenue, would be the stage for their first runaway spectacle. It was ideal because the casino's main entrance fronted Tropicana Avenue and not the Strip. There was a set of regular glass doors and one revolving door. Exiting the casino, you came down a flight of a dozen steps, or a sloping walkway off to the side, to a driveway leading to Tropicana Avenue eastbound less than a hundred yards away. The "Trop," although an upper end casino was not a monstrosity in size and therefore very accessible to through traffic on its three lanes passing the entrance.

John and Gunther had decided that the optimum time to pull their stunt was during peak casino hours, when the tables would be hopping with action. They didn't want John's big bet, which was going to be a stack of twenty black $100 chips, to be the only bet of the sort when he laid it down on a blackjack table just ten feet from the revolving door. They had observed the front of the building for three consecutive evenings between nine o'clock o'clock and midnight. During those hours there was a steady flow of incoming and outgoing traffic, both on foot through the entrance doors and in automobiles along the driveway. Cars and taxicabs would enter the property from Las Vegas Boulevard, the Strip, drop off people in front, then roll down the driveway that emptied out eastbound on Tropicana. They had never seen any of the three lanes clogged up for more than half a minute, which really didn't matter because there was always room for a motorcycle to slip through, between any vehicles stopped there.

There appeared to be only one problem: where to place the Vespa before positioning it at the bottom of the staircase. As the precise moment of John's rapid departure from the casino could never be determined with exactness, neither could Gunther be sitting on the Vespa outside the main entrance waiting. Surely he would be accosted and asked to move by either security or parking attendants, who had to keep the area clear to maintain the smooth flow of traffic so vital to casinos.

It was at this planning juncture that the soon-to-be runaway artists realized they needed help with the operation, mainly another participant.

Enter Rene and Raul Lopez. Identical twins whom Gunther knew from dirt bike rallies he used to ride in during better days when he had a dirt bike. Rene and Raul both worked as clerks in the same 7-Eleven convenience store, though the boss never knew it. Officially it was Rene who'd filled out the employment application and received the paychecks, but depending on which brother felt like it, that brother reported to work. Of course there were occasional problems when picking up past conversations with the boss, but what could he expect from a Mexican clerk, anyway. To minimize that problem, the Lopezs both made believe that their English wasn't very good. Both were, however, born in Las Vegas.

There was no question that John was the leader of the operation. Gunther really didn't want to know what went on inside the casino. His job would be to drive the Vespa once John jumped onto the back seat. He was content to leave the planning and logistics to John. Despite the short time they had known each other, Gunther trusted John and, like virtually everyone else who crossed his path, liked him.

John assigned two distinct responsibilities for Rene and Raul. Rene would be the "blocker." At the moment of truth when John swiped his losing chips off the table and headed for the door, Rene, who would be standing next to that door, would come into the casino, pass by John from the opposite direction, and block anyone who tried to chase him, most likely a pit boss coming out of the pit. They knew that dealers could never abandon their table for any reason, thus it would not be a dealer trying to prevent John's escape. The tactic Rene would use to block a would-be pursuer was simply to get in that person's way, impede his progress toward the fleeing John. It would most likely be a clumsy move, bumping into the pursuer with an "Oh, I'm sorry" or any other mumbling of an excuse for having upset him. The key was that Rene would protect the space from the table to the door. Once Rene was outside the door on his way to the Vespa, his security would fall to the fourth man on the team, Raul, who would be coming up the steps as Rene descended them, ready to interfere with any pursuer who somehow bypassed or was not slowed by Rene.

Blocking, however, was not Raul's major function. As he was to be called the "signal man," Raul's job would be to signal Gunther when it was time to bring the Vespa to the door. The order in which the move would go down commenced with John's laying his bet on the table. Then Rene, who could clearly see this, would brush his hand through his hair. Raul, who would be strategically positioned outside the door at the top of the landing, could see Rene's signal through the glass of the revolving door. Once he read it, he would immediately descend the steps and walk twenty feet around a bend, where Gunther, sitting on the Vespa in a deserted corner of the lot, came into view. Raul would then take off his ball cap, the signal for Gunther to approach; a possible escape situation was imminent. Having signalled Gunther, Raul would return to the bottom of the steps, now ready to perform his second task as the outside blocker. In fact, his role in the scam was the most vital. He was the link of communication between John, designated "the runner," and Gunther, designated "the driver." His vantage point included each person involved in the runaway. If he fucked up, the odds of disaster increased dramatically.

With Gunther waiting on the Vespa at the bottom of the stairs, the chain of signals would now reverse and come from the outside in. Raul, knowing that Gunther was there, would mount the steps and make eye contact through the door with Rene. By rubbing his chin distinctly, he told Rene that Gunther was ready and everything was a go. Rene would then rub his chin inside the casino for John to see. This told John that Gunther was ready. He could now place the bet with the security of knowing his escape driver was there. Since John was the main figure of the scam, the final call of placing or not placing the bet was his. However, once it was placed, he had to swipe it and go if it lost. That was the point of no return.

It was decided that the debut Tropicana move would climax in a runaway, no matter what unless there was some unforeseen reason which made that impossible. What this meant is that

John would keep betting after winning hands, only to grab the chips and run on the first loser. But not in a haphazard manner.

Reflecting on Gunther's concern about how they would cash out the chips, John implemented a process that simplified it and put their expected profits at minimal risk. Instead of replacing bets immediately after winning hands, which served to bulk up John's pockets with chips and risk those chips if John were to be caught running out on the loser, chips won would be cashed out immediately after the hand. But not by John. Once John was paid at the table, he would meander through the casino and then exit unseen from a side entrance and then work his way across Tropicana Avenue to the Marina casino. There, he would find the keno pit and await the arrival of his teammates, including Gunther, who would be given the signal from Raul that John won the hand, then simply drive the Vespa down the driveway onto Tropicana and make his way to the Marina.

Once the entire four-man team was assembled in the keno pit at the Marina, the winning chips would be distributed among Gunther, Rene and Raul. They would each cash out roughly $700 in profits, a relative small amount by Vegas standards that would not draw any attention from casino personnel. Then after the cash was obtained, everyone would come back to the Marina, where John would be waiting. The money would be passed to Rene and Raul, who would each hold half of it for the duration of the operation that night. By making them the "bankers," their profits would never be at risk because the only persons subject to capture and arrest during the commission of the runaways were John and Gunther.

The money safely in the possession of the twins, the entire operation would revert to a repetition of what had taken place. Each person would take his position at the Tropicana, inside the casino and out. Then when John received the signal from Rene that Gunther was ready and everything was a go, he'd put down the bet. If they were fortunate enough to have another winning bet, they would meet up again at the Marina keno pit and go through the same cash-out process. In the event of a loss and an escape, Gunther would pilot the Vespa to the Denny's restaurant, but not *the* Denny's. Rather another one located farther north on the Strip near the Sands. Although neither John nor Gunther knew at that time that the Dunes Denny's was a haven for casino rip-off artists, they figured it wouldn't be a good idea to meet where they often hung out after committing a rip-off.

Gunther did mention to John a problem that might arise with John's method of making those big bets in that fashion on blackjack tables. This would not be the case in roulette, where anyone betting two grand on red or black was considered by pit bosses to be a harmless sucker.

"The problem", Gunther said, leaning against his parked Vespa in the Boulevard Mall's rear lot," is that when you make a bet that big and then leave the table after playing only one hand, the pit bosses are going to think you're a card counter. Even more so when you come back a second time and make the same bet."

Gunther was right. A well-known trick of professional card counters, then the longtime public enemy number one of casinos, was to signal the "big player" member of their team to the blackjack table when an inordinate number of tens and aces remained in the card shoe. When this happened, the card counter had a significant advantage over the house, therefore, the big player was at the most opportune moment making his big bet. Often the bet was made on only one hand and almost always in the middle of the shoe, because strong favorable "counts" for card counters could not exist at the beginning of a six-or eight-deck shoe. Thus a blackjack player stepping up to a table and betting a stack of black $100 chips where most players were betting red $5 and green $25 chips would draw heat from the casino. Then when he left after only one hand, the pit bosses would think the favorable count had evaporated. And then seeing the return of the big player in the middle of the same or another shoe, it would be assumed that the plus count had resurfaced again.

"So what would they do?" John asked, standing opposite the scooter from Gunther. They had come to the mall so John could buy a pair of sneakers at Sears. Since his arrival in Vegas he had but a single pair of uncomfortable shoes. For the task that would be at hand, they agreed that running shoes were necessary. John found a modest pair of sneakers with a name that sounded as far away as Nike, Reebok and Adidas as you could get. He paid $9.99, a paltry amount for sneakers even in 1980.

Gunther nodded with pursed lips and hiked his shoulders a bit. "First thing, as soon as your bet hit the table, there'd be a ton of heat. Two or three pit people might come over and stare you down. They might even have the dealer reshuffle the cards right in the middle of the shoe. They only do that when they're suspicious someone's card-counting."

"So, if they go ahead and reshuffle the cards on me, that doesn't change my odds of winning the hand, does it?"

"No, but it might test your patience and nerve."

"Would they have any reason to call security and have a guard stand behind me while playing, like we saw with the Texan at Vegas World? I mean, just because they think I'm counting cards."

"They'd only call for security if they decided to eighty-six you?"

"Eighty-six me? The assholes would have me thrown out of the casino for counting cards. What is it, illegal?"

"No, but the casinos treat it that way. They hate counters like they're the plague."

"But they wouldn't mobilize to throw me at after one hand?"

"Doubt it."

"Then there's no problem!" John said, suddenly lifted again. He patted the rear seat of the Vespa as if he'd just scored something. "All we need is the one hand. Either we win two thousand or I run out the door."

"Speaking of what..."

"Which," John corrected.

"What?" Gunther asked, not in repetition of the mistake but with uncertainty as to what John had meant.

"You say 'speaking of which' in that sense, not 'speaking of what.'"

Gunther did not need a grammar lesson; he needed the cash to buy a Harley. "Okay, whatever. But what I wanted to know is how you're planning to cash out the twenty black chips if you loose the bet and end up running out of the casino. Or even after losing the bet after having won a few bets. In either situation, you still have to cash out twenty $100 chips that are going to have drawn a lot of attention."

John rubbed his forehead, but not because he was stumped by Gunther's reasoning. He'd already been thinking of that and figured the best way to handle it was in the same manner they handled winning chips after each winning hand: distribute them among Gunther and the twins and have each cash out six or seven chips. In that fashion there'd be three cash-outs: two for $700, one for $600. With all the black-chip action in Strip casinos, no one would be able to match their particular black chips to those John had run out of the casino with. That kind of problem could develop, though, when and if large denomination chips were used.

"I guess that would work," Gunther said.

"So then it's cool," John said with a coaxing pat on Gunther's shoulder. "That's how we'll do it. If by chance at any time my bet takes heat, we'll just call it off. I'll take the bet off before the dealer starts dealing."

"Make sure you do," Gunther said with urgency. "Remember, if that happens, you have to act fast. Once the dealer deals the first card to the first player, you can't remove your bet."

"Even if no one's seen any cards?"

"Doesn't matter. That's the rule. When the dealer waves off the bets or says 'No more betting,' the inverse also takes effect. Meaning you can't take your existing bets off."

"That's a bitch?"

"That's the rules."

"What would they do if I scooped up my chips just after the dealer dealt the first card to the first player, and I'm sitting all the way at the other end of the table?" Which is where John realized he would never want to be. While watching countless rounds of blackjack over the past ten days, he'd noticed that the person who received his cards first on the blackjack table was the last player whose bets the dealer attended to at the end of the hand. Therefore, if John were standing across from that player, he would receive his cards last, but once the dealer was finished playing his own hand, he would turn his attention to John's bet before any of the others. Logically, John would have more time to grab his losing bet off the layout if he were on the opposite side.

"They would make you put your bet back in play," Gunther answered.

"And if I refused?"

"Drag you to the back room and have you arrested."

"Well, then I guess it would just have to be a premature runaway, because I ain't going to no back room."

The back room was the cold, gray security room where casino security took suspected cheaters and undesirables for interrogations. In the old days, beatings inside them were routine.

Perhaps John thought they were not yet a thing of the past.

"I wouldn't worry about it," Gunther counselled. "It's unlikely that a security guy is gonna come up behind you and stand there as you play. But you may have to deal with one passing by while making his rounds."

John chuckled. "That's no problem. If I have to take off, I'll be gone so fast that any guard not waiting in advance to tackle me will have no shot of stopping me. People can't react that fast to shock."

"Then let's do it," Gunther said with a burst of enthusiasm. He put his hand out.

"Let's do it," John said, shaking it.

The big night was a steamy Saturday night in the Nevada desert, the Strip awash in a billion baubles of bright neon. Gunther wore his leather vest and pants despite the stifling heat, as always. John was dressed in a sports shirt and jacket, also bought at Sears, and shiny but cheap white sneakers. Both Lopezs wore polo shirts, though neither Rene's nor Raul's were of the Ralph Lauren variety.

About to leave Gunther's apartment, Rene and Raul in one of their beat up Plymouth Dusters, Gunther and John on the scooter, John realized that Gunther was putting on a riding helmet for the first time since he'd known him.

"Don't you have one for me?" he asked the biker.

"You don't need one."

"Are you serious?" A tinge of resentment filled John's voice. "I'm gonna be the one on the back of this thing when you're doing wheelies or whatever else during our escape."

Gunther couldn't help but laugh. "It's not for that, John. Don't worry about me crashing. Just hold on loosely and you'll be all right."

"Loosely?"

"No reason to strain yourself squeezing. You just relax back there and leave the biking to me."

"So why the helmet then?"

Gunther turned and half-rolled his eyes at him. "You forgot one thing. People are going to see you run out of the casino and us make the escape. They're going to see the Vespa..."

"So. You've already got a phony tag on it." This was true. Gunther had a collection of used motorcycle tags he either shoplifted from souvenir shops or stole off other parked bikes.

"*So*! What about me?"

"What?"

Gunther removed the helmet and humorously patted his bald head. "If I wear the helmet, no one could give an accurate description, at least up there. Get what I mean?"

John couldn't put much of a dent into that logic.

"Speaking of *which*, you don't think you should wear a ball cap on your head? With all those cameras they got in there."

"I thought of it, but wouldn't it look funny seeing a guy wearing a sports coat with a ball cap? At least in New York it would." John would have never considered that ensemble panhandling on Park Avenue.

"Here it's fine. Guys dressed up wear ball caps all the time. In fact, during major sporting events you see more guys in suits wearing caps than not."

"Okay, we'll stop by my dive and get a cap."

"I got plenty of 'em. I think I got one that will go great for the occasion."

"What's it say on it?"

"The Tropicana."

"C'mon!"

"I'm not kidding. My last girlfriend bought it one night I was in there gambling. She left it over. Never came back for it. Besides, I think it's best you wear that cap. You'll blend right in.

Lots of guys will be wearing Tropicana caps." Gunther's eyes dropped to John's jacket. "Can't say the same for the jacket."

John noticed that Gunther was cracking wise more and more often. He was really loose. Seemed like he was enjoying it before they even started. John attributed that to Gunther's thinking that his new Harley 1200 was suddenly in reach.

They sat in the Marina keno pit, discussing strategy a final time before the big inaugural runaway move. Rene and Raul had already gone inside the Tropicana and bought the twenty $100 chips John would need for his bet. It was best, John had decided, that he not be seen in the casino before he placed his monster bet on the blackjack table. They could have gotten four $500 purple chips instead, which would be a lot easier to grab off the table than twenty blacks. But Gunther had explained that purple chips drew attention in the casino, and in the event of a runaway might be very difficult to cash out. Purple chips in action were tracked by casino personnel, and usually there weren't many of them in play on the tables. The casino cage might be given the order not to cash purple chips and hold up anyone at the counter trying to do so.

"Okay, you guys ready?" John asked after a final rehashing of details.

They all sounded off in the affirmative with unbridled enthusiasm. Their atmosphere was as charged as the huddle of a championship high school football team. Gunther proposed a beer before they got going but John preferred to waive the celebrating until they made some cash.

"Then let's go!" Gunther said.

Five minutes later, each man was in position at the Tropicana. The casino was jammed up with its Saturday evening glitz. The constant casino murmur hummed along with the clinking and blipping of slot machines. John, wearing his Tropicana ball cap, had to wait for a spot to open up at the blackjack table closest to the door. He was thinking how it was a joke; that end table was *so* close to the door. A couple of quick strides and he'd be outside, rushing down the steps to the Vespa. Hopefully, that wouldn't be necessary on the first bet. Wouldn't it be nice to win a few before he had to bolt?

The spot that did open up after several minutes was in centerfield, smack in the middle of the table. John glanced inconspicuously toward the revolving door and saw Rene, then through the glass panes and was able to see Raul, who then slid out of view to give Gunther the signal to bring the Vespa to the base of the stairs. When Gunther, tucked in an out-of-the-way slot between two parked limousines, saw Raul remove his ball cap, he revved up the Vespa and scooted up to his spot at the base of the stairs.

Seconds later Raul emerged back into view through the glass. He was grazing his chin at Rene, who in turn grazed his at John, who now knew Gunther was in position for the escape. The moment of truth had arrived. John placed his huge stack of black chips in the betting circle and remained standing. The other six players at the table, all betting $5 red chips, looked up at John as though he'd just gotten off a flying saucer, so strange it was to see such a mountainous bet at a $5 table.

The dealer on the game was an older gentleman with tons of refinement and experience. He immediately called over the floorman when his eyes took in the monster bet. The Tropicana motif was island tropics; all the floormen and pit bosses were clad in tropical-style, multicolored button-downs and trousers. The floorman who came over to watch John was about thirty and seemed in pretty good shape. He parked himself next to the dealer, leaning against the table. His eyes went from John's stack of black chips to John and back to the stack. John realized he'd be there for the duration. He'd been hoping for either a woman or an old fat slob who presented less of a challenge to his escape but wasn't overly worried due to the detailed planning of their operation. Everything was so well planned that even a track and field star bolting out of the pit after him had very little chance. Plus he'd be slowed by having to hurdle the velvet rope that cordoned off the pit – and then Rene would be there to greet him as soon as he was on the other side.

The floorman smiled his Vegas casino hello, and of course got John thinking that he had read his thoughts and knew John would make a run for it if he lost the bet. But John overcame the paranoia and returned his smile, wordlessly using the charm that had served him so well in his panhandling days. Then his eyes dropped to his chips in the betting circle and watched the dealer place his first card in front of them. It was a 10. Then he dealt himself a 9. If he laid another 10 on John, John would be in good shape. If not, John might have to grab and run sooner than later.

When John received his second card, he got ready to go. It was a 6. The dealer had dealt him the lousiest of all dog hands – a sixteen. Against an up card of 9 he had little chance. John stood pat. He could have hit the hand with the same percentage against him, but they'd agreed beforehand not to risk busting in any situation because dealers removed busted-out losing chips immediately. John did not want to be forced into a competition with the dealer to get to the chips first. The last thing they needed was a collision between John's hand and the dealer's, where chips would be flying and John would be running out the door with nothing more than a jammed finger.

John waved his hand palm-down to indicate he was "good." The dealer turned his attention to the three players yet to act. They all stood with pat hands. Then he turned over his hole card, an 8, making John an instant loser. It was time to go but John didn't have to panic. The dealer had to pay off two winning $5 hands on John's left before he could take John's chips. That was a gaming regulation. Regardless of the amount or size of a bet, it had to be treated in its proper order. This gave John more than a full second to make his move.

He shot Rene a final look and noticed that he had taken a step forward in anticipation of John's impending gallop. Without further hesitation, John swiped the stack of black chips off the layout and started for the door. As soon as he turned away he began laughing. He didn't know why but he couldn't stop. Probably some innate childish reaction to putting one over on the casino.

The dealer and floorman both yelled, "Hey!" in unison as soon as it hit them that John was really running out of the casino with the chips. Then the floorman galvanized into action and started to give chase. Rene approached quickly to block him out. As John slid into an empty slot in the revolving door, he heard Rene's voice saying "Oh, I'm sorry...excuse me..." Rene had successfully hindered the floorman's progress.

John was out the door and down the steps in a matter of seconds; Gunther perched on the Vespa a few yards away. Just an instant before John had both feet level on the pavement, he did the unforgivable; chips began slipping out of his hand! In his haste he had neglected putting the chips in his sports jacket pocket as he should have the moment he grabbed them off the felt. Now three of them were trickling down onto the driveway and rolling away from the Vespa.

John swore loudly as he bent down to pick them up, attracting curious glances from people walking up and down the steps. Two of the chips John recovered easily but the third seemed to have a mind of its own as it took off spinning on its side downhill in front of the Vespa.

"Forget it!" Gunther hollered through his helmet, revving up the scooter. "Let's go!"

The floorman in his palm-treed shirt was now out the front door and coming down the steps. Raul bumped him going up but couldn't hold him forever, and John didn't see him coming because he was totally consumed with recovering that third chip. Gunther was still hollering when John finally got his fingers on it. He let the Vespa roll downhill to nullify the gap John had created between himself and the back seat of the scooter. The floorman had gotten dangerously close and a pit boss and security guard were just now shooting out of the main doors next to the revolving door.

Finally John hoisted himself onto the seat. Gunther released the clutch, throttled the gas, and with a pop and screech the Vespa lurched forward. At that instant, there was a harsh thumping sound followed by a scream. The floorman, apparently very agitated by the gall of John's actions, had lunged forward to take a fisted swing at John's head, but instead smashed his unprotected knuckles against Gunther's unforgiving helmet. John turned his head back in the direction of the casino as they descended the driveway. He watched the image of the floorman shrink until Gunther nosed into traffic on Tropicana Avenue.

Half an hour later, with everyone gathered at the Denny's next to the Sands, Gunther said, "See, I told you, John, it was a good thing I wore the helmet."

Word about that kind of blatant move, visually and audibly shocking (a guy swiping chips and running through a casino and out the door amid a chorus of panicked "Hey!"s), travels rapidly to all the casinos on the Strip. It was for that reason John and Gunther decided to do the next runaway immediately. The only delay was cashing out the black chips John had run out of the Tropicana. Gunther, Rene and Raul took a cab back to the Trop, had the cabbie wait in front while they went inside and got the cash, then motored back to the Denny's where John waited.

Since it was imperative to get the ball rolling again as quick as possible, a wise decision was to attempt the second runaway at the Holiday casino, which was just a hundred yards down the Strip from the restaurant. They had already cased the casino and its surrounding grounds and had deemed it one of the best for their operation. Even though it was mid-Strip with no convenient perpendicular sidestreet, ingress and egress were rather uncomplicated, with Las Vegas Boulevard only thirty feet from where the Vespa would be waiting.

Everything was laid out the same; each person would repeat his role from the Trop. The blackjack table John laid his twenty black chips on was ten feet from the door, another joke. Rene hung by the door like he was watching the action in the busy casino. Raul was just outside it. Gunther on the Vespa was rearing to go but hoping not too soon. The beauty of this design was that they'd be using a side door. There was hardly traffic moving through it. On the inside, besides the occasional security guard making his rounds, there was absolutely nothing that would impede an escape.

John had decided to abandon the ball cap. What was the difference, he reasoned, if they had him on videotape wearing the cap or not? He had no plans on getting caught and had no criminal record to which they could compare his photograph. Besides, if he kept doing runaways wearing the cap, they would be looking for a guy wearing a cap. Gunther agreed, so the Trop cap was tossed in the trunk of Rene's car.

A friendly Mexican pit boss named Miguel greeted John as soon as John's mighty stack of black chips appeared in his betting circle, again in centerfield on a full table. "How're the tables treating you?" he asked amiably.

"I could use a little luck," John said with his ingratiating smile.

"Well, good luck to you then, sir."

"Thank you, Miguel."

John turned his attention to the cards the dealer removed in succession from the shoe and snapped in a horseshoe arc onto the layout. A handsome king of diamonds landed in front of his chips. John stared at the red and blue paint on the card and prayed for another. He was then treated to a one-eyed jack, giving him a hard twenty. Very strong hand against the dealer's up card of 7. If the dealer had a 10 or an ace in the hole, John would be instant winners. If not, the dealer would have to draw out until he reached seventeen or busted.

Each player played his hand. When it came time for the dealer to play his, John felt a nervous twinge in the pit of his stomach. The dealer flipped over his hole card, a 9. He had sixteen and had to hit.

John tensed up like desert cactus. Please, he thought, anything but a 4 or 5.

The dealer pulled a card from the shoe and placed it next to his 9 and 7. It was a 6! Just enough to bust his hand and make John a winner.

John let out all his nervous energy in a joyful scream. Rene immediately flashed a "chin" through the door at Raul, the sign that John had won the hand. Raul removed his ball cap, giving Gunther the same good news. On receiving it, Gunther revved the scooter and drove off to park and wait until he was signalled back to the door for John's next bet.

Miguel the pit boss smiled warmly. "Nice hand, *amigo*. You got us good."

"Thanks," John said, thinking he'd get them better.

The dealer paid him four pretty purple chips, $2,000. John scooped them from the table with the twenty blacks and headed straight for the casino cage. He cashed out the purples, then walked through the casino to the sports book, where he met up with Rene. He gave Rene the cash, then proceeded back toward the table he'd just won on. Rene scurried back to his spot by the door and "chinned" Raul. Outside, Raul took off his hat, prompting Gunther's new arrival at the door.

John stepped up to the same blackjack table and saw someone had taken his spot while he was gone. The next spot over was open. Given the adrenaline rush of winning the previous bet, John couldn't care less from which spot he made his bet. He laid down the $2,000 in chips.

Miguel welcomed him back. "Good luck again, sir."

"Thanks," John said and smiled.

The dealer dealt John a nineteen, then drew out to eighteen for the house, another winning hand for John and a second reprieve from running out the door. Again he was paid with four purple chips.

"Would you like me to change your black chips into purples?" the dealer asked.

"That's all right, Robert," John said quickly, noting the dealer's nameplate. "They're my lucky black chips." John didn't give two shits about luck. He was thinking that he didn't want the team to be stuck cashing out purple chips after a runaway. He remembered that Gunther had warned him about casinos keeping track of their purple chips.

John carefully gathered his black and purple chips off the layout and went directly to the cage. At the same time, Rene flashed the "won" signal through the door outside to Raul, who again took off his cap to urge Gunther's retreat back to the waiting position. John cashed out the four purples, then met up with Rene in the sports book and handed him $2,000 for the second time in five minutes. Finally, the team's set-up signals bounced from Rene to Raul to Gunther, who again brought up the Vespa. It took but five minutes for them to be in position for John's third bet at what was becoming their lucky table.

Again seeing John's tall stack of black chips in the betting circle, Miguel said amicably, "You really like to hit and run," apparently not the slightest bit suspicious that John might be a card counter taking pot shots in the middle of the shoe, let alone that he might bolt out the door with $2,000 in losing black chips.

"Yeah, I do this all the time," John said cheerfully. "Keeps me in action longer."

"I'll bet," Miguel agreed, as if he liked to do the same thing.

The dealer acknowledged John with a smile, then surveyed his imposing black stack along with the puny red and green piles on the layout.

Blackjack! This time John received a $1,000 bonus for his ace and jack.

"This must really be your lucky night," Miguel gushed. Then when he saw John was again leaving after the single wager, he inquired with puzzlement, "You're going to leave right after a blackjack? Why not stay? You might hit a lucky streak."

John loved it because now he really had him. Miguel had bought his act – lock, stock, and barrel. Believed he was just a happy-go-lucky gambler who liked cherry-picking his spots for his huge bets. "That's okay. I like winning 'em one at a time."

Miguel shrugged. "More power to you."

The third payoff to Rene in the sports book was $3,000.

John's fourth hand at that table was dealt by a shapely California-blond relief dealer with pretty painted fingernails. She smiled when she busted her hand and paid him $2,000. She smiled wider five minutes later when she paid him again. John appreciated both smiles with a $25 tip.

He had now won five hands in a row! Rene's pockets were lined with $11,000 in cash, and the night was still young. John still carried the $2,000 in Holiday black chips and could hardly wait to get them back in the betting circle. Maybe this would turn out to be the dream streak that every gambler strived for. Maybe not, but whatever the case, John was certainly enjoying this.

The original dealer, Robert, was back from his break when John arrived for bet number six. "How's it going?" he asked.

"Couldn't be better," John replied happily. "I'm five for five."

Miguel came over. "Are you going to go for ten straight?"

John couldn't help but notice that Miguel seemed awful cheery for a pit boss whose pit had lost eleven grand, even chummy with the lucky gambler who'd won it. He imagined how Miguel's demeanor would change once he ran out the door with $2,000 in chips that were supposed to go into the dealer's rack. "Why not?" he said in a carefree tone. "Ten straight would make my day."

"Are you going to keep doing it one hand at a time?"

"Only till I lose," John said, which of course was no lie.

When John saw his pair of 8s staring at him from the layout along with the dealer's king, he realized quickly that the loss might be coming sooner rather than later. He reminded himself that he had to swipe the chips and run if it did. Having won five hands in a row, it might be easy to freeze up when losing the sixth, in a state of contentment that could be summarized by "What the hell, I'm still up eight grand."

But letting that happen would be a lapse that might cripple their entire operation before it really got off the ground. So when the dealer flipped over his hole card, a 5 that gave John a sudden rush of hope, but then slapped down a 6 for a perfect twenty-one, John swiped his stack of black chips like a bird of prey snatching a snake out of a pond and dashed toward the door.

He heard absolutely nothing behind him. Evidently Miguel and Robert were too stunned to react, or maybe their brains needed more time to process what happened. After all, it wasn't easy to believe that a guy who won five hands in a row and $11,000 would balk at letting the casino win back $2,000 of it, to the point of grabbing the chips and running out the door.

But that's what John had done, and as his palm reached for the handle, the chips safely tucked in his jacket pocket, he broke out into the same fit of laughing he'd displayed running out of the Tropicana.

The second he burst through the door, Gunther revved up the Vespa and John jumped on. He wrapped his arms around Gunther's lower torso as the scooter lurched forward and disappeared into the Saturday night traffic on Las Vegas Boulevard.

Two days later, Gunther had his Harley 1200. It wasn't brand spanking new but it was a beauty. With shiny red fenders, mirrorlike silver chrome and gold-spoked wheels, Gunther's new Shovelhead twin-engine motorcycle looked like it came out of Easy Rider, though even with the helmet Gunther did not look like Peter Fonda. The bike was so impressive that when John first saw it, even he considered using the money from his cut of the profits to buy a Harley and split Vegas to join the Hells Angels.

The cut they'd agreed on was that John and Gunther each got 35 percent while the Lopezs split the remaining 30 percent. This was deemed fair, as it was only the runner and driver who were risking their asses, not only of being captured but also of being injured or even killed during an escape. Despite Gunther's skills driving his new Harley, an accident instigated by other motorists during a chase could always claim them.

The new Harley would see its first runaway action the next weekend. Although aware that their flagrant casino moves would have caused some serious steam in the form of intercasino communication, John and Gunther figured that as long as they planned their runaways with care, they would stay one step ahead of casino security, who would not be able to mobilize in time to stop them.

The key was to take as little notice as possible when John laid down the bet. At the time in Vegas, twenty-four-hour video coverage on every table did not exist in casinos. The cameras inside the omnipresent bubbles jutting from casinos' ceilings rotated between four tables. Thus it was unlikely that either of the two runaways were caught on tape, although it was certain that some footage of John at a table was collected, especially at the Holiday casino where he'd been at the table six times.

They figured the word was out on a guy betting stacks of black $100 chips. This would mean that casino surveillance departments would have notified pit personnel to be on the lookout for anyone making that kind of bet and to notify them in turn when this was spotted. Then a set-up could be implemented to catch the runner in the act. And the driver as well, assuming they had footage of Gunther on the Vespa from either the Tropicana's or Holiday's outdoor surveillance cameras.

John came up with a great idea to subvert casino measures taken against them. Instead of making the same black-chip bets, he reasoned, why not use cash instead?

Gunther saw the good sense of it immediately. Casinos allowed gamblers to wager cash on the tables, provided it did not exceed the limit. A player could throw a wad of cash on the table just before a blackjack dealer was ready to deal or a roulette dealer ready to spin the ball, and announce, "Money plays!" The dealer would then call out, "Money plays up to the limit!" Then when the outcome was determined, the dealer would count out the cash. If it exceeded the limit, the excess would be returned to the player. The cash that stayed in play was then either paid or dropped in the table cash slot in accordance to whether it won or lost.

The beauty of this change was severalfold. Firstly, by using cash they didn't have to worry about cashing out chips after a runaway. Once the cash was swiped off the table, they didn't have to return to that casino, saving both time and exposure to risk. Secondly, removing cash from the layout in a hurry was easier than removing chips. Paper bills would not slide out of the hand and roll on the ground as chips did, evidenced by John's little mishap at the Tropicana.

But perhaps the most significant advantage of using cash was that if ever caught during an escape, neither the runner nor the driver would have any chips on his person from the casino they would be charged with ripping off. A good lawyer would certainly be able to work with that as no prosecuting attorney would be able to prove that the bills found in possession of the runner were those that had lain on a casino's blackjack table.

It was the north end of Caesars Palace that served as the arena for the inaugural Harley-cash runaway. John found a roulette table fifty feet from the rear doors and threw down $5,000 cash on red, announcing, "Money plays!" The dealer followed the script and cried, "Money plays to the limit!" and let the little ivory ball rip. It spun for several revolutions then dropped in number 34, red. The dealer counted out John's bills and paid him $5,000 in purple $500 chips. John proceeded directly to the main cage in the front end of the casino, avoiding the rear cage in view of the pit he'd just won at, and cashed out. The cash was passed to Rene, then the runaway team set up for another cash bet on the same roulette table.

It lost, John snatched up the cash and came flying out the door amid a loud cacophony of people shouting "Stop him!" and "Get him!". He jumped on the shiny red, silver-chromed Harley, and Gunther piloted them away underneath the moonlight into the neon showers of the Strip.

From there it was on to the Dunes. John lost his first $2,000 bet at a roulette table in the Oasis casino, a small oval-shaped dome that sat on the corner of the Dunes' property that fronted Flamingo Road and the Strip. For that move, Gunther had hidden himself in shrubbery at the edge of the building, then roared right up to the open arcade of the Oasis at the crucial moment to scoop up John. It was an extremely ballsy move that saw Gunther invoke his riding skills by jumping over a small pond and performing a wheelie while John held on for dear life.

But John loved it. He couldn't get enough of the escapes, laughing like a devil in the midst of each one. It grew to the point he actually enjoyed the runaways more than the tranquility of getting the cash. The adrenaline rush each time was more than he'd bargained for.

An hour after the Oasis, John ran out the main entrance of the Riviera, having swiped $3,000 in crisp $100 bills off a blackjack table after his hand lost. But not before he won two previous hands at the same table for $6,000 in profits.

At morningtwo in the morning the happy foursome began celebrating. They went to the Brewery, at the time Vegas's hottest nightclub, and partied until dawn with some of the town's hottest women. The next day they all suffered hangovers but it had been worth it. The day after that, Raul, posing as Rene, went to the 7-Eleven where Rene was the employee of record and told his boss to "take this job and shove it."

The following week John and Gunther spent rearranging their lives. John rented an apartment in a luxury complex called Paradise Villas. Gunther abandoned his hovel near UNLV for a new two-bedroom on the same floor as John's. As soon as they were settled in, they began mapping out their plan of attack for the immediate future. Over the next six months, Las Vegas was to be hammered by the casino runaway team with its Harley. On weekends they hit the busy casinos, often working the day shift in broad daylight to mix it up a little and avoid specific patterns. There were of course a few close shaves.

One midafternoon at the Hacienda, at the south tip of the Strip, a Metro patrol car pulled into the casino's lot the precise instant Gunther and John skidded by it on the Harley. The cop at the wheel of the cruiser might have ignored them had a Hacienda security guard on their tail not frantically thrown his arm in the direction of the fleeing casino thieves. The cruiser flipped a U-ee and flared its red and blue lights. But he was no match for a Harley Shovelhead 1200 with Gunther behind the handlebars.

A month after that, also on the day shift, John laid down a $2,000 bet at a table close to the door at the Union Plaza downtown. The table was close to the door but not the closest and John had so much confidence boosted by the feeling of invulnerability that he was willing to increase his amount of risk. When he put down the cash, an athletic-looking floorman seemed to get suspicious as the dealer began dealing the cards. John noticed the floorman move toward the direction of the door while watching his table. He interpreted it as the floorman's getting ready to intervene in case of a run, as if he'd suspected John would do exactly that if he lost the hand.

John prayed that he'd win the hand. If he lost, he could always let the dealer sweep the bills. But that thought emptied out of his head as fast as it had entered it. Surrendering was not in the spirit of the bet-and-run team, as they now referred to themselves.

The dealer drew a 9 to his twelve and reached out for John's bills; they were no longer there. John was off in a maddening dash for the door. But the floorman had the angle and sprinted toward him like a football safety cutting off the field from the ball carrier. No way John was going to be able to elude him, and John was a relatively small guy.

But his adrenaline was pumping him into a Hercules. When the floorman's arm latched around John's shoulder, John swatted it like a fly, then threw a cross-body block at the floorman that sent him careening into the glass, shattering it. John made his way through, hopped on the bike, and cried out to Gunther, "Move it! This one could be a serious problem if we're caught!"

They got away, but this particular runaway caused a lot of heat in the desert. The next move they set up two weeks later at the Aladdin drew tons of heat the second John made his bet. The pit boss instantly picked up the phone on the center podium, no doubt to alert surveillance and security. John, as much as he didn't want to, aborted the move, scooped his bills off the layout and exited the casino, getting into a cab instead of mounting Gunther's waiting Harley. Gunther understood what had happened and calmly drove away. The team met up at Gunther's Paradise Villas apartment and evaluated the situation.

The result was their decision to hit the road. Like Peter Fonda and Dennis Hopper did in *Easy Rider*, Gunther Rintz and John Roy biked up to Reno. Rene and Raul Lopez took a plane. They met up in a motel and planned their course of attack against "America's biggest little city."

Reno proved to be an excellent stomping ground for the bet-and-run team. Its main downtown casino area was laden with little crooks and alleyways that afforded good cover while Gunther waited on the Harley and better ins and outs during escapes. They had one major near-disaster when a pedestrian cut suddenly in front of their escaping Harley, causing Gunther to lose control when he veered sharply to avoid him. The bike wiped out and both driver and runner were spilled harshly into the street, but without injury. John, who was helmetless, managed to protect his head at the expense of bruises to his hands and wrists, but no bones were broken. They hopped back on the Harley and disappeared through a few nooks and crannies before the Reno police had the chance to grab them.

They earned $20,000 in Reno, then returned to Vegas. They let a month go by before returning to work. In the interim, Gunther performed the body work needed to get his Harley in the sparkling shape it had been in before the wipeout in Reno. It was agreed by each team member that all expenses related to the maintenance of the bike would come off the top of their bankroll. Nobody got chintzy.

The first move after the layoff was slated for the Sahara, another prime Strip casino with a beautiful escape route fashioned somewhat after that at the Tropicana. Like their inaugural casino, the Sahara sat at an intersection between Las Vegas Boulevard and a major sidestreet, Sahara Avenue, again the southeast corner. The escape route was basically the same, perhaps even easier at the Sahara. Gunther would be positioned on the Harley outside the main entrance, from where he had only thirty yards to drive straight ahead to the right hand turn onto Sahara Road eastbound.

But when John laid his twenty $100 bills over the betting circle, he picked up on something weird: too little steam. *Some* steam always accompanied a large cash bet on a blackjack layout, especially when it was put there in the middle of a shoe, where it was often presumed to be the wager of a big-time card counter signalled to the table by an unknown cohort. But here, there was no steam at all. Everyone was just a bit *too* cool for John's comfort. When the dealer had called out, "Money plays up to the limit," neither the floorman nor the pit boss, who'd both been leaning in idle conversation against the podium in the center of the pit, turned his head to acknowledge John's $2,000 bet. It was as though he were wagering the table minimum. John wondered if the Sahara had already been alerted about their gig and was playing the tune of a set-up.

The dealer dealt the hand. The non-steam intensified as each player received his first card. The floorman and pit boss were still chatting away as if they didn't give a shit. None of the bosses in the neighboring pits were on the phone. There was absolutely no intensity anywhere in the casino. John didn't like it at all.

He looked down the pit on both sides – nothing. He looked back at Rene, who would be turning the corner to block a pursuing floorman's path, and saw nothing near or behind him that indicated steam. He looked through the doors to Raul outside. Raul was taking off his cap – and then John saw the Harley rolling to the door. There were no steps to go down. It was a flat dash of about twenty feet to the door, another ten feet to the bike – and gone.

But John was growing more and more uncomfortable with this overly relaxed atmosphere. The players all had their first card; the dealer was about to deal the seconds. John had to make a decision. Fast. Were they setting him up?

He never game them the chance. Before the dealer snapped John's second card onto the layout, John took off, taking everybody – including Rene – by surprise. It takes the human brain a full second to comprehend when it processes a sudden, unexpected image and a fraction of one to send a signal in reaction. John was almost at the door when he heard a cacophony of "Stop him!" and "Call security!" Suddenly, two guys in street clothes – who'd been sitting at the very same blackjack table John had stood at! – gave chase. It *was* a goddamn set-up. And it wasn't only a set-up inside the casino; it stretched outside. Three of the four valet parkers in uniform outside the Sahara's main entrance were security agents in disguise. All three had been caught off guard and weren't ready by the time John was outside the door. It was only the *real* valet parker who reacted quickly enough to jump back into the car he had just pulled up to the main entrance for a now protesting customer and follow them down Sahara Avenue.

It was like a real chase scene in the movies. John was barking at Gunther, "Faster! Faster!" Gunther, incredibly cool under pressure, barked back, "Relax! Relax!" He made a series of stunt-like moves along Sahara, and when they turned left against oncoming traffic onto Maryland Parkway, they finally lost the valet parker wanna-be hero.

They escaped by the enamel of their teeth.

Back at Gunther's apartment, they realized that they must have been under surveillance before they'd gone to the Sahara, which meant that it was very possible his apartment was no longer safe. Same thing for John's as it was just a few doors down from Gunther's. So they abandoned both and holed up in the apartment the Lopezs shared on the other side of town.

They knew they were done with the runways in Vegas. At least for a while. The logical conclusion was to hit the road again. At the time, there were no casinos between Nevada and Atlantic City, so if they wanted to take their daredevil show elsewhere, it would have to be at that eastern seaboard resort. Las Vegas to Atlantic City, however, was a long haul, even on a beautiful Harley Davidson motorcycle. So they travelled together as a team, took a plane to Philadelphia and rented a car at the airport, which they drove to Atlantic City.

In 1981, a handful of casinos had already sprouted up on the town's famous boardwalk. But there were a few factors that made the runways a bit more difficult than in Las Vegas. The first was that the casinos, much larger than those in Vegas, were set deeper inside the hotels that housed them. No tables were right up against the doors, so John would have a longer way to run to get to the getaway bike, which would be the Kawasaki 450 they rented for the occasion. Also, only boardwalk escapes were feasible. All other main and side entrances of casinos were just way too far from the tables.

Another negative factor was that the New Jersey Casino Control Commission did not permit cash wagering on gaming tables, thus they would have to revert to using stacks of black chips. A final facet working against them was that Atlantic City in general saw more street crime than its Nevada counterparts, especially in the vicinities near casinos. Just a block off Pacific Avenue, the thoroughfare through the city's casinos, was Atlantic Avenue and its inherent twenty-four-hour street crime. John and Gunther certainly didn't want to mix with any of it.

The first east coast runaway happened through the boardwalk exit of Caesars Boardwalk Regency, the Atlantic City version of Caesars Palace. John had bet his stack of twenty black chips at the table closest to the boardwalk doors, still a hundred feet away. He'd won the first hand, got paid the $2,000, cashed out and dumped the cash to Rene. He then promptly lost the second hand, grabbed up his stack, flew out the back door to where Gunther waited on the Kawasaki.

The boardwalk escape was more dangerous than those in Vegas since motorized vehicles not belonging to official agencies were not permitted under any circumstances anywhere on the boardwalk. There were also substantial police patrols: some on foot, others on bicycles, still others on motorcycles, and even occasional automobiles inching their way slowly through the incessant crowds strolling amid the casinos, arcades, amusement piers and taffy stores. Thus the coordination of the on-the-road bet-and-run team had to be perfect. Gunther could not be sitting for more than a minute anywhere on the boardwalk. He would be accosted in no time by police and given a ticket, or worse the cops might stumble right into the path of an escape.

When John had given the chin indicating he was ready to place the bet, Rene had signalled beyond to Raul near the doors, then Raul exited the casino, walked along the boardwalk to the first perpendicular sidestreet where Gunther sat on the bike behind a garbage dumpster. Then Gunther moved cautiously onto the boardwalk while Raul hustled back inside Caesars to give Rene the "go" signal. Rene then chinned John that they were all in position.

Gunther had been on the boardwalk around a minute when John came flying through one of Caesars' rear exit doors and jumped on the back seat. Gunther took off but had to navigate carefully through the throngs of people in order to reach the sidestreet on the other side of Caesars. They had only gone thirty feet when they heard hysterical shouts behind them from Caesars' security guards hurtling through the doors. But when John turned around and saw the angry men, he realized they did not see him. The endless waves of weaving and twisting bodies in both directions were such that the guards had no clue. Gunther was able to bob and weave underneath the flocks of singing sea gulls to the edge of the building, then glide down the wooden ramp and disappear inland.

Later that afternoon, John made similar dashes from the Sands and Bally's. They'd been fairly lucky and picked up $6,000 in profits for their trouble. At night they went to the far south end of the casino run and had escapes from the Golden Nugget and Tropicana, both without having won a single hand.

But the real problem came the next day, another beautiful spring afternoon in the town beside the boardwalk. After winning six hands in a row, breaking their all-time streak set back in Vegas at the Holiday casino nine months earlier, John bolted on the first loser after his record-setting $12,000 win at the Claridge. The escape was clean, though they decided to let some time pass before cashing out the $2,000 in black chips John had run with. They'd wait until the next shift when the heat cooled.

But the Claridge had been very pissed off, and by that time the word had been out about the daring bet-and-run team. They knew about the motorcycle escapes. When Rene was standing on line at the casino cage to cash out half the black chips, Raul behind him, he noticed something strange. The woman in front of him had just laid four black Claridge chips on the counter in front of the teller, presenting them for payment. But they were different black chips, not the same as those he had in his hands. He double-checked to make sure, and was then certain. The rims of the woman's black chips were speckled red; Rene's were speckled yellow. Rene told Raul to hold off cashing out while he checked the black chips in several of the tables' chip racks. Good thing he did. He found they were all speckled red. What the hell had happened? Rene and Raul left the casino without cashing out.

It was Gunther who figured it out. "They pulled all the blacks off the tables and locked them up in the cage," he explained when they gathered in the boardwalk breeze, leaning on a railing with a bird's-eye view of the beach and ocean. "I'd heard that casinos have backup series of chips that they use in instances such as this. I wasn't sure they really did, but now obviously I am."

It was true. All casinos had a complete series of reserve chips for all denominations. The main reason for this was to be able to remove the primary series of chips when doing so would foil or snare a criminal operation, without having to suspend casino operations. One instance where this was routinely done was the case of chip snatchers, those desperate (usually losing gamblers) people who grabbed a handful of $500 or $1,000 chips and tried to get out the door. Few did, but those lucky ones got very unlucky when they tried to cash out their ill-gotten chips and were stunned by the handcuffs biting their wrists before they realized what hit them.

"So what do we do?" John asked. "Just eat the two grand?"

Before Gunther could come up with a viable answer, John had another of his brazen ideas. "We gotta come up with a good story as to how we got those chips," he said. "They can't be the only primary black chips on the loose."

John's idea grew into a plan to send Rene to the Claridge cage with ten of the twenty chips. If the teller cashed them out indifferently then Raul would follow behind and cash out the ten that remained. If questioned, Rene would say that his girlfriend living in Mexico had forgotten to cash them out before leaving town and authorized him to do so. No matter how it worked out, they were confident that Rene couldn't be busted because he was not the person their surveillance department would have on tape. Even if it could be proved that only twenty black chips were unaccounted for, which would be proof that the chips Rene had in his possession were part of those wagered on the runaway, there would still be some wiggle room for Rene. He could get out of hot water by saying some stranger approached him on the boardwalk and offered to sell him $2,000 worth of Claridge chips at whatever discount for whatever reason. That Rene had been inside the Claridge when the runaway went down was not a problem. He'd been wearing a ball cap and had never been near the table John had victimized.

It turned out they had been right about Rene not getting busted – but it cost them two thousand bucks to find out. No sooner had Rene placed the ten yellow-speckled black chips on the counter than the woman teller scooped them off, disappeared into the back and returned with the cage manager *and* the casino manager. They grilled Rene as to where he got the chips. Rene played it cool and recounted the rehearsed girlfriend-from-Mexico story.

"What's your girlfriend's name?" the casino manager asked glibly.

Rene shot off the first that came to him: Rosa Ramirez.

"What's her birthday?"

Rene was as taken aback by that as he'd been by the guy's first question. He stuttered and stammered then finally managed to blurt, "January first1st, nineteen-sixty1960," because it came to him like the first page of the calendar.

The casino manager smiled as he made out a receipt in the name of Rosa Ramirez and passed it to Rene. "Give this to your girlfriend," he said smugly. "She can come claim her thousand dollars anytime she likes within thirty days. She must have documented ID with proof of her birthday."

"No *problema*," Rene squeaked, just wanting to get his ass out of there while he still could.

When he turned to leave, the casino manager cracked wisely, "If you can come up with a Rosa Ramirez with a driver's license saying she was born on January 1st, 1960, we'll give you another thousand dollars for the ten black chips you're holding out."

Needless to say, their bet-and-run scam had worn out its welcome in Atlantic City.

That night drinking beers on the hard, wet sand of the shoreline, John and Gunther chucked the remaining chips in the ocean. They did it with a laugh.

The bet-and-run scam continued on and off until Labor Day weekend, 1982, when John ran out of a casino with a losing bet for the last time. That farewell bet-and-run move was made in the Dunes. When it was all said and done, the scam netted some $400,000.

Two months later, I met Gunther at the Denny's Dunes. A bunch of casino grifters were milling around the tables telling war stories and his came out. I thought their bet-and-run scam was hilarious. I wanted to meet John, but Gunther said that he had returned to New York. From time to time after that, I would run into Gunther at the Denny's and say hello. When several months went by without seeing him, I began wondering what had become of him.

But that fateful April day in 1983, when I saw John dart across the front of the Denny's with the entire Dunes security force in tow, I should have guessed that Gunther was nearby on his Harley.

CHAPTER 2

THE GREAT CASINO IDENTITY THEFT/CREDIT SCAM

When the crime of the twenty-first century began taking shape in the mid-1990s, one of its first testing grounds was in casinos, but only those that issued its gamblers credit lines. The crime was identity theft and the earliest organized identity thieves were the cold-blooded Russian gangs that plied their trade in the United States before leaving it for the cloak-and-dagger safety of the Internet. Not far behind them was the good old Cosa Nostra, the Italian Mafia that with Bugsy Siegel had pioneered Las Vegas in the late 1940s and retained its foothold ever since, still maintaining a stranglehold on several illicit enterprises such as loansharking, prostitution, drug-trafficking, and its mother lode of dirty cash: illegal bookmaking.

Droves of Italian–American mobsters migrated to Vegas with each passing decade. They came from every major US city and Mafia family. In the 1950s, they brought in their already corrupt unions and established them at the heart of every hotel-related business from construction to hauling trash containers. In the 1960s, they began large-scale casino-skimming operations, sneaking duffel bags filled with cash out of casino count rooms before it could be counted. By the mid-1970s, while count rooms got skimmed downstairs, organized Mafia burglary rings cleaned out hotel suites upstairs.

But in the early 1980s, a new Clark County Sheriff named John Moran made it his business to oust the mob from Las Vegas. And he quickly put noticeable dents in its breastplate of criminal activity. By the end of 1982, Moran's first year in office, Las Vegas Boulevard had been ridded of the brigades of streetwalkers that had freely solicited sex for thirty years. A few years later, Moran, working with joint FBI and Metro organized crime task forces, put Tony Spilatro and his "Hole in the Wall Gang" out of business. The moniker came from Spilatro's crew's m.o. of drilling through walls in hotel rooms to gain entry to neighboring rooms on either side, where cash, jewelry and other valuables were purloined while the absent guests gambled, dined or took in a show downstairs.

By the end of the 1980s, the mob had taken a vast array of hits from law enforcement on every front. With the barrage came an invasion of corporate raiders. Before 1990, Vegas casinos had virtually fallen from Mafia control and reinvented themselves into legitimate corporate entities whose boards had chairmen that dined with presidents and kings. Thus the mobster population actually began decreasing as the town underwent its most explosive expansion in not only its own history but also that of any other American city.

In December 1995, unconcerned by the changing image of Las Vegas, two members of the Cosa Nostra immigrated there while scores of others passed them by in the opposite direction. Their names were Joey and Frankie Roselli. They were brothers in their early forties with completely different physiques. Joey was a strapping six-footer with a full head of thick black hair. Frankie was half a foot shorter with wispy, receding strands and a goatee that partially camouflaged his baldness. Each was as gruff as the other and both were made-members of a New Jersey Mafia crime family. "Made-members" got that way by killing somebody.

But the Rosellis did not arrive in Vegas to do any killing. They came to attend a wedding: not one of the thousands that took place in the town's storied little wedding chapels, but rather the first that joined the hands of identity theft and casino credit. It was to be the most spectacular wedlock Las Vegas had ever seen.

The idea had come to Joey the previous January, while watching the Super Bowl with Frankie in the living room of Joey's spacious New Jersey home. Their wives and kids were vacationing in Florida while the men tended to family business. Joey had been extremely pissed off because he lost the $100,000 he'd bet on the game long before it ended. Always a sucker for the underdog, he'd bet the San Diego Chargers, the weakest team in years to qualify for the Super Bowl. What really got his goat was that Frankie had bet the San Francisco 49ers, who had a three-touchdown lead against the lowly Chargers before halftime. That Frankie was gloating over his measly $5,000 win didn't help matters.

Barely thirty seconds after the game, Joey's bookmaker, who was also his Mafia captain, called to say he would stop by to pick up the hundred grand on Tuesday. Joey slammed the phone down in disgust.

"Why you always bettin' them damn underdogs?" Frankie asked from his easy chair, as he always asked on Sundays during football season.

Joey sunk back further in his plush leather sofa. "Because I'm a fuckin' idiot. That's why. You woulda thought I'd've learned my goddamn lesson by now, wouldn't ya?"

"Well, if you gotta bet every Sunday, maybe next year you should be bettin' the goddamn favorites." It wasn't bad advice. Joey's football picks next year could certainly not get worse.

But he had other thoughts on his mind. Contrary to public perception of Mafia soldiers and the fact that he was less than well spoken, Joey was an avid reader. He devoured *Time* and

Newsweek in addition to sports magazines. He also faithfully read the *Wall Street Journal*.

That's where he'd learned about the incipient proliferation of identity theft. The Russian mob, which he hated, was manufacturing credit cards with stolen identities faster than his own mob could hijack trucks and rob warehouses. What appealed to him about this new "paper" crime was that it entailed no violence and seemed to be a risk-free enterprise.

During the post-game wrap-up show, Joey zapped off the TV. He saw the surprised expression on his brother's face. "Frankie," he announced as if he'd finally found the wager that was a lock winner, "I'm gonna tell you how we're gonna make a major score. And we ain't gonna give none of the profits to the *capo*."

"That's against the code of conduct, ain't it?" Frankie said with a tinge of trepidation. Screwing the *capo* could mean a bullet in the head.

"The fuck it is, but what's the goddamn *capo* givin' us?"

Frankie nodded. "He sure ain't payin' off your gamblin' debts."

"You can say that again."

"So what racket's gonna make us rich, Joey?"

"The casinos."

Frankie looked at his brother like he was half-cocked. "You think we're gonna win moolah at the casinos?"

Joey shook his head with a wiseguy grin. "We ain't gonna win jack shit. We're gonna steal it."

"With guns?"

Joey shook his head in the same style. "With credit lines."

"We ain't got no credit," protested Frankie.

"No, we don't. But we're gonna pull off a big credit scam."

Frankie had been a mobster for a long time but still could not fathom what his older brother was talking about. He stared at him blankly.

"Listen, Frankie, credit lines in casinos are easy to get, easier than friggin' Visa cards. All we gotta do is come up with some phony dope for their credit departments, you know, whole life histories and shit, and then we just go there and sign markers. Then we get the money and we don't pay back no markers."

Joey explained the basics of obtaining casino credit. People seeking it went through the same process used by everyday financial institutions screening applicants for bankcards, although certain requirements were unique to casinos. An application had to be filled out and submitted to the casino's credit department. It contained the personal information requirements found on bank applications: full name, Social Security number, date of birth, past and current addresses, and that vital piece of security information: your mother's maiden name. All that data was then entered into the nation's central credit databanks to ascertain its veracity.

The second section of the application demanded your employment history. You had to list jobs, businesses owned or any other relevant financial information that showed you were creditworthy. You had to provide proof of salaries and other forms of income you stated on the application. Casinos took great pains to verify your financial security. They were not in the business of loaning money to gamblers only to find out later they were deadbeats who couldn't or wouldn't pay it back. Which amounted to exactly what Joey had in mind: taking a free shot at the casinos.

Thirdly, you had to provide details about your bank accounts and specify from which you intended to pay your markers, the legally negotiable instrument that resembled a check and was made out to the casino's order and signed by the gambler before he received his chips. The grace period for payment was normally thirty days. If not satisfied, dunning letters and phone calls demanding payment quickly followed.

"I understand all that already," Frankie said, moving into the kitchen to stir the spaghetti in the pot and whip up the sauce. "But how the hell we gonna convince any casino to give me and you credit? The way my fuckin' wife spends money, I can't even pay off my MasterCard."

Joey laughed and went into the kitchen, where he couldn't resist dabbing his finger into the simmering pasta sauce. "Shit," he said, "at least your wife taught ya how to cook. Mine ain't good for nothin'."

"I'll make you some eggplant Parmesan tomorrow."

"Frankie, you know the IDs we got in the safe-deposit box in the bank?"

"You said never to touch that unless we needed to get outta the country in a hurry."

"Well, I didn't know about identity theft then. We're gonna use them names because they belonged to guys who were upstanding citizens with perfect credit histories. They probably never been to Vegas, so nobody out there knows 'em. We get credit in their names and bust out the casinos. Whaddaya think?"

Frankie had his own finger in the sauce. When he finished licking it, he smiled and said, "I like it."

"What, the sauce?"

"No, Joey, your idea!" If we can get rich off it, I think it's a great idea."

Six years earlier, when the federal government began its relentless pursuit of John Gotti and other New York and New Jersey mobsters, there had been tremendous heat on the Rosellis' criminal activities. The feds were shaking the branches of their illegal businesses and lots of incriminating evidence were falling to the ground. Prosecution under the RICO statutes seemed imminent. The Rosellis had become very concerned and begun making preparations to flee the country. The key to escaping resided in phony identity, not fake identity but *real* fake identity. This meant identity documents verifying not only who they were but also histories of membership in society that included good banking and credit records.

The Rosellis had paid $25,000 each to a Princeton University student for the packets. The student, whose father was also a New Jersey mobster, had simply scoured the obituary pages of major newspapers for those who'd died young and wealthy and left behind good reputations and probable spotless credit histories. It was easy enough to determine the social status someone had from an obituary. From there, the student manipulated public vital records offices, the Social Security Administration and TRW, which at the time was the major credit reporting bureau for the United States. This was all before the Internet age and was done without a single keystroke on a computer.

"So if we ever need to get outta the country again," Joey said, "we'll just get a hol' of our boy to give us new sets of ID."

The next day, the Rosellis got to work. They went to the bank, entered their safe-deposit boxes and removed the passports, driver's licenses and birth certificates that hadn't seen the light of day in six years. The passports were still valid but the driver's licenses had to be renewed. The same afternoon they went to the Department of Motor Vehicles and renewed them. When they got back to the house, Joey made his initial fact-finding call to the MGM Grand credit department. He asked the MGM switchboard operator to put him through to the casino's VIP services, figuring that if he came off as a very important person, they would take him for one.

A woman identifying herself as Barbara came on the line.

"I'd like to apply for casino credit," Joey said politely, in a tone and manner that was completely foreign to him. "I would like to get some information on how to do it."

"I can take all the information from you now and pass it on to the credit department. They'll get back to you within three business days."

"I don't have all my records with me," Joey said quickly. "Can you tell me what I'd need?"

"Sure. They require your full name, date of birth and Social Security number. Then your current address and telephone number, and of course employment and banking information with proof of income. You must also specify a bank account to be used for remittances to the credit department. That account must have a history of activity dating back at least six months, with an average balance deemed appropriate for whatever credit line you're seeking."

Well, whatever the hell that meant, Joey would make sure the money was there, but now he knew they had at least a six-month wait for approval because they didn't yet have the bank accounts.

"Is there anything else I can do for you, sir?" Barbara asked.

Joey said no and thanked her. "Okay," he said to Frankie in his normal voice, "we got some work to do."

That work entailed bringing two dead men back to life and re-establishing them in the financial credit world. Their names were Charles Kent and Bill Hearn. They had been residents of the state of Florida, where all their fiduciary accounts had originated. Even though they'd been dead for a decade, that fiduciary world did not know that. Neither did the credit world. When people died, their financial histories were usually consumed by the next of kin or they simply dissolved. In neither case was the country's credit system notified.

Joey became Charles Kent. The physical description on Kent's license matched Joey's to a tee, right down to the dark brown eyes. Same for the physical traits indicated on Hearn's license, on which was laminated Frankie's mug photo with the goatee.

With their passports and driver's licenses in the names of their alter egos, they marched into three different banks and in each opened accounts in both Kent's and Hearn's names. In a branch of the First Bank of New Jersey, Joey deposited $9,900 in cash into Charles Kent's new business account. Down the road at a Valley Bank branch, Frankie made an identical cash deposit in Hearn's new business account. In the two other personal accounts in both names, they made only minimal deposits. The reason for making the large deposits in different banks was to avoid any coincidences that might red-flag them on computer screens in Las Vegas casino credit departments. Two persons applying for credit at the same time using the same bank might alert examiners that something was up.

Each week like clockwork, Joey and Frankie made large cash deposits into the business accounts, always less than $10,000, the amount at which banks were required to notify the IRS of cash transactions. The last thing a pair of mobsters setting up a huge scam involving banks needed was to be entangled with the IRS.

The next order of business was to set up exactly that: their business. Kent and Hearn would each have their own enterprise – a real operating business entity. At first they'd contemplated hiring an answering service whose employees could confirm spoon-fed information to credit departments calling for verification of employment histories and salaries. At the time, the cell-phone revolution was just on the horizon and answering services still flourished. Therefore, using them was certainly a viable mode of operation.

But it was Frankie who came up with a better one. "Why not open a real freakin' business?" he suggested over a plate of calamary in a Little Italy clamhouse. "With real employees and everything."

Joey stopped twirling the load of pasta on his fork. "Whaddaya talkin' about?"

"I mean we start up a real business. You know, like an import–export company. Only we don't really import or export nothin'. We just make them casinos out there in Vegas think we do. We even rent an office somewhere and hire a secretary."

Joey's dark eyes came alight as he absorbed what Frankie had said. It was simply brilliant. Instead of having to depend on answering-service people, who had many clients' lines to answer and were therefore prone to mistakes, they could hire someone to answer only their phone. When the casinos' credit departments called for verifications on Kent and Hearn, the person in their employ would furnish the information they'd been instructed to by their phony bosses. Joey could picture it happening clear as day. It was the perfect set-up. Then once the scam he envisioned was over, the business would be abandoned.

They would need two separate companies, one each for Kent and Hearn. In Fort Lee, New Jersey, an upscale town just across the George Washington Bridge from Manhattan, they rented a thousand square feet of office space that contained two offices and a reception area furnished with a built-in circular counter. They had a phone line installed, ordered file cabinets, desks and swivel chairs for the offices. All this before having either a business name or stated business interest. In fact, when the commercial leasing agent asked what business they were in, Frankie cracked that they didn't know yet.

But within days they decided they would be international investment consultants, Kent in the Fort Lee office and Hearn in the second office they rented in Manhattan. The choice of affairs was well suited to deflect suspicion and foot traffic into their offices. As international businessmen they would not be expected to be in the office much, which would allay suspicions on the part of an employee who actually did work on the premises. Secondly, an international investment consulting firm would hardly attract passersby to have a look inside. Had they decided to front as a travel agency or garment concern, people looking for vacation packages or department store buyers for new clothing lines might roll in off the streets.

The last stage of the set-up was finding residences for Vegas's soon-to-be high rollers. They would have preferred to use post office boxes instead, because all they really needed was home addresses. But post office boxes could be easily identified as such, and they couldn't have credit departments thinking they slept with their mail. The next idea was renting cheap apartments – it wasn't like they'd be living there. But the problem was that street addresses could be matched to specific levels of the socio-economic structure. It would not look good to examiners if someone applying for a large casino credit line lived in a low-income area. Another thought was to rent rooms in houses in exclusive neighborhoods, but then they'd have to contend with other tenants who could always cause problems and even turn into police informants and trial witnesses. No, they would have to splurge for their fictitious residences just as they had for their offices.

Posing as Charles Kent, Joey Roselli leased a condominium from a private owner in the Horizon House, a stylish Fort Lee high-rise set on a ridge with spectacular views of the Hudson River. He took the smallest one-bedroom but it still went for $1,700 a month. Frankie found his digs in a similar building but at $400 less because it was located in Edgewater, New Jersey, another riverfront town but not quite as trendy as Fort Lee. Both apartments would contain but a telephone, and the lines would always be on call-forward to the Rosellis' real residences. Not a solitary piece of furniture would be placed in either, as it was decided that the set-up apartments would only be entered when necessary. Since the mailboxes were in the lobbies, the only time that might be was when management needed to enter the apartments for some reason. In the event of such occasions, they would just tell curious management personnel that the apartments had been rented for their kids who were away schooling in Europe and wouldn't be moving in for six months. As long as the rent got paid, nobody cared anyway.

Six months. That was the key. While the balances in Kent's and Hearn's business accounts steadily climbed over that period, the Rosellis kept building up their elaborate sham. The business operated by Kent in Fort Lee was named Jade East Global Investments, Ltd. Joey had paid county fees to incorporate and obtained a business license, which he hung on the wall of one of the inner offices. He even registered with the Chamber of Commerce. Frankie did the same for Hearn in Manhattan. Their second entity was called Worldwide Western Investment Group. They'd arrived at that name after being frustrated by repetitive business-name searches that told them the name they had entered was already taken. So by correctly thinking that Worldwide did not go with Western, they finally found an available one that sounded good even though it was thoroughly ridiculous. How could something worldwide be western?

Next they put help-wanted ads seeking a receptionist/secretary in the newspapers. Joey conducted the interviews on behalf of Jade East Global while Frankie handled those for Worldwide Western. Joey hired a personable Latin woman named Maria. Frankie gave the job to Fran, a part-time student working to pay for her night classes. They explained to each secretary that their duties were mainly to answer the phones, take messages, sort the mail and, most important, simply show up. They were told that no one would be looking over their shoulders. They could do whatever they wanted as long as they were punctual in arriving at nine o'clock and not leaving before five o'clock. They could listen to the radio and even watch TV. Joey had retrieved two Sony televisions from their warehouse of stolen goods and put them in the offices.

Before Maria and Fran reported to work the first day, Joey

and Frankie realized that they had to create the impression that their offices were somehow involved in affairs pertaining to what their businesses were supposed to be. The first thing they did to satisfy that requirement was to take out subscriptions to the *Wall Street Journal, Forbes Magazine* and other periodicals of a financial nature. These were delivered to the offices. Then to create the incoming mail usually associated with business offices, they unleashed a constant barrage of mailings to each office. Not just from New York and New Jersey. Every other week, either Joey or Frankie would fly to a different American city just to drop these letters in an airport mailbox. When they arrived at their offices, they would be postmarked from all over the country. When their wives took a two-month trip to Europe, they carried hundreds of letters in their suitcases. Thus Jade East Global and Worldwide Western received its share of international mailings. All this was done solely for the benefit of Maria and Fran, neither of whom would find any traces of similarity with the incoming letters. Joey and Frankie used an assortment of envelopes: different sizes, shapes, colors, printing and handwriting, all with the names and addresses of the senders, which were real companies they selected from directories.

The final coup de grace was the phone calls Maria and Fran received in their offices, no fewer than a dozen each. Maria in Fort Lee would take a message from Mr. Sukahara in Japan, who wanted to know whether he should invest in a certain Asian stock. Then it would be Mr. Wilfredo from Brazil asking about a diamond venture in South Africa. Or Mr. Williams from Memphis seeking advice on a certain pharmaceutical company's financial standing.

Naturally all those calls came from either Joey or Frankie, aided by their talents imitating foreign accents and a voice-changer gizmo bought from a spy shop. At the end of each business day, or every two or three business days, Joey called Maria

Maria in his normal voice to get his messages, as did Frankie to get his from Fran.

In the first two months, they often stopped by in person to see how the women were doing. One time in Fort Lee Joey got a shock. Stepping off the elevator into Jade East's reception area, he found Maria in the company of two Fort Lee police detectives. Joey's heart missed a few beats, but he began breathing easier on learning the cops were there investigating a burglary that had occurred in a neighboring office. They wanted to know if Maria had seen anyone suspicious in the corridor.

The six months went by without a hitch. Joey stopped betting on sports and Frankie cut out gambling altogether. Why bet, he reasoned, when he would be stealing from the casinos. When December rolled around, Joey received a surprising question when he stopped by the Jade East offices. While he was pretending to go through the mail she'd just handed him, Maria asked, "Mr. Kent, when and where is our office Christmas party going to be?"

Joey stuttered only slightly, as he was as quick on his feet as they came, then said, "I'm sorry, Maria, but this year we're not having one because too many of our employees are Jewish."

Maria's face took on a bizarre expression but she didn't complain.

On December 7, 1995, the fifty-fourth anniversary of the attack on Pearl Harbor, Joey called VIP services at the MGM Grand. The woman who answered had a familiar voice and when she said her name was Barbara, Joey remembered it was the same woman whom he spoke with six months prior.

"My name is Charles Kent. I'd like to apply for casino credit, please."

"Have you ever had a credit line with us before, Mr. Kent?" Barbara asked.

This was the one and only danger facing the Rosellis in their scam. As Charles Kent had been dead for ten years and a resident of Florida, it was unlikely that he ever did have an MGM credit line. Joey had contacted the college kid who'd sold them Kent's and Hearn's IDs. The kid said that he'd obtained copies of both their credit reports while putting together the document-packets and that neither contained accounts that might have related to casino credit. But it was not foolproof. Seven years had passed since he'd done the research. Plus he couldn't be sure if casino credit accounts even appeared on credit bureaus' reports. This was the one chance they'd have to take. If the information Joey gave conflicted with what was in the MGM databank then the scam would be blown out of the water before it set sail.

"No, I haven't, ma'am," Joey answered smoothly.

She took down all the information that she'd said she would six months earlier. Joey gave the Fort Lee addresses of Kent's residence and office, along with the phone numbers. He gave his birthdate, Social Security number and Kent's mother's maiden name, which happened to be as Italian as his: Costello. He gave her his banking information and specified that his First Bank of New Jersey business account would be used to write checks in payment for markers not picked up before leaving the casino. She informed him that on his first visit to the MGM, he needed to bring a voided check from that account. Just for their files.

Then after all the personal and business questions were finished, Barbara popped the big one: "How much credit would like, Mr. Kent?"

Joey thought of the balance in Kent's business account. Like a devout churchgoer making his Sunday donations to his faith, Joey had made his Monday deposits to his bank account. For six months. There was now over a hundred grand sitting impatiently idle but ready to do great harm to Vegas's coffers. He figured that since that particular account would be used to pay the markers, and that its average balance for the six months would have been around half its current balance, $50,000, he'd ask for half of that.

"I guess I'd like a twenty-five-thousand dollar line," he said.

"Very well, Mr. Kent. I will submit your application to our credit department promptly. They should get back to you before the week's out."

"Thank you, ma'am."

"Thank you, Mr. Kent. And we hope to see you soon."

Joey replaced the receiver and said, "*Goomazigon*!" The word had no real translation into English but meant something like the Yiddish word "*putz*," which also had no real English translation. "She's got a pair of *cugnones* hopin' to see me soon."

"You think they'll give you twenty-five grand?" Frankie wondered. "That's a big line."

"Not when you have a hundred in the bank."

"Then I guess you want Hearn to go for the same."

Frankie called VIP services at Caesars Palace. He went through the same rigmarole as Joey. Gave the same basic information and ended the call by asking for a $25,000 credit line. He was told as well that the credit department would get back to him within the week.

It got back to him the next day.

The call was made to Hearn's dummy apartment in Edgewater but was forwarded to Joey's house where the Rosellis were basing operations. The gentleman on the line informed the man he believed to be Bill Hearn that his creditworthiness entitled him to a Caesars Palace line of up to $50,000! How much did he want?

"I might as well take the full fifty," Frankie said into the phone. Then to make light of the situation added, "My wife's gonna kill me if I blow it all the first trip."

The Caesars credit executive laughed and explained that on

his arrival to the hotel he should immediately page the casino host, who would "take care" of him. Mr. Hearn would be given RFB privileges, which meant his room, food, and beverage (except champagne) costs would be taken care of by the casino, as long as he showed the pit bosses the required gambling action. He reminded Frankie to bring proper identification and an unsigned blank check from the account he'd be paying markers against. Frankie assured him that not only would he bring the ID and the check but also that "my gambling action will even entitle me to free champagne."

Joey and Frankie marvelled at both the swiftness of Caesars' decision and that Hearn had been given a $50,000 line. They had already known that both Caesars' and the MGM's credit departments had called their offices to verify information on the applicants. Fran at Worldwide Western had informed Joey that the woman who'd called from Caesars had asked only how long Mr. Hearn had been with the company and what his function was; she had not inquired about earnings nor had she sought any information as to what type of investment portfolios Worldwide Western handled. Following Frankie's instructions, Fran had informed the caller that Mr. Hearn was the president and had been with the company for fourteen years.

Maria had also not been asked for information about Mr. Kent's salary. The call she received from the MGM credit manager had gone basically the same way Fran's with Caesars had. It had lasted all but two minutes, she'd told Joey. Just long enough to say that Mr. Kent was the CEO who'd been with Jade East for a decade.

That the MGM credit manager's forwarded call made its way to Joey's house just a day after the call from Caesars was no surprise. However, it was Barbara from VIP services calling, not one of the high-ups from credit services.

"Congratulations, Mr. Kent," she said gaily through the line, as if Joey had won the goddamn lottery. "Your application has been approved up to fifty-thousand dollars. How much of that would you like to start with? You know, you can always begin with less and then have your credit line raised to the fifty thousand at a later date."

She had the right idea but not quite the right means of carrying it out. What Joey planned to do was start with the fifty grand on Day One and get it raised to a hundred as soon as possible. The monster plan was already taking shape in his head.

"Thank you, Barbara," he said, for the first time getting on familiar terms with her. "I think I can handle the full fifty."

"Very well, Mr. Kent, that is no problem." She then gave him the same rap about paging the casino host once he arrived at the MGM.

A long stretch Cadillac limousine rolled to a stop under the bright eruption of golden light filling the main entranceway of Caesars Palace hotel in Las Vegas. The chauffeur parked behind a second black limo against the white marble pavement fronting the steps that led to an armada of pearly glass doors into the casino. With the help of a Caesars' valet, the limo's rear door swung majestically open and out stepped Frankie Roselli in the company of a glamorous woman who was a head taller than he.

Her name as far as Caesars was concerned was Estelle Hearn, the wife of their newest high roller, Bill Hearn. But her real name was Louise Roselli and she was Frankie's real wife, a dynamite cook who had been dragged out of her kitchen to participate in her husband's credit scam. She was also quite glamorous. Just shy of forty, with her brunette mane and voluptuous body, she could still compete with any of Las Vegas's bejewelled lovelies, even those half her age. She had big breasts and long, tanned legs that were beautifully toned from three afternoons a week at the gym. Frankie liked to call her "princess."

The glowing $3,000 Sonia Rykiel dress she wore with her Salvatore Ferragamo Tunisia embellished sandals certainly were fit for a princess. However, the heart underneath it was as larcenous as any high-class hooker's. Her husband the high roller wore an expensive, exquisitely tailored Armani suit that he'd bought in a New Jersey shopping mall the day before they came out to Vegas. Hand in hand, the couple had all the air and sophistication of contemporary grace. Only they knew that beneath all the dazzling glitz, they were nothing but a pair of high-rolling con artists.

On the top step before the handsome doors, Frankie paused to light a cigarette with his Dunhill. He had taken up part-time smoking just for this occasion and those to follow, if only to bring into evidence his gold lighter and French cigarettes. After a puff, he blew out the smoke and escorted his wife into the dark seduction of the casino. Cheers from crap tables wafted up from the pit, accompanied by the constant tooting and blipping of slot machines.

They stepped into the sunken, domed pit and walked through sentinels of horseshoe-shaped blackjack tables. Then skirted around one end to make their way to the main casino cashier cage. Frankie picked up a house phone and asked the operator to dial the executive host's office. Jackie Leonard, Caesars' big honcho host, was expecting him. When he came right on the line, Frankie said with the arrogant confidence of the Strip high roller, "Jackie, Bill Hearn here. I'm in from New Jersey."

Jackie Leonard spoke with the jazzed-up familiarity that casino hosts allowed themselves to bestow on complete strangers. It was a privilege in the casino business. It was also a polished method for ingratiating people out of their money.

"Been expecting you, Bill. How was your flight in? Stewardesses take care of you all right?" He chuckled obnoxiously. "If not, we'll find you some better ones on the ground." The host, so caught-up in his own bullshit, had forgotten that his newest high roller was in town with his wife.

But Frankie played along with the gig. He'd rehearsed it. He knew their entire stay there would be scrutinized by a wide array of personnel, everyone from hosts to pit bosses to unseen surveillance people. He had to be sharp. One little fuckup and they'd get on to him real fast.

"Thanks, Jackie," he said real chummy, "But I'll take the broads some other time. This trip I'm stuck with the wife."

"I'm very sorry to hear that, Bill, but we all learn from our mistakes." Jackie continued pouring it on, and they hadn't even met yet. Frankie gave him his best version of a fake laugh.

"Hey, Bill, you ever hear the slogan "What goes on in Vegas stays in Vegas?"

"Sure thing, Jackie. I'll take you up on it next trip." But Frankie was the unusual mobster. He'd never cheated on his wife. "Hey, Jackie, could you come over to the cage right away and get my credit fixed up? I'm really itching to play a little before I take the lady upstairs." That was the cue to cut the bullshit and get down to business.

"I'll be right over," Jackie said. "We'll take care of everything, and you got full RFB."

"Great, Jackie. Thanks."

Jackie Leonard looked like a beautifully polished bowling ball that someone rolled down an interstate alley from Chicago and into the glitter of Caesars Palace. He was all smooth hustle, with that worked-up personality that could be turned on faster than a light switch. His suit was charcoal gray and expensive. His black shoes were shiny but not as shiny as the elastic skin stretching his sleek face. The dark hair was slicked back to oily perfection. But still, he was one of those guys that no matter how much he spent and groomed his body, he could not escape that he was pudgy and crusty like an Italian loaf of bread. The name Jackie Leonard was as phony as he was.

Before Frankie could open his mouth, Jackie swept him into an embrace, his heavy arms locked around his shoulders. "Bill, it's so nice to see you at last!" He said this as if they'd been pen-pals for centuries and had finally crossed a desert without water to see each other. Once he released him, Jackie didn't waste any time getting Frankie closer to the gambling tables, where he thought Frankie was itching to lose his money. He escorted Frankie to the VIP window at the cage.

"How are you, Mr. Leonard," the woman cashier greeted the host.

Jackie just nodded. Then he said to her, "This is Mr. Bill Hearn from New Jersey. He's a new player at our casino, and I want you to set him up right away. He has full RFB privileges in the hotel."

The cashier went into the rear of the cage and removed some paperwork from a file. She laid Hearn's file card on the counter in front of Frankie. "How do you plan to pay off your markers, Mr. Hearn? Cash or check?"

"I will pay by check within thirty days," Frankie said with the guarantee in his tone. He had rehearsed well.

"May I see some identification please?"

"Would you like my driver's license or passport?"

"Either will do, sir."

He gave her the New Jersey driver's license with his photo next to the name Bill Hearn. She compared the photo to his face and wrote the license number on her file card.

"Have you brought a blank check for the account you'll be using to pay off markers?"

"I have." He slid it along the counter to her. She paper-clipped it to the file card. Then she had him sign two separate signature cards. Each time he signed a marker, she explained, the signature on it would be compared to the one on the signature card. She told Frankie that he would be required to give casino personnel in the gambling pits his date of birth when requesting a marker. She let him know that his birthdate was the first line of defense against someone impersonating him and fraudulently obtaining credit from the casino. Frankie thought how he would love to let her know that his birthdate was his first line of *offense* in fraudulently obtaining credit from the casino.

Finally, she informed him that his brand-new credit account at Caesars Palace would be activated in fifteen minutes, at which time he could sign markers as he pleased up to the limit of his credit line.

As soon as business at the cage was done, Jackie began his less than tactful retreat. Other high rollers had to be met and pampered. "Well, Bill," he said, "I wish you the best of luck during your stay. I hope you beat us for fifty grand."

Frankie thanked him while mumbling under his breath, "Count on it."

Fifteen minutes later, he and Louise were standing at a busy crap table watching white-dotted red dice skitter across the green-felt layout. People were cheering and hollering with their fortunes. They looked like the typical Vegas high roller and his wife. A sexily-clad cocktail waitress sauntered over and took their drink order. Frankie ordered the typical high-roller scotch on the rocks while Louise opted for her favorite apple martini. The waitress flashed her artificial smile and was gone.

The time had arrived to commit their first casino crime, the actual obtaining money under false pretenses. Frankie called over the pit boss, who'd been shooting the breeze with another casino employee at the podium inside the pit.

"Yes, sir?" he said promptly.

"Give me a marker for five grand," Frankie said without preamble.

"What's your name, sir?"

"Bill Hearn."

"Date of birth?"

For the tiniest fraction of a second, Frankie almost slipped and gave his real date of birth. But "April 6th, 1950" slid off his tongue gracefully. The dead bastard was a few years older than he, no big deal.

The pit boss instructed the table's boxman to have the dealer cut out five grand in black $100 and purple $500 chips and pass them to Frankie. A few moments later, a pit clerk with a clipboard in her hand approached. Attached to it was the credit slip Frankie had to sign. It was saw-toothed and looked just like a bank check. He signed it, thanked her, and she walked off.

Before they had arrived in Vegas, Joey taught Frank about a low-level scam casinos were constantly on guard for. It was people feigning to be high rollers when in reality they were just hustling comps (freebies) from the casino. He showed him how they used "offset" procedures to con the casino into thinking large sums of money were being wagered when in fact the bets only cancelled out. A favorite method for offsetting was done on crap tables, where one guy would bet on the "Pass Line" and another the same amount on the "Don't Pass Line." Most people doing that, Joey said, were sure to be caught before they even got a lousy hot dog out of the casino, let alone a free room.

In order for their mammoth casino-credit scam to work, they would have to perfect that offset procedure to the point where they could implement it for thousands of dollars on every roll of the dice without giving themselves away. But Joey had explained that craps was not the ideal casino game to do it on. "Baccarat is better," he'd said, "because there you usually got the same amount of people bettin' on player and on bank," the two main bets in the game.

Joey knew everything about baccarat, had been a junkie for

it. He told Frankie that it was the game of choice for super high-rolling jet-setters and therefore the perfect stage for their scam. Baccarat salons were always tucked in exclusive corners of casinos. They were all elegance with glittering chandeliers above the groomed heads of the casino's best-dressed players. By the time Frankie spoke to Jackie Leonard on the house phone, the host already knew he was a baccarat player.

Although Joey had said that baccarat was the best game to implement the offset procedure, they decided to stage their first bout of phony gambling at a crap table. The reasoning behind it was that in the fancy baccarat salon they'd be under more scrutiny, therefore, any mistakes they made would be more perceptible to casino personnel. It was best they learn the casino ropes at the crap table before venturing onward to baccarat.

Frankie placed two black chips on the Don't Pass Line. Louise, merrily laughing as though she were having the time of her life, did the same. At the other end of the table stood Joey with his wife Sherry. They were dressed unobtrusively so as not to draw attention from the pit. Their chance to doll up would come later at the MGM. Around the horn of the crap table, about midway between the couples, were Vito and Tony, two younger wanna-be mobsters from the Rosellis' neck of the woods looking to make their bones. Joey had recruited them for the scam because more trusted people were needed for the offset procedure. They would have used their own kids, but they were under twenty-one and might be ID'd by casino security.

Following the offset procedure, Vito and Tony placed identical bets of $100, four green $25 chips on the Pass Line. Joey and Sherry followed suit. The total effect of their betting scheme was that they had $400 in black chips on the Don't Pass Line and $400 in green chips on the Pass Line. This was a perfect offset. When one bet won, the other lost, except for 2.8 percent of the time when one bet lost and the other pushed (tied). In that case, they'd lose half their total wager. This was the only money the casino would win from them, and they treated it as a business expense. The entirety of all other expenses would be comped by the casino.

Having Frankie and Louise bet the Don't Pass Line, on which only 10 percent of crap players wagered, was strategic. Since Frankie was the high roller being watched by the casino, he should be the one betting the side least often bet. In this fashion, he was the oddball. Only he would be noticeable to the casino's eyes. Had the situation been reversed, where he was betting the Pass Line and his cohorts the Don't Pass Line, *they* would stand out to pit personnel. A sharp pit boss might notice that their $400 was offset by Frankie's $400, especially if his bet was the only large one on the Pass Line. The coup de grace of this scenario was that they had four people offsetting two. Normally, as Joey had explained, people using this method of trickery to fleece the casino worked in pairs, one offsetting the other, which was very easy to spot. And, for added disguise, the Rosellis could always shift the offsetting alignment. They could have three offsetting three, even one offsetting five, adjusting each bet so that the total on each side remained the same, or close to the same.

Joey, as he was the most knowledgeable about casinos, had to constantly watch over their operation. Their success – and freedom – hinged on his ability to feel any heat they might draw from the casino and to evaluate it. One thing he knew was that once casinos caught on to scammers of any genre, their surveillance departments immediately galvanized into a full investigation spearheaded by their multimillion-dollar video systems. "They watch you in the dark and you don't ever notice," he'd told Frankie, Vito and Tony on the plane.

The two recruits and wives only had to follow Joey's and Frankie's leads. They had no decisions to make. The crucial part for them was to remember the signals that Joey and Frankie flashed around the table. The way they handled and played with their chips sent signals for specific betting patterns. For the wives, memorizing the signals perfectly wasn't of supreme importance as they could talk freely to their husbands and thus be told directly what to do. But Vito and Tony disguised the fact they were together and pretended both couples were strangers. They had to comprehend the signals with 100 percent accuracy. It was also imperative that Frankie and Louise never let on that they knew Joey and Sherry.

Things went well on the crap table. They each varied their bets while maintaining the overall offset. Frankie gave the impression of a carefree high roller with lots of cash to burn. The cocktail waitress brought the scotch on the rocks needed to refill his tank. He socialized with fellow gamblers, joked with the pit bosses, did everything to bring as much attention on himself as possible. After two hours playing craps, he reached his destination, which was to go broke. The fifty black chips given him by the casino had returned back to the house reserves. But around the table, his partners had won $4,800. The cost of their first gambling skit was $200.

Frankie playacted his disappointment at losing five grand in front of the pit bosses and promised he'd return "to win back my money and then some." This parting gesture was made to give the impression he was a lousy gambler who did nothing but lose his chips. Louise scolded him on cue, saying for everyone to hear, "Darling, I hope you're not gonna blow fifty grand in here." Then Frankie made some affected crack for her to keep her mouth shut, and they left.

After the session, the team met up in a dark lounge inside the Flamingo Hilton across the street from Caesars. They evaluated their first act and agreed it had gone great. The casino bosses loved Frankie's action and had completely bought his high-roller act. Tony, who'd been the last to depart that crap table, heard one of the bosses comment on Frankie's play, calling Hearn a real steamer, a term casinos used to denote bad gamblers who chased losing bets.

"You played your parts perfectly," Joey said to Frankie and Louise. "I don't see no reason why we shouldn't march right into that baccarat pit."

The time was ripe for the second stage of the operation. Their goal for the weekend was for Frankie to lose $50,000, the entire amount of his casino credit line. The reason it was necessary that he ended up a loser was that he couldn't repeatedly sign markers when winning. Doing that would make casino bosses suspect he was hoarding chips, and maybe even lead them to think he was doing what they actually planned on doing, but at a much later date.

The Caesars Palace high-roller baccarat room was tucked into a private alcove off the main casino, enclosed by an elegant royal gray railing and a uniformed security guard. Comfortably nestled in their velvety chairs around the long oval baccarat table, underneath big chandeliers, was an assortment of immaculately dressed men and women of different colors and races who all wore expensive jewelry and spoke several foreign languages among themselves and English to the dealers. The green-felt table was guarded at each end by high towered chairs. Seated in these chairs were the two laddermen who verified the dealers' payoffs and gauged the players' large bets at the table. Their hawkish concentration was only thinly disguised by their evening dress, and it seemed much more intense than anything I had seen in the casino's main pits.

The first two chairs that came available on the big table were taken by Vito and Tony. The action was high; the table minimum was $200, the maximum $8,000. Instead of risking $400 on each hand of baccarat, Vito simply offset Tony's $200 bet on banker by wagering $200 on player. As Joey had said, the bets on player and banker were equally distributed, unlike in craps where one side proliferated with most of the action. Here, they didn't have to worry about who bet which side. They had adopted a strategy whereby everyone occasionally changed sides and fluctuated the size of their bets. Once they were all positioned around the table, there were literally dozens of combinations they could use to attain the desired amount of money bet on each side.

Frankie and Louise were last to be seated. Buoyed by the confidence carried over from the craps pit, Frankie summoned the pit boss, who instantly shuttled up from behind the tuxedo-clad dealers to place his hand on Frankie's shoulder.

"Yes, Mr. Hearn?" Frankie enjoyed being serviced like royalty, and he was impressed that the boss knew his name. Word must have come from the crap pit prior to his arrival in the salon: a big baccarat player named Hearn was on his way. Despite his shortness in height, Frankie felt high enough to touch the ceiling above the chandeliers.

"I'd like a marker, please," he said with authority.

"How much, sir?"

"Twenty thousand." It was time to get the show on the road.

The pit boss nodded obediently, then instructed the dealer to issue Frankie $20,000 in chips. "How would you like that?" the dealer asked.

"Just give me five-hundred- and one-thousand-dollar chips."

The dealer's polished fingers dipped into his rack and removed stacks of princely $500 purple and $1,000 yellow baccarat chips. He pushed twenty purples and ten yellows across the layout to Frankie. As at the crap table, the pit clerk appeared with her clipboard. Frankie signed the chit and thanked her.

His mission was to lose the twenty grand as fast as he could, without making it obvious. He couldn't just bet the table max of

$8,000 because the others offsetting his bet would appear obvious. Also, at that betting rate, he could be broke in three hands, which would look peculiar to casino personnel. High rollers did not comfortably sink into their velvet chairs around the baccarat table only to leave broke five minutes later. Thus for the duration of the scam, they had to maintain a delicate balance between exhausting credit lines and how long they took to accomplish that.

They all had black chips they'd bought for cash. Before entering the casino, Joey had distributed $10,000 to each player besides Frankie. No one would run out of money. Whatever bet Frankie made, they would offset it with the totality of their bets. Louise would only bet when Frankie instructed her to. When betting high, he could use her to partially offset him. Sometimes gambling wives liked to bet against their husbands, although it was usually a smaller amount. In any case, her betting against Frankie would draw no suspicion from the casino. Pit bosses saw this "connubial play" often enough.

Frankie had placed his first $500 bet on the player betting circle when the distinguished-looking pit boss came around and placed his bejewelled hand on his shoulder. "Would you like tickets for the show tonight?" he asked graciously.

"Who's playing?" Frankie hadn't noticed the neon marquee when they'd arrived in the Caesars limo, which had picked up the couple at the airport. Of course they hadn't flown into Vegas. Joey had dropped them on the arrivals curb, where they'd met the limousine. All for appearances.

"Julio Iglesias."

Neither Frankie nor Joey was a big fan of Julio's, but maybe their wives wanted to go. "What time does it start?" Frankie asked.

"Ten o'clock."

Frankie looked at his gaudy diamond-studded watch. "That

gives me two more hours of gambling." He exchanged a glance with Louise, who nodded happily. "Sure, we'd love to see Julio."

"How many tickets would like?"

"What?" Frankie's first thought was that the boss somehow knew he and his wife were not alone.

"Perhaps you have some guests you'd like to have accompany you."

Wow! Not only was Frankie relieved, but the offering of additional tickets knocked him right out. If one thing was evident up to that point, Julius Caesar himself must have believed he was a high roller!

And Frankie went with it. "You know what," he said to the pit boss, "I'll take six, if you will. Two couples I know from Palm Beach are staying at the Mirage. I'd love to invite them."

"No problem, Mr. Hearn. Six tickets to the show will be waiting for you at the box office. If there's anything else I can do for you, just let me know."

Frankie thanked him, and the boss patted his shoulder before walking off.

Two hours later, Frankie was ahead $9,600 on the baccarat table. The total amount of money lost by Joey, Louise, Sherry, Vito, and Tony was $9,900. This $300 overall loss was added to the $200 they lost playing craps. The $500 total loss for the evening was in line with what they had expected. Joey had made calculations based on estimates of the total amount of money they would put into play coupled with the house advantage working against them. In fact, he'd made similar calculations for projected losses in the long run. He'd said rather amusingly, "If this thing lasts long enough, we could end up losing a million bucks."

But if they lost the million, they'd have ten times that in profits.

Going into the Circus Maximus showroom, around a bend from the main casino, was not as easy as it appeared. Not when you're scamming the casino for big money. Since Frankie was the high roller accompanied only by his wife, it was vital to the security of their operation that they not be seen in the company of their cohorts who'd played baccarat with them. What enabled them all to see the show without being together was that the tickets left for Frankie at the box office were not part of a seating arrangement. They were casino VIP tickets. You presented them to the showroom host at the door, with a gratuity, of course, and he led you to the best tables in the house, usually right up against the stage.

Thus Frankie went alone to the box office, picked up the six tickets, then passed them to everyone outside the casino. They re-entered as two unassociated couples and two men by themselves at five-minute intervals. Being the high roller, Frankie slipped the host a $50 bill and was led to the front row. According to plan, Joey tipped $20 and with his wife was seated a few rows behind Frankie and Louise. Vito and Tony tipped $10 each and sat at the opposite end of the same row as Joey and Sherry. When the show ended, they gave the casino more baccarat action, then called it a night.

Before embarking on the scam, the Rosellis had rented three apartments in Las Vegas, all with cash and under phoney names. One was for Joey and Sherry, another for Frankie and Louise and the third for Vito and Tony. But Frankie and Louise were obligated to sleep in their Caesars hotel room since they were supposedly in from New Jersey for the weekend. Part of the charade was to live completely the Vegas life of a high roller. If they left their hotel room vacant, suspicion would fall on Frankie if the casino got wind of it. Not that staying in a luxurious hotel room was a terrible inconvenience.

It was two in the morning when Frankie and Louise arrived

at the room. Room? It was a magnificent suite! Upon opening its double baroque doors, a beautiful living room with dangling chandeliers, plush carpeting and an array of lavish furniture overwhelmed them. There was a movie screen on one wall and a small collection of impressionist paintings on the others. In the center of the room was a handsome, blue blue-baize regulation-size pool table.

Stepping inside, Louise said humorously, "If we have a fight, who gets the bedroom?"

"I'll choose you for it."

"You want to flip a coin?"

"No, let's do odd-finger."

"Okay."

They shook up their fists, and she called, "Even." Frankie stuck out his index finger; so did she.

"Well," she said with a laugh, "maybe you'll get lucky and we won't have a fight." Just a little Mafia husband-and-wife comedy.

The following afternoon, they played three hours of baccarat. Frankie managed to lose $25,000. Then after dinner he lost $30,000 more, which wiped out his credit line. Mission accomplished. Their actual losses to exhaust his credit were $1,700. This was a little more than they had wanted to lose, but it was unavoidable. Whatever losses they incurred would come back to them exponentially.

Frankie and Louise checked out of the hotel. At eleven o'clock they dropped Joey and Sherry at the airport. Joey had junked his casual attire for a stylish Ermenegildo Zegna suit that clung elegantly to his powerful frame. Sherry had tossed her halter top and jeans for a flowing silk dress that was every bit as snazzy as the one Louise had worn at Caesars, though she was not the natural beauty her best friend was. Minutes later, a long stretch limo pulled curbside and scooped them up. This one was from the MGM, another behemoth Strip gambling resort waiting to extend high rollers credit.

The MGM host who greeted Joey at the casino cage turned out to be a hostess, and she had a lot more class than Jackie Leonard at Caesars. She was a good-looking Eurasian woman with high cheekbones who introduced herself as Vanessa. They engaged in some small talk, much of which was her familiarity with Fort Lee, New Jersey. She said she had relatives living there. She even mentioned particular restaurants and clubs she knew. Joey played along assuring her that all those restaurants and clubs were the best and his personal favorites. One, coincidentally, was an Italian eatery named Armando's, where Joey had once taken Maria to lunch after a "tough" morning at Jade East's offices.

Vanessa led Joey to the VIP area of the casino cage and instructed the teller to process his credit account. He showed his New Jersey driver's license in the name of Charles Kent and handed over the blank check. The teller had him sign the signature cards, then advised that his account had been instantly activated and he was free to sign markers as he pleased. Joey thanked the teller, told Vanessa it was a pleasure meeting her, and headed up to their penthouse suite overlooking Las Vegas. Its view was panoramic. Looking down on Sin City, Joey truly felt like he was king of the world.

When the scam team descended on the big table in the MGM's grandiose baccarat salon, not one of its members modelled the same appearance as they had at Caesars. In step with Joey and Sherry's stellar fashion upgrade to play the leads in style, Frankie and Louise downgraded theirs to jeans and T-shirts. Frankie wore zeros (glasses with no ocular power) and Louise had colored her hair and donned a windbreaker. The high-rolling couple from Caesars did not know each other at the MGM. Joey knew that casino people liked floating around visiting other casino people at their workplaces. He figured it best to avoid someone from Caesars recognizing Frankie and Louise in the MGM. Caesars would not take pleasantly to the news of their high roller gambling elsewhere.

To complete the makeover in obscurity, Vito wore a ball cap and Tony slicked back his hair. Neither resembled himself from the night before. Glancing at his entire crew, Joey smiled with satisfaction. Each was playing his part well. He had unlimited confidence in their ability to pull off their scam at the MGM.

Joey as Charles Kent asked for $10,000 in chips to get started. The pit boss instructed the dealer to cut them out while a clerk brought Joey the marker to sign. As they'd done at Caesars, they worked their offset system very effectively, constantly changing their schemes like a good football team changed its formations. It took the rest of Saturday night and all day Sunday to exhaust Kent's credit line at the MGM. They only lost $900 of their own money.

At that point, Joey decided to try and rush things up a little. He paged Vanessa on the house phone and asked her to come to the baccarat salon. She obliged immediately.

"I've had a run of bad luck," he said to the attractive hostess. "I was wondering if you could up my credit line to seventy-five thousand?"

Vanessa smiled graciously but declined. "I'm sorry, Mr. Kent, but our policy is to evaluate play and payment history before issuing credit increases. Obviously your play warrants the increase but we must wait and see how things go from here." The insinuation was that not all credit players were timely payers.

Joey told her he understood and would be back soon.

That was fine. The whole premise of their casino credit scam was to pay off markers punctually while getting the credit limits for each high roller raised repeatedly in Caesars and the MGM up to a ceiling point. Then they'd stiff them on the markers and abscond with the cash. What that ceiling point would eventually be and how long it would take to get there, they didn't yet know. However, they were prepared to dig in for what might be a long credit war against the casinos. One that would take place in several locales besides Las Vegas and force them to make a tremendous outlay of cash.

The last phase of the weekend mission was turning the chips they'd accumulated into cash. As Frankie and Joey had lost $85,000 in credit between Caesars Palace and the MGM, their cohorts had recouped more than $80,000 of it. That was a lot of chips to cash out. It was also the most difficult and dangerous phase of the operation, which Joey and Frankie understood quite well from having spent their entire lives dealing in illicit cash businesses.

The golden rule was to never cash out $10,000 or more in chips at one time. At that number, casinos, like banks, were required to prepare a cash-transaction report for the IRS. Needless to say, the Rosellis did not want any federal agency becoming aware of their activities, even if they were being conducted in phony names with phony IDs. Any reports sent to the IRS could lead to all kinds of federal investigations, any of which might expose their operation.

So they made numerous trips to the cage with planned precision. Each time, less than $2,500 was cashed out. At that amount, Joey knew from legitimate casino experience, tellers asked people cashing out where they'd been playing. If you answered "In the baccarat salon," they called the baccarat boss to verify you'd played there. They gave a good physical description and told the boss how much in chips you were cashing out. The boss then gave his approval over the phone – if satisfied that the player in question was legit. If not, he came right to the cage to see you. If he did not recognize you from the baccarat room, the payoff would be held up while you were questioned.

The Rosellis needed none of that. Not only because their action was a sham but also that each person cashing out aside from Frankie and Joey was always a winner. Repetitive winners make casinos very suspicious. So if Louise, Sherry, Vito and Tony were making constant trips to the casino cages with large winnings, the bosses would want to know who these people were and how they were winning all the time.

In keeping the cash-outs limited to less than $2,500, the only question tellers asked was "Do you have any markers to pay?" In the subordinate players' cases, a negative response was truthful, so there was never a problem. But when it was Frankie's and Joey's turns to cash out chips and answer the same question, their response was "Yes, I have markers but I'll be paying them by check." This was fine and appeared normal in the casino since the value of the chips they were cashing out was just a small fraction of the amount they owed it.

After that first Vegas weekend of the casino scam, Joey flew back to New Jersey to "do the books." He wrote a check for $50,000 to the MGM from Charles Kent's checking account. Then he took a check from Bill Hearn's, previously signed by Frankie, and filled in the amount. He mailed them to Las Vegas – Kent's from Fort Lee, Hearn's from Manhattan. One practice they adopted was to make sure all the casino payments were made from the cities where the gamblers did business, thus the credit departments would see the envelopes postmarked from those cities, which would jibe with normalcy. They were thinking that a curious investigator noticing new credit players sending in payments from cities other than their own might become suspicious and launch an investigation.

Joey had learned how casino credit departments handled the collection of unpaid markers. Firstly, they did nothing for two months. Gamblers were given a thirty-day grace period to pay their debts, just like banks offered to credit card holders. But the casinos were more discreet. They did not bother you with a late notice until a second month without payment had elapsed. Then they sent a reminder. When that did not produce payment, they sent a third letter two weeks later. Only after three full months did the credit department make a phone call to a player's business or residence. This was because gambling debts were highly likely to be sensitive interfamily issues. Husbands could lose wives and vice-versa due to gambling losses. Businesses got wrecked, people committed suicide. Heck, casino gambling debts in Nevada were not even legally collectible until the mid-1980s.

When they finally did telephone, they politely reminded the customer about his "unpaid obligation to the casino." In the Rosellis' case, the debtors wouldn't be answering phones since both the scam apartments and offices would have already been abandoned. But not actual telephone communication. That would become the function of an answering service. Joey and Frankie would receive the messages and then call back the casino credit departments to say they needed more time. That routine would buy them another month, maybe two.

Then when repetitive calling brought no fruition, casinos took to dunning letters demanding payment that were sent by certified mail. When they were informed by the postal service that "Alice doesn't live here anymore," they'd finally realize they'd been had. That would not be for a minimum of six months after they got busted out, even longer for casinos in Puerto Rico and the Caribbean. It could be nearly a year after the crimes were committed before the FBI got involved. By that time, all traces to the fictitious impostors would be galactic dust. The fallout would only lead investigators to the dead people whose identity they stole and whose credit they abused.

The next weekend back in Vegas, Frankie as Hearn had no trouble blowing $50,000 at Caesars, most of which the team recouped on the other side. But at the MGM, Joey's luck as Kent ran too good. No matter how they maneuvered the bets, Joey couldn't lose. Too bad it couldn't happen when he'd been gambling legit, he'd thought fatalistically. Even one of the pit bosses had commented on his incredible lucky streak. But naturally that boss hadn't known that Joey's partners betting against him lost more than he won.

Before leaving the MGM, Joey made sure to pay his lone marker at the cage. It only amounted to $10,000 as he'd won consistently from the very first shoe of cards and couldn't take another marker. Since nearly all credit gamblers leaving Vegas as winners squared up before heading to the airport, Kent had to do the same. The most crucial aspect of the scam was never to exhibit behavior deviating from what casino bosses saw every day.

They played the casinos slowly like a precious violin. The key was patience. Whereas banks set rigid credit limits and were pains in the ass when it came to issuing increases, casinos freely increased your credit line if you faithfully paid your markers and did nothing to arouse suspicion.

Under Joey's invaluable guidance, they laid down the greatest credit scam in casino-gambling history. In cyclical fashion, they applied for credit in most of the major Vegas casinos and then expanded to Atlantic City, Puerto Rico, the Bahamas and Aruba. There was no time for Reno, Lake Tahoe or any of the smaller US gaming areas. They jetted from one place to the other, working the casinos while VIP services paid for their flights.

In the Caribbean, they had a great time doing it. They went jet skiing, parasailing, scuba diving, and sipped daiquiris while watching sunsets. The best part of it was charging everything to the casinos. They gladly paid.

The casinos in Vegas couldn't do enough to keep their high

rollers happy. Before long, they were not only paying the Rosellis' airfares and picking them up at airports but also sending them gilded invitations to gala casino functions, with offers to fly them in for these as well. A few even offered to send them on paid vacations to non-gambling venues! They would have gladly gone but didn't have the time. As Hearn's and Kent's credit lines went up, so did casinos' desires to please them.

When they weren't gambling at a particular casino, they could be found dining in one of the hotel's gourmet restaurants, soaking up the sun's rays around its marble-tiled swimming pool, or relaxing in whichever luxurious penthouse suite they occupied. All this came at the casinos' expense. They paid for their every indulgence while the Rosellis robbed them blind. Louise loved messages. They paid for one every weekend. Her facials, too. When the men played golf, there were no greens fees. They even paid for lessons with hotel golf pros. Joey wondered how far casinos would go to court high rollers. One thing for sure, he took more pleasure out of bilking casinos than in any other racket he'd had going in the Mafia.

One morning over a champagne breakfast at the Monte Carlo, Joey said, "Frankie, we're gonna make this operation even bigger."

"Don't you think it's big enough?" Frankie asked dumbfounded.

"We're gonna give 'em the double whammy."

Both Frankie and the women stopped sipping champagne and gave Joey their undivided attention.

"Remember what I told you about getting new ID from that kid in Princeton if we ever had to get outta the country?"

Frankie nodded, while the women displayed a little panic at talk of getting out of the country. Obviously it would not be by conventional means.

"Well, forget that. We're gonna stay a while. Right here in these casinos. I'm gonna call that kid at Princeton and get two new sets of ID. Why not get some more credit under two more phony names?"

Frankie looked at Joey and then at his wife. Joey's wife looked at Joey and then at Frankie's wife. Nobody voiced an objection.

After a few phone calls, Joey found out that the kid from Princeton was now in grad school at Harvard. But that didn't mean he didn't want to pick up some extra cash for two more sets of fake ID.

Six weeks later, they had their new ID packets. Joey's second alter ego was Brian Caldwell, a dead stockbroker who'd been a bigshot on Wall Street. Frankie's was Frank Lawrence, a native of Rhode Island who'd had a car dealership. Frankie wasn't too thrilled that the person whose identity he would assume had the same first name as him, but figured at least he couldn't get the names mixed up. A few times when pit bosses at the tables had addressed him as Bill, Frankie forgot he was Bill, and they'd thought that maybe Bill was hard of hearing.

With driver's licenses and passports in Caldwell's and Lawrence's names, Joey and Frankie set about creating false business and residential fronts for their second pair of phony high rollers. Both took residences in outstanding sections of Long Island. Caldwell opened a consulting firm in Manhattan called Caldwell Associates. Frankie's idea for Lawrence almost turned into a Woody Allen-esque skit. On a whim he called his business Lawrence Headhunters because he'd seen the term while flipping through a newspaper. Joey liked it as well because it figured to attract only resumes from people seeking jobs, no foot traffic.

Well, they were right about that, but what they didn't count on was a deluge of mail not only from job-seekers but also from many of the nation's top firms – whose employee requirements were satisfied exactly by the job-seekers sending resumes. It appeared they stumbled onto a *real* business! Frankie actually suggested pursuing headhunting like a real recruiting firm, but Joey reminded him that the only heads they hunted were at the opposite end of a gun.

Now they had a foursome to attack the casinos. As the months rolled by, they balanced out the Vegas attack with a multi-front offensive establishing beachheads in Atlantic City and the Caribbean. The scam became an overlapping process of gamblers raiding the system. As Kent and Hearn continued gambling in their respective casinos, Caldwell and Lawrence, sporting the same faces with different names, activated credit lines in other casinos. They marched up and down the Vegas Strip as a tandem of casino credit-playing monsters with incredible endurance, backed up by their army of well-trained soldiers. Amazingly, they never took heat. As long as the markers got paid, the bosses in the casinos treated Joey and Frankie as their most valued high rollers.

Soon pit bosses on all three shifts were routinely welcoming them with phrases of familiarity like "Good to see you again, Mr. Kent" and "Good luck this time in, Mr. Hearn." The Rosellis accepted it all gracefully and continued staging their acts as carefree high-rolling losers, all the while recovering their visible losses in the dark at the other end.

After three more weekends at Caesars Palace as Bill Hearn, each of which Frankie was largely greeted by the casino host, Jackie Leonard, he informed him that he'd like a credit increase to $100,000. Leonard advised him that he thought this would be no problem and brought Frankie's request to Caesars' credit executives. They knew Caesars would delve into his short history as a casino credit-player and like what they saw. Hearn was both a consistent loser and quick payer. Each Monday morning after a weekend of losing tens of thousands at the baccarat table, he sent off the check from New York. Then why not, they would ask themselves, grant Hearn the doubling of his credit line so he could lose twice as much?

They followed this logic.

And so did Joey and Frankie. After two months of this charade, Caesars upped Hearn's line to $150,000, regardless of the fact his bank account only contained $50,000. They were sold by their elaborate set-up and Hearn's seemingly endless capacity to lose and then pay. Having a credit line of $150,000 in Caesars Palace propelled Hearn to the distinction of being considered a casino "whale." That was the special term reserved for super high rollers, the cream of the cream of the crop, that small group of elite gamblers for whom any casino would bestow every artificial luxury imaginable, in anticipation that each whale in return would leave a million bucks in the casino's coffer every year.

While this barrage went on at Caesars, other casinos got the same treatment. The Rosellis would spend six hours in Caesars, where Frankie signed markers, gambled and lost as Bill Hearn, then six more at the MGM, where Joey, as Charles Kent, did the same. Then it would be off to the Hilton, where Frankie as Frank Lawrence set in motion the same revolving-door credit scam. Next the Monte Carlo, where Joey racked up markers as Brian Caldwell, followed by the same rounds on another shift. They seldom worried about personnel from one casino coming into another and spotting them at the baccarat table. Vegas had become so huge, its football field-sized casinos so thronged up with people, that the odds of this occurrence rivalled the town's biggest long shots. And even if they did get spotted by a Caesars Palace pit boss coming into the Hilton baccarat room to chat with an acquaintance, he'd probably only say or nod his hello to Joey or Frankie. Discretion was a cardinal rule observed religiously in the flashy and often secretive world of casino gambling.

When Bill Hearn, after two years of faithful gambling in the Caesars Palace baccarat room, during which casino bosses bestowed on him every casino gratuity imaginable, had finally reached that credit-line plateau of $1 million, he simply busted out the casino. This means that he bade the pit bosses and Jackie Leonard farewell, and never returned. Nor did he pay his markers. Through their elaborate cash-out procedure, always avoiding the scrutiny of the IRS, they turned all the Caesars chips they'd accumulated into cash. By the time the Caesars scam was over, they'd cleared more than $800,000 from its casino. The net profits from the seven other Vegas casinos they bilked ranged from $500,000 to $700,000. The total take from the worldwide casino credit scam was upwards of $10 million. Not bad for a couple of phony high rollers!

Chapter 3

A Woman to Dye For

On a hot July day in 1992, an innocent blond girl from a Wisconsin farm, who was about as hot and spunky as Patricia Arquette, walked inside the Dunes Denny's and asked the manager, "Can I get a job waitressing here?" The manager could not believe what he saw or heard but hired her on the spot. He told Dawn Blankenmyre she could have whatever shift she liked. Dawn, who'd been used to getting up early in the morning to milk the cows, chose the day shift.

She did not come to Las Vegas seeking stardom, riches, or anything else. Her boyfriend did. Like so many pretty, naïve midwestern babes, Dawn stood by her man in Wisconsin and followed him out to Vegas. Hardly there a month, the boyfriend dumped her for a cocaine-sniffing showgirl. Dawn was devastated but the toughness she'd nurtured as a small-town farm girl kicked in when she needed it.

In her first three years in Vegas, she lived in the same modest apartment on Swenson Street, dated half a dozen men, and had a fling with a major international film star while she briefly worked as a cocktail waitress at the Las Vegas Hilton. She was basically a good kid. Even though she made much better money running drinks to high rollers than breakfasts to Average Joes, she quit the Hilton because she got sick of all the unwanted sexual advances from food and beverage managers and casino jerkoffs on the floor.

Working the counter and tables at Denny's, Dawn had her share of regulars, both local Las Vegans and tourists who preferred Denny's to hotel coffee shops. One of those tourists was a guy named Jeff Engelhart. He was ten years older than she, cute as hell, especially with his dimples when he smiled at her. Jeff had been raised in New York, gone to UCLA, then moved permanently to Los Angeles, where he became an optometrist and opened up a fashionable eyewear shop in trendy Westwood. Unfortunately, his shop was not a big money-maker. More unfortunately, whatever money it did make ended up in the coffers of Vegas's casinos.

That Jeff was not permitted by law to prescribe drugs or surgery hardly meant he'd never messed with chemicals. In his grammar school years he shunned sports cards and action-hero cards for science books and chemistry sets. He spent lots of kid-time mixing this solution with that, forever curious as to what chemical reactions he might concoct. The only thing that kept him from becoming a full-fledged ophthalmologist was his addiction to gambling. Instead of studying in his UCLA dormitory, he devoted his time to playing poker in L.A.'s cardrooms. While continually losing, he racked his brain to find ways he could beat the games.

Being more than a mere novice in chemistry, it was quite natural that the idea of marking cards with chemical solutions came to him. He tried several compounds, applied them to the backs of playing cards in his apartment. Most of the solutions did the job marking cards, but the problem was that he wouldn't be the only one who saw the markings. He found this out when playing in a few "friendly" games in the dormitory recreation room. One of those resulted in a broken nose that by the time he met Dawn was the only real imperfection in his face.

They'd been going out more than a year and seeing each other every weekend when Jeff told her he had a serious question to ask her. Dawn thought he was going to pop *the* question and immediately started thinking of a diamond ring she'd seen in a jewelry store at the Fashion Show Mall.

"I think I found a way to beat Las Vegas," he announced over dinner at Piero's on Valentine's Day.

Dawn had been expecting him to pull out a ring, but he pulled out a deck of cards. She knew he had a gambling problem, but to the best of her knowledge there were no blackjack tables in the restaurant.

"With those?" Dawn indicated the deck of cards lying on the table.

"Not with those, but you're getting the idea."

"It's another scam."

Jeff laughed. He loved the fact that in spite of her wholesome beauty and bubbly personality, Dawn had a larcenous heart. He'd found that out when she told him about the credit card she'd once found while working at the Hilton. It was a Visa Gold. Instead of turning it in to the hotel's lost and found, Dawn went on a shopping spree. "Why not?" she'd said. "The woman who lost the card probably belongs to some high roller who loses even more than you in the casinos."

If her using his losses in comparison didn't exactly make him feel special, he sure as heck appreciated that she'd been able to milk the card for five grand in designer clothing from stores like Neiman Marcus and Saks.

"Yes, it's another scam," he admitted proudly. "This time it's the goods."

"It's got to do with cards."

"You bet."

"Is that all? Only cards?"

"You have twenty-twenty vision, right?"

She looked at him strangely. "As far as I know. I haven't had an eye exam lately." She smiled seductively. "Want to give me one?"

"So then you've never worn contact lenses?"

"Why would I? I already have blue eyes."

"Well, maybe you'd prefer having green eyes."

"What do you mean, Jeff? I've always been told I've got beautiful eyes."

"You do. I'll explain it when we get home." Home was her Swenson Street apartment, where they stayed together whenever Jeff was in town.

They finished their lobster, had scrumptious cheesecake for dessert, then went dancing at the nightclub in the Rio Suites Hotel. While dancing, he whispered in her ear, "Yes, Dawn, I do want to marry you, and once we get the scam off the ground, I'll buy you the engagement ring."

By the time they got home it was almost dawn. Too late for Jeff to discuss the scam. He crashed, and Dawn hurried without sleep to work at Denny's. When she got home late that afternoon, Jeff was anxiously waiting on the couch in the living room. On the coffee table were several decks of cards. Next to them was a contact lens case and a bottle of saline solution.

"What's that?" Dawn asked.

"Playing cards, contact lenses and saline solution."

"I can see that! I mean, what's it for?"

"Have you forgotten what I told you last night at Piero's?"

"That you wanted to marry me?"

"I told you that at the Rio when we were dancing. I'm talking about what I told you at dinner."

Dawn smiled grudgingly. "Well, if I take part in your scam, I'm gonna hold you to the marriage."

"I promise that after our wedding in whichever little white chapel you want, we'll go to the Golden Nugget's coffee shop and have layer cake with champagne." That particular layer cake was considered Vegas's best.

"You better."

He held out his hand. "Scout's honor."

"In that case, it's a deal." She came over to the couch and jumped his bones. After a barrage of nibbling his face, he stopped her. "Dawn, not now! I want you to do something now."

She popped into a sitting position. "I was just trying to do it. I guess you didn't notice." To say Dawn had a rapacious sexual appetite was like saying Wisconsin's milk products were just okay.

Jeff sat up and grabbed a box of cards from the coffee table. He removed the cards from the box and spread them facedown into an arc on the table. With his fingers he peeled five cards off the arc and slid them toward him. They were completely detached from the rest of the pack and not overlapping. Each card was plainly visible.

"I want you to look at the backs of these five cards." He touched them to make sure there was no confusing which cards he meant. "What do you see?"

"I see the red backs of five Bicycle playing cards." Dawn was certainly no dummy. Moreover, she was no stranger to playing cards. Like tens of thousands of Las Vegans, she had an affinity for poker, both the video and live version. At the time, online poker was just someone's dream. Though far from a degenerate gambler, Dawn was familiar enough with blowing her tips in the downtown gambling joints.

"You don't see anything abnormal on them, right?"

"Should I?" Dawn picked up a card and examined its back closely. She shrugged. "No."

"Good," Jeff said. He picked up another Bicycle box and removed the cards. This time their backs were blue. He spread them into a similar arc and separated five cards. Dawn was already examining them.

"I don't see anything abnormal with these, either," she said. "Am I supposed to?"

Jeff smiled like someone in charge of a procedure that was going exactly as he'd wanted. "Dawn, now I want you to take that contact lens case and solution with you into the bathroom and insert the lenses."

She suddenly shrieked. "No way!"

"Come on, Dawn. It's no big deal."

"That's easy for you to say. You're a goddamn optometrist."

"Dawn, I promise. It's painless."

"Now you sound like a dentist. I've never worn contact lenses before! I told you that! I've never even touched my eyes. The mere thought of it turns my stomach."

Jeff couldn't help but laugh at her adolescent resistance. She was so goddamn adorable. She was twenty-two but at the moment, despite her sex appeal, she didn't look a day over thirteen. "I'll show you how easy it is." He stretched out his eyes in exaggerated fashion and touched both simultaneously with his forefingers. "See?"

She cracked up and planted a big one on his lips. "I love you."

"Enough to put the lenses in your eyes?"

"I'll try."

"It's easy. They're soft lenses. Just put the right lens on the tip of your right index finger. Put two drops of saline solution on it and insert the lens into your right eye. Do the same with the left lens using your left hand. There's absolutely nothing to it. Believe me."

Dawn leaned over the table and opened the lens case. It was an inch long with a screw-on cap on either side for each lens. She unscrewed the right-side cap and saw the green lens swimming in solution. "That's awfully green," she said almost ominously. "Isn't it gonna look phony in my eyes?"

"It's the same color green that I sell in my shop all week long."

"To women who just want to have green eyes?"

"Guys, too. You'd be surprised. Half of them don't even need lenses. It's completely out of vanity."

"Can't you tell me why you want me to wear these lenses? What kind of scam is this?"

"Baby, you'll see soon enough. Now, please, go in the bathroom and put them in your eyes."

"Which side of the lens goes against my eye?" she asked. "I'm totally ignorant about contact lenses."

Jeff smiled. "It's a valid question. But with these particular lenses it doesn't really matter. If the lens pops out, try it again. If it pops out a second time, then flip it and reinsert it. Naturally they're gonna feel uncomfortable in your eyes at first, but after a few minutes you'll get used to it."

She screwed the cap back on, gave Jeff another kiss and hopped off the couch. "Okay, here goes!" She grabbed the bottle of solution and started toward the bathroom.

"Make sure to close the drain before you start," Jeff called out behind her. "You lose one of those lenses, no sex for a week."

"That's unfair," she protested as she stepped inside and closed the door.

"Okay, four days," he yelled back.

Dawn Blankenmyre stared at her imagine in the mirror. What she saw was not her extremely pretty face but the expression in her blue eyes. Looking into them, she knew that she really loved Jeff Engelhart.

She put the first lens in her right eye. It went in easily, swam a little but stayed on the eye. It felt a little strange, like Jeff had said it would, but not terribly. The left lens fell off her fingertip and into the sink. She scooped it off the metal lid of the drain and carefully placed it over her eye. It came out and folded over on her cheekbone. She cursed, clumsily gathered it up and reinserted it. This time it stayed put. Good thing she'd closed the drain.

Suddenly the blue tile of the bathroom took on a strange green tinge. The white sink was also now a shade of green. Dawn experienced the awkward sensation of looking through night-vision goggles. She had never worn them but recognized the greenish haze through which soldiers and terrorists in movies see while stalking their prey in darkness. The lenses also seemed to have a slight ocular power and there was a tiny blur at the inside periphery of the vision field, on each side of the bridge of her nose. She blinked and arched her brows for several moments, trying to adapt to the strange lenses in her eyes, wondering for what mad reason she was wearing them.

She came back out to the living room. Jeff hadn't moved from the couch.

"How do they feel?" he asked.

"Strange. Like there's an ant crawling around each eye."

"You'll get used to it."

"Can you tell me now why I'm wearing them?"

"Sure. Come over here and sit down."

She sat next to Jeff and looked at the two decks of cards on the coffee table. They were still spread in arcs with five cards detached from each one.

"Notice anything different on them now?" Jeff asked.

"Wow!" Dawn sighed. On the center of each of the five red- and blue-backed cards was a pale bluish-greenish tinge the size of a fingerprint. It looked like a small prism of light being filtered from background color, like in bas-relief. "Did you just paint those cards with something?"

"I did," Jeff said smugly. "But about ten minutes before you came home."

Dawn looked at the cards, then back at Jeff. Her mouth

dropped open when she understood. "You can't see those markings without the lenses, right?"

Jeff nodded. "I'm looking at the same cards you are right now. To me, they appear perfectly normal. Those green tinges are invisible."

"So this is how we're gonna beat Vegas?"

He nodded with a broad smile.

"And just what am I supposed to do."

"You, sweetheart, are going to mark the cards."

"What! Are you crazy! Have you forgotten that I have a job? If I get caught in any card-marking scam, not only will I be fired but I'll never get another job in this town."

He put his hand on her knee. "Dawn, you won't get caught. And as far as your job working at Denny's goes, I think that you will very soon be quitting voluntarily."

Dawn stared at him for several seconds. "What am I getting into with you, Jeff?"

"An exciting adventure, Dawn."

"I don't know, Jeff."

"Listen, why don't you fix yourself something to eat. I'll explain the whole thing to you afterward. Then if you really don't want to do it, it's okay; I'll understand. But at least hear me out."

Dawn nodded. "That's fair enough. Should I leave the lenses in?"

"They're starting to feel a little better, right?"

"Yeah. Now it feels like the ants have stopped swimming and are taking a rest."

"That's better. Leave them in. By the time you're done eating, you won't even know you're wearing them."

"Well, I don't know if I'll ever get used to looking at green walls and floors, but what the heck, I've been thinking of painting this apartment for a year." She came over and kissed him, then went back to the bathroom to take a shower.

Jeff Engelhart was not the first person to conceive of a method for marking cards whereby the markings on the cards could only be seen through special lenses. He was, however, the first to develop a marking solution that with the proper lenses was equally distinguishable on the backs of both red and blue playing cards.

The evolution process started with the cobalt-based solutions that innovative cheaters applied to cards and could see with specially adapted sunglasses. The problems with this were several-fold. Firstly, sunglasses alone bred suspicion in casinos if you wore them anywhere but at the poker table. Even there, these types of sunglasses did not look like normal ones. Their lenses were tinted red, which was a giveaway to those in the know. They became known as pink-eyes.

With the advent of contact lenses, the "readers" evolved into red contact lenses that held the promise of being undetectable to others. But such was not the case. Even though the lenses contained but a small red circle the size of an eyeball, it was enough to give a filmy reddish appearance that made people wearing them look bizarre if not extraterrestrial. Whites of the eyes being red was normal and could be ascribed to either a cold or being stoned. But black eyeballs tinged red didn't cut it.

There were other problems with these red lenses. One was that there was a difference in their sensitivity to the light of markings on red versus blue-backed cards. Another was that they were just plain difficult to see out of, especially against red backdrops. With some of them, you couldn't see anything on a stop sign besides the white letters that spelled "stop." The vision field was often too dark, and people wearing them found themselves bumping into things right in front of them they couldn't see. In a California cardroom, a guy wearing contact pink-eyes walked smack into a pregnant woman and knocked her over, causing a big enough stink to get him arrested for assault. The only way he could get those charges dropped was to admit he was wearing the lenses.

Blue-tinted lenses reduced some of those problems to some degree. They were certainly easier to see through, but still encountered some problems with filtering the spectrum of light from marked tinges through the overall color of the card's back.

Then there were the problems with the marking solutions. Regardless of the lenses through which they could be seen, they still could be compromised either during or after the fact. Any suspicious person not wearing the proper lenses could stick the marked cards under infrared light and see the markings light up like a Christmas tree. But if someone came up with a marking solution that disappeared without a trace once the card-marker finished his business at the tables? And if he could marry that to contact lenses that did not appear bizarre on the wearer's eyes?

These were the problems facing Jeff Engelhart when he set out to develop both the perfect solution and readers. He was determined. He knew that if he succeeded he'd be able to scam Vegas out of millions. And it wouldn't be poker, where marking cards was such a well-known scam. It would be blackjack. There were still dozens of casinos in Nevada that dealt handheld games. They could all be destroyed if you could mark the cards.

Jeff worked on the solution first. He researched base metals and chemicals in a tireless fashion that rivalled Nobel laureate scientists working on cures for insidious diseases. He concentrated on cobalt elements and fused together metal and non-metal components, dissolving them in each other to compose compound substances, one of which he hoped would result in his magical disappearing solution. The key was that the solution had to disappear in a relatively short period of time, not more than an hour. Just as important was that it left no remnants that changed the texture or appearance of the card. It could not be sticky nor could it emit an odor.

After hundreds of relentless hours in the laboratory in the back of his Westwood eyewear shop, Jeff finally developed a solution that passed the test. Its "paint" showed up just as well as any previous solution and gradually disappeared ten minutes after application. How long it would take to completely disappear depended on conditions under which the cards were marked: mainly temperature and humidity. Jeff estimated that fifty minutes to an hour would be an accurate range – and perfect for the scam.

Next he turned his attention to fabricating the contact lenses. He specifically addressed the problems of overall vision and outward appearance. He eventually developed an infrared lens with heightened visual acuity that he was able to tint green, thereby doing away with the red-dot-over-the-eyeball problem. Vision through the lenses was far from perfect, but good enough to avoid bumping into things when wearing them. They also filtered the tinge from the markings equally well off red- and blue-backed cards. The tinge could be seen from a distance of ten meters, generously longer than the length of a poker table.

Now that he had mastered the equipment needed for the scam, the remaining questions to be resolved were the method of applying the solution to cards in casinos and the transportation of it. He was aware of the omnipresent surveillance cameras. Any movements appearing unnatural to observers monitoring video screens, either at gaming tables or on the floor, would attract their close attention. You couldn't take a bottle of marking solution out of your pocket like a handkerchief to blow your nose. Nor could you daub the solution onto the card with a paintbrush. You had to use your fingers and be very discreet.

At the outset, Jeff had not envisioned using Dawn or any other woman in the scam. It went against general principles, especially if you were involved romantically with the woman. The first tiff between you and your *new* ex-girlfriend, and she was knocking on the authorities' doors, clamoring about the little scam she knew about. Instead, Jeff had thought about doing it himself using cigarette boxes. He would pad the inside of the boxes with solution, then as he removed a cigarette he would rub a finger on the solution and transport it to the cards he touched. The first problem with that was that he'd never smoked a cigarette in his life. He drank like a fish, but sticking the solution inside a beer bottle wouldn't quite cut it. Handling a box of cigarettes would be foreign to him and just might attract the attention of surveillance inspectors upstairs. Ultimately, it was just too much for one person to carry out both the card-marking and playing of the hands.

Gradually he focused on using Dawn. First and foremost, he could trust her. She loved him, and he was pretty sure he loved her back. She was also one cool cookie. If she had the stones to saunter through department stores using a stolen credit card to purchase thousands of dollars worth of merchandise, she could handle the pressure of what he had in mind. She had even told him that the high she got from copping the merchandise was almost as intense as an orgasm. Jeff was also into orgasms, so he figured Dawn wouldn't need much foreplay to get her to help him rip off the casinos.

It was much easier for a woman to transport and access the solution than for a man. Women carried pocketbooks and were constantly rummaging inside them. Whether lying on the beach or playing poker, how much time could elapse before a woman went into her handbag? She could remove her cosmetic case and dab on some rouge, all the while working the solution onto her fingertips. Thus the first part of the m.o. would be to place the solution in her pocketbook.

But where? He couldn't just stick a glob of the stuff along its insides like he'd imagined with the cigarette packs. That might create a soggy mess and run onto everything else in the bag. She couldn't use an empty bag either, as that might be noticed curiously by pit personnel on the floor or surveillance people above. Jeff racked his brains to find the right means. It hit him one night as he sponged crumbs off his kitchen table.

A sponge! That was it! A woman could easily carry a sponge in her handbag. The solution could be dripped onto the sponge, which would not absorb it like a paper towel would. Then the damp sponge would be recessed into the bag in a spot easy to access. Just a touch would be enough to transport solution from the sponge to the finger that would mark the cards.

When Dawn came out of the shower and towelled off, they began to seriously plot what Jeff hoped would be the scam to "dye" for. He inserted a pair of the same contact lenses without the benefit of a mirror. Then he opened a small half-ounce bottle that contained the solution. He tilted the bottle and squeezed several drops onto the spongy yellow side of the small sponge that Dawn had brought from the kitchen. He explained that the woolly green side was not to be used. "Save that for scrubbing," he said seriously.

He gently passed his fingertip over the sponge and dabbed the back of a red card with it. "Make sure you mark the card right in the middle. Just give it a normal touch. You don't have to press down on it like when giving a fingerprint."

"I've never been fingerprinted, I'll have you know," Dawn said. "I'd like it to stay that way."

"Okay, but just touch it softly, like this." Jeff touched the sponge again and transferred the solution to the card.

Dawn's finger glided over the sponge and then dabbed a blue card. Through the contact lenses, they saw the greenish tinges they'd put on the cards. They went through ten cards each, Jeff on the red deck, Dawn on the blue one.

"How often do I have to rewet the sponge?" Dawn asked.

"You don't. All you have to do is wet it like I showed you.

The sponge will maintain enough solution for an entire marking session, which will last twenty minutes or so. But you will need to touch the sponge every few minutes because the air will dry out the solution on your fingertip. Each time you go to your bag to touch the sponge, make it look like you're doing something else commonplace. Take a cigarette or a piece of gum. Dab your lips with lipstick, anything feminine."

"It's a good thing I smoke," Dawn observed. "Why not just put the sponge in a jacket pocket?"

"You could do that, but I think going into your handbag is better than using your pocket. It's more out in the open. A pocket is more suspicious than a pocketbook."

"That's cute."

"What?"

'"A pocket is more suspicious than a pocketbook.' Sounds like a con woman's old saying."

Jeff laughed. "Maybe it is."

"Okay, I'll start by using my pocketbook."

"There's only one thing a bit difficult with this," Jeff cautioned. "You have to learn how to pick up the cards and either mark them or not mark them every time the same way. We'll be playing only handheld games. Obviously, players can't touch the cards when they're dealt faceup out of a shoe. So the first thing we need to see is how you pick up the cards." He scooped up the deck. "I'll play dealer. I'll deal you the cards and you pick them up." He dealt her two cards.

"I can pick them up the same way I pick up my two cards at Texas hold'em," Dawn said with confidence as she swept up the two cards."

"Not exactly," Jeff advised. "You touched the top card with your forefinger. That's the habit you have to break when gripping your cards. The solution is going to be on that finger. You don't want to touch the card with it until you're expressly marking it."

He slid two cards along the table and lifted them up, his forefinger barely off the card's surface but in line with the middle of it. "The trick is to not make it obvious that you're avoiding contact on the card with your forefinger. If it's sticking out, they'll notice it."

"Who will notice it, the dealer?"

"More likely the eye in the sky. You know, the black bubbles they got all over the ceiling hiding the cameras."

She slid two more cards toward her, emulating Jeff's grip as to not touch the cards with her forefinger.

"That's good. Now, if the top card is either a ten or an ace you mark it. You just touch the back of it in the middle with your fingertip, then you rest your finger slightly off the surface, like this." He showed her. "The reason for not leaving the fingertip on the card you just marked is so you don't develop the habit of feeling comfortable with it on the card. Otherwise you might start mistakenly marking cards. When you scratch the cards against the felt for a hit, you do it the same way every time with your forefinger off the top card's surface." He scratched the cards along the table; she followed along with those in her hand, her forefinger slightly raised off the cards."

"That's perfect."

"What if the bottom card's an ace or 10?"

"Ignore it," Jeff said strongly. "Never rotate the cards or shift them in any way. You mark only one card per hand, the top one of the two you pick up. You never touch a hit card or double-down card. You play your hand, then tuck it under your chips when you're pat, or toss them over if you bust...Okay?"

"I think I got it."

They practiced for three hours. Jeff was glad to see that Dawn appeared to be taking it very seriously. So much so that she hardly looked at the TV during *American Idol*. When they'd finished, Dawn asked, "Are we going to be sitting at the same table marking the cards together?"

"Not to begin with. You will be marking; I will be playing – but not until after you've left the table. As most of the time the tables will be full, I will be taking your seat. After you've sufficiently marked the cards, you'll leave the casino and wait for me at some predetermined spot. Then I'll sit down and play, and join you when I'm finished."

"Why must I leave the casino?"

"Because if anything goes wrong, the last thing we want is for them to grab both of us up. Then they'd have a conspiracy rap on us, which is the most serious criminal charge involved with cheating casinos."

"Sounds like you've been watching *Law & Order*.

"I went to the library and researched Nevada's gaming statutes."

"Wouldn't it be more effective, though, with two people marking the cards?"

"Yes, but I just told you that we can't do it together."

Dawn reached for her cigarettes on the table and lighted one. "I understood. I have a friend I worked with at the Hilton. She's really cool. She might want to get involved in something like this."

"Isn't she the one you told me about who parachutes and hang glides?"

"Yeah, that's Donna. She's a real daredevil babe, big-time risk-taker. Her fantasy is to be the Sharon Stone character in *Basic Instinct*."

"Well, that's just fine, but for the moment, let's leave wannabe psychotic killers out of this."

"No, really. She'd be great if you want another person."

"Dawn, let's just start with you and see how it works out, okay?"

Dawn blew out a puff of smoke and got back to marking the cards. When Jeff fell asleep, she was still practicing.

On Dawn's day off two days later, they drove out on I-15 to the Nevada Landing casino in Jean, Nevada. It was twenty-two miles from Vegas and happened to sit right in front of a minimum security state prison, whose inmate population consisted of more than a few convicted casino cheaters. Jeff did not mention this to Dawn. His sole reason for going out to Jean was that the Nevada Landing was an out-of-the-way casino whose pit personnel were less on the ball than their Vegas counterparts and therefore likely less inclined to notice any faults Dawn made marking cards. It would be a good training ground where they could refine their operation before going for the cash in Vegas. Jeff decided that he wouldn't even play; Jean would just be a test-run for Dawn marking the cards.

Inside the casino, Dawn went directly to the ladies' room, into a stall, where she sat on the toilet and opened her handbag. Among her cosmetics case, pocket mirror and lipstick was a brand-new yellow sponge, its backside green wool. She removed the sponge and the half-ounce bottle of solution. Very carefully she squeezed two-dozen drops onto a silver-dollar sized area in the middle of the yellow spongy side. She then recapped the bottle and put it back in the handbag. Finally she laid the sponge on top of the items in the bag, the woolly side against the leather lining. It was important to keep the sponge stable in order to facilitate her touching the solution onto her fingertip with the greatest ease. She didn't want to be rubbing the wrong side of the sponge or searching for it.

The last phase of her preparation was to insert the lenses. She was now a pro at it, popping them in and out as though she'd been wearing contacts for years. She'd considered putting the lenses in her eyes before entering the casino, but it was better to prepare the sponge with solution when not wearing them. Although her eyes had adapted to the lenses, vision was still a little cloudy and very green.

She left the stall and moved to the basin. At that moment, another woman walked in, and they briefly made eye contact. Out of nerves, Dawn was spooked, as if that woman might be an undercover gaming agent, but she realized it was only her imagination at work. She knew she had to overcome the fear. She had not let on to Jeff that she really was scared shitless. She was aware that she, not he, was carrying all the evidence of the scam on her person. If she got grabbed up and searched, the solution and the sponge would be found in her pocketbook.

They'd throw away the key.

She looked through the green haze into the mirror at her reflection and breathed deeply. When she came back out to the casino, she spotted Jeff standing behind a single-deck blackjack table with two open seats. He looked at his watch. That was the signal telling her to sit at that particular table. If for any reason Jeff wanted her to stop marking the cards before twenty minutes were up, he would interrupt the game to ask the dealer a question. That was the cue for her to leave immediately and go wait for him in the car, which was parked in the front parking lot. As Dawn also wore a wristwatch, she would time the duration, and when finished go out to the car just the same. If the casino changed the cards while she was at the table, she would begin marking the new decks but still halt the session at the end of the allotted time. When they moved into the playing phase, strategies for deck-changes would be implemented.

Dawn took the end seat to the dealer's left. She would be the first player in the dealing rotation. Jeff stood behind a player at the opposite end of the table, where Dawn could easily look up at him without being obvious. She needed his presence there to boost her confidence.

Jeff had selected this table because the dealer was a middle-aged woman who certainly didn't appear to be gay. He did not want to have a young man or a bisexual woman dealing to her at this early stage. As Dawn was so attractive to either sex, such a man or woman might take too much notice and risk putting her ill at ease.

Dawn wasted no time getting the solution onto her left forefinger. As she sat down, she went directly into the handbag and touched the sponge, then removed a cigarette from the open Camel box. The move was perfectly natural. She placed the cigarette between her lips and lighted it with her right hand.

The dealer acknowledged her with a matronly smile and dealt the round. Dawn picked up her two cards with her left hand. Jeff noticed that her forefinger was lifted a little in exaggeration from the card, but it wasn't terrible. The dealer certainly hadn't noticed. Jeff also noted that her forefinger had never touched the back of the top card, thus it should not be a 10-value card or an ace.

Now holding the cards an inch above the felt, Dawn scratched them on the layout to indicate she wanted a hit. The dealer hit her with a 9, then Dawn tossed her cards faceup on the table. They were a 6 and a jack. The top card had been the 6, so Dawn had correctly not marked it. The dealer swept them off the table and placed them in the discard rack at the edge of the table to her right.

On the second round, Dawn again did not touch the top card with her forefinger, though it was still raised a bit too much from the card. At the end of the hand, Jeff saw that her top card had been a 7.

On the third round she touched it.

Jeff watched her fingertip tap the center of the top card and then resume its position slightly off it. He was pleased with her action and more so when the card revealed itself to be an ace. Over the next fifteen minutes, Jeff watched her fluently mark the cards. She went into the handbag on five occasions, each time appearing completely natural. One time she removed a piece of gum, another her pocket mirror to take a peek at herself, a third for another cigarette. Jeff noted that the three other women at the table went in their handbags just as often. In all, Dawn did a terrific job. All her movements were naturally feminine. The only fault was the slight exaggeration of her forefinger in the air. Jeff knew that was easily correctable.

Dawn was also a capable blackjack player. She knew basic strategy well and therefore when to hit, stand, split and double-down. Jeff was amused that she won a hundred bucks during the stint at the $5 table. She left after exactly twenty minutes and went outside to the car.

A minute later, Jeff walked into the men's room. Inside, he popped in the lenses. He had decided not to wear them while watching her performance on the table so that he could clearly see her every movement. He came right back out and crossed the casino floor back to Dawn's table. He stood behind another woman on the table and looked at the backs of her cards as she tucked them beneath her chips. Clear as day, he saw the same blue-green tinge from the solution. It was right smack in the middle of the card. Apparently Dawn had not erred in applying the solution at the center.

Jeff stayed watching at the table for only five minutes. It was enough time. His observation counted seven marked cards. They were all splendidly done, the fingerprint-size marking centered on the back of each card. He also noted that the luminosity of the markings had not faded in the span of seven cards, so he was able to conclude that his predictions concerning the frequency of Dawn's touching the sponge were accurate. As all casinos were climate-controlled, there shouldn't be much difference in atmospheric conditions that might cause significant changes to procedure in any single casino.

Jeff went outside to the car and found Dawn in the passenger seat listening to Steppenwolf's *Born to be Wild*. "You were great," he said, and gave her a kiss. When he pulled back, she grabbed his head and gave him a bigger one.

"I know," she said exuberantly.

"Just one thing. When you pick up the cards, your marking finger is raised a little too much. See if you can bring it down a bit. It shouldn't be more than" – he made a slightly open oval with his thumb and forefinger – "this much off the card. Just a few centimeters."

"I'll do better next time."

"You did fine, Dawn. "You're" – he listened to the lyrics...*born to be wild* – "born to be wild!"

"I am, baby! You think this is gonna work?" she asked excitedly.

"We're gonna make a killing off this."

He kissed her again, then opened the door to get out.

"Where you going?" she asked.

"Back inside. I gotta see if the solution disappears."

He stood behind the table again. He could still see the markings on the seven cards when one of them appeared, which was just about every round because there were only fifty-two cards in the deck. But they had already begun to fade. Seeing that, for the first time in a casino and not on a coffee table or in his Westwood shop's laboratory, gave him a titillating thrill. Even though he knew the markings would disappear, it was still incredible when they did.

Half an hour later, the markings were gone! Without a trace. And then, as if part of the script, the floorman came over and scooped the cards off the table, replacing them with a new deck. Jeff smiled inwardly. Had the floorman changed the cards earlier, they would have had to go through the whole marking process again.

Jeff was as happy as a kid in a candy store when he came back to the car. He got in, grabbed Dawn by the shoulders and shook her joyfully. "You're the best!" he exclaimed. "I'll have you out of that Denny's in no time."

"No time" would be soon in coming. Jeff had pondered how and where they'd proceed with his new card-marking business. There was still an adequate number of casinos left in Vegas that dealt blackjack from the hand. Card shoes had become the preferred method of dealing, mainly to prevent players from touching the cards. Each major casino on the Strip had around six handheld games, and there were more downtown. Jeff, however, felt that Reno would be better for their first blackjack attack. There were more handheld games up there, and Jeff wanted to see how the casino bosses in Reno handled his action before he took it to Vegas.

They flew up on Dawn's next two days off. In the interim, they had gone back to Jean and then on to Whiskey Pete's at Stateline, where Dawn had marked a hundred cards in each casino. She'd made the adjustment with her forefinger and was now perfect as far as Jeff was concerned.

On the flight, Dawn had been reading *Vogue* and put it down to whisper to Jeff what she thought was an intelligent question. "Why do I have to wear the lenses? If you're the one playing, you're the only one who needs to see the markings."

Jeff's laughing outburst took her aback.

"What's so funny?"

He gave her a playful kiss. "I love you."

"That's not funny!"

"I know, but you forgot one thing. If you weren't wearing the lenses while marking the 10s and aces, how would you know which 10s and aces you'd already marked when the same cards came back to you after you'd marked them?"

Jeff's interrogative sounded confusing, but after a few moments she got it. "Oh," she said with a touch of embarrassment and slumped back into her seat with the magazine.

When they entered Harrah's in Reno on a Friday afternoon in the fall of 1995, they found a casino with dozens of accomodating handheld games, both single- and double-deck. As single-deck was more advantageous, Jeff chose one with a $10 minimum and $500 maximum. Dawn took the lone empty seat in centerfield (middle of table) and got to work marking the cards. She bet the $10 minimum each hand so as to bring as little attention on herself as possible. The dealer was an old-timer who'd probably seen a million hot babes on his tables over the years. Dawn shouldn't have a problem with him.

She didn't. In twenty minutes at the table, Dawn managed to mark twelve of the twenty 10-value cards and aces. She then exited Harrah's and went directly to a non-gaming watering hole called Sam's, without cashing out her chips. Jeff slipped into her vacated chair and bought in with five $100 bills. He asked for $200 in $25 green chips and three $100 black chips. He would keep his betting range from $50 to $200, small enough to avoid too much notice. Higher stakes would come shortly.

Jeff had worked out a certain strategy for playing marked decks from which he would not deviate. First and foremost, he would not make any outrageous plays that might tip off the pit that he had advance knowledge to the cards. There were two main points during the deal where that knowledge would come into play. The most advantageous was knowing the value of the next card to be dealt. How often he would be able to see the marking depended on dealers' individual styles: how they held the pack of cards; how they shifted it when dealing hit cards. This information was most valuable when sitting in the first seat to the dealer's left, called "first base." At that position you were the first player to receive a card. If you knew that the first card you'd receive was an ace, you had a 58 percent advantage on that hand. You would then make a big bet before the deal. Likewise, if you knew that first card coming to you was a 10 or face card, your advantage was 13 percent. You would bet big, though not as much as you'd bet when it's an ace.

The second utilization of marked cards was that you would always see the marking on the dealer's hole card, 100 percent of the time because the card would lie flat on the layout until the dealer covered it with his up card. That advantage alone was worth more than 2 percent, and would be especially helpful in "insurance" situations, when you had the option to bet the dealer had blackjack when he showed an ace.

Advance knowledge of the next and hole cards also governed how you played your hands. With a hand of eleven and knowledge that the next card was a 10, you would double down. If that next card was a 5, you would not. Similar double-down decisions could also be made with knowledge of the hole card. If your hand was a mediocre nine against a dealer's up card of 8, you would not normally double down. But if you knew the dealer's hole card was also an 8, you certainly would. However, as important as these playing strategies was the implementation of camouflage. You had to keep your advantage concealed. For example, if you had a hand of eight against a dealer's 10 showing, and you knew his hole card was a 6, you would have a large statistical advantage in doubling down, but couldn't because doing so would be an unusual play and attract the attention of the pit. Therefore, Jeff had to work within the parameters of intelligent play governed by prudence and lack of greed.

This first dealer was a terrific "shower." He held his pack of cards horizontally at all times, giving Jeff an uninhibited view of the green markings on the red backs. His first bet was $50. He received a queen and a 4 against the dealer's 7. The hole card was not marked. When the dealer arrived at his hand, Jeff could see no marking on the top card of his pack. He could thus presume with reasonable accuracy that it was not a 10-value card or an ace. Basic strategy called for a hit, and with no knowledge to contradict that, Jeff scraped his cards on the felt. He received a 6 and stood pat with twenty. The dealer's hole card was a 9, and he busted.

After the dealer took the card that busted him, Jeff saw the green tinge on the top card of the deck. He knew it was a 10-card or an ace. Had he been sitting at first base, he would have increased his wager. Another improvement he would make to the operation was to have Dawn elongate the marking for aces so that he would be able to distinguish the huge advantage of an ace from the smaller one of a 10-card.

His hand was a soft seventeen, an ace and a 6. The dealer's up card was a 5, and his hole card was marked. Jeff knew the dealer's hand was either fifteen or soft sixteen, an ace and 5. Since the chances were 4-to-1 that it was fifteen (the same odds that the hole card was a 10-value), Jeff doubled down. He drew a king that did not improve his hand. The dealer flipped over his hole card; it was an ace. He hit his soft sixteen with a 3 and beat Jeff's hand.

No big deal. The scam was not perfect and would not win every hand. But it would, Jeff knew, destroy the casino's blackjack tables once it ran at its optimum level.

Jeff played on for three-quarters of an hour, at which point the markings on the cards completely disappeared, and won $400. He never made exaggerated plays. He greatly concealed his advantage by resisting money-saving plays that would appear foolish not only to pit bosses but also to other players at the table. On one hand he had a pair of 6s against the dealer's 9. When it was his turn to act, he saw that the top card was marked, thus there was an 80 percent chance it was a 10-card that would bust his hand. But he had to take it because standing with twelve against the dealer's 9 conflicted mightily with basic strategy. Pit bosses would notice the deviation, as would other players. If the unusual play led to the dealer's winning the hand when he otherwise would have lost it, Jeff would be subjected to criticism by the rest of the table, which would only draw more attention to him.

Jeff found Dawn drinking a beer at Sam's.

"How'd we do?" she asked jubilantly.

Jeff gave the thumbs-up sign. "Four hundred ahead," he said. "That's just the start. He took a stool on the other side of the small cocktail table. "Your markings were perfect. You're so good that I think we can take the next step."

"For me, that's going to be another beer," Dawn enthused.

Jeff grabbed a waitress and ordered two longnecks. "You know how you're marking the cards with that simple touch?"

"Yes."

"Do you think you can make the markings a little more pronounced when the card's an ace? You know, like this." Jeff showed her on the table by dragging his forefinger a few centimeters across an imaginary card. "The marking only has to be a little more distinct on the aces."

Dawn laughed. "Why would you think that's a problem?"

"I just didn't want to overwhelm you with too much the first time."

"I appreciate that, Jeff. Speaking of which, I have another idea to improve our game."

Jeff was all ears.

"I noticed someone at the table playing two hands. Why don't I play two hands as well? That way I can mark more cards."

"You're learning quick," he said with an admiring tilt of his head, thinking that in the same twenty-minute period she'd be able to mark at least sixteen of the twenty relevant cards. Her doing that would also greatly increase their efficiency at double-deck games. "You think you could handle that?"

"I got this far, didn't I?"

Their second card-marking stint took place at the mammoth

Silver Legacy casino. Dawn sat at a table with a young, slick guy dealing a double-deck. They no longer had to be concerned that unwanted attempts of flirtation would make Dawn nervous or interfere with her marking the cards. She grabbed the first-base position and played two hands. Jeff watched from three tables down the pit. He alternated his glance between Dawn's table and the pit personnel. Besides the occasional male gawking at her beauty, no one took special notice of her. Jeff had at first worried that the attention to her looks would increase the chances of pit bosses catching on to her. But he had come to realize that it actually lessened it. The general macho attitude of the casino business only served to give Dawn more cover.

Pit bosses looked at gorgeous women gambling as showpieces belonging to gentlemen high rollers. They would apply the logic that a beautiful woman already had it all, so why would she get involved in a casino scam? In fact, that logic was sound. Few women needed or wanted to get involved in casino cons. What made Dawn's beauty even more trusting was that she had no tattoos and was very well spoken. When pit bosses and other players at the table engaged her in conversation, she looked her interlocutors in the eye and replied with politeness, all the while able to carry on marking the cards.

Jeff was quite anxious to play at first base. He would be able to exploit the knowledge of the next card before the deal to increase his bet. When he sat down, the position next to him on his left was open, but Jeff opted to play one hand.

He bought in for $1,000 and started off betting $100 per hand. As the dealer prepared to deal the third round, Jeff saw the marking on the top card that would be his first card. It was clearly wider than the previous markings with a smudge that corresponded to Dawn's intentional design. It was an ace. Jeff increased his bet to $200. He had a 58 percent advantage over the house.

The dealer laid a queen of hearts on the ace, giving Jeff blackjack and a $300 win on the hand. If that wasn't enough, Jeff saw another ace coming his way on the next round. As he'd bet $200 on the prior deal, he could now double that to $400 while giving the pit boss the impression he wanted to ride a streak off the blackjack. He would've liked to bet a grand, but that would be pushing the envelope.

Jeff knew he had another blackjack before the dealer did. That's because he saw the 10-card marking on his second card before the dealer slid it off his deck. He won $600 and attracted the attention of the pit boss. But not his suspicion. The boss only wanted to offer him and a guest dinner for two at the Silver Legacy's steakhouse and two tickets to see Mariah Carey in the casino's showroom. Jeff felt ripples in his stomach at the thought of a succulent steak, and then thought of all the great shows they might see on the house in Vegas.

Jeff chatted with the pit boss as he played. He had no trouble maintaining his friendly demeanor while performing his task. His cheerful attitude enhanced the cover of their operation even more. Jeff only had to glance at the cards in the dealer's hand just before the deal and then again when it was his turn to act. Unlike card counters, he did not have to constantly watch the cards. Whereas card counters had to pull back when engaged by pit personnel, Jeff could continue playing, all the while giving the impression he was hardly interested in keeping track of the cards.

Jeff got on a hot streak, and the black and purple chips began piling up. When the markings started fading after twenty-five minutes on the game, Jeff had reached bets of $600 per hand and was ahead more than four grand. He was getting ready to leave the table and meet Dawn at Sam's, but then the unbelievable happened. A new player had sat down in the last spot at the opposite end of the table, called "third base," and played two hands.

It was Dawn! She had not left the casino and decided on her

own to return to the table and start marking the cards again. This was perfect, even though Dawn had made that decision on her own and acted on it without consulting Jeff beforehand. This was a breach of their security. But considering that Jeff had not wanted to leave the table so quickly in front of the pit boss, her timing could not have been better. He also knew that remarking the cards once the original markings disappeared would have no effect on the cards' texture. All Dawn would have to do is mark the aces and 10-cards that had lost their original markings.

It worked like a charm. Twenty minutes later, two-thirds of the aces and 10-cards were marked. In the interim, Jeff had maintained $100 and $200 bets, playing basic strategy. He could not all of a sudden drop to $25 or $50 bets after having wagered $600 on the last several rounds. During this time, he'd watched Dawn and marvelled at how smooth she was marking the cards. He hardly noticed her going into the handbag to touch the sponge. She spoke and laughed with other players at the table, even with him to avoid singling him out for non-conversation. A new woman dealer had come to the table. She also displayed the top card of her deck to Jeff's satisfaction.

Jeff's chips continued piling up. He hit blackjacks and double-downs on $500 and $1,000 bets. Soon he bet the table maximum of $2,000, when he knew his first card was a 10 or an ace. Then *he* spread to two hands, and they really kicked ass! They quit after the markings disappeared for the second time, with a $15,000 profit. Then they had a fantastic dinner and let it all hang out during Mariah Carey's performance.

Dawn's innovative move gave tremendous new potential to the scam. Jeff instantly saw the value of a revolving-door card-marking operation. They would have to be careful, but if they played and marked their cards right, they could sit at the same table and clean up for several hours. Jeff would have to make decisions as to how long they would stay on any given table, based mainly on how much they were winning and the degree of heat those wins were taking.

The next day, they played long and hard at Harold's Club, Bally's Reno, the Eldorado, and again at Harrah's. At each casino, Dawn found a handheld game where two spots on the table were open. She marked the cards for twenty minutes before Jeff arrived at the table. If no other spots were open, Jeff would sit next to Dawn, who would "courteously" surrender her second spot to the "stranger." He would then play while she continued marking.

Some dealers were not as good as others. Several of them, often tall men whom Jeff began referring to as "stiffos," stood erect behind their games and held the deck in perfect vertical fashion, even when peeling off hit cards to players. This prevented Jeff from seeing the top card, which was always the next card. However, when that happened he still had the advantage of knowing the dealer's hole card, which was enough to secure a worthwhile edge against the house. Since dealers worked forty-five minutes on and fifteen off, whereupon they were replaced by relief dealers, and often rotated between tables, Jeff seldom had more than two stiffos in a row.

They earned $22,000 on Saturday's day and swing shifts. Everything had gone spotless save one little scare. While Jeff was playing at Bally's Reno, with Dawn still at the table marking, a pit boss who had a natural suspicious air about him happened on the table just after Jeff made a blackjack on a $1,000 hand. A double-deck was in use on the game, and when Jeff made the play, more than half the cards were in the discard rack. This meant that if the deck were rich in aces and 10-cards, it would be a very favorable situation for card counters looking for that exact situation.

The spooky pit boss's first move at the table was to grab the cards in the discard rack and riffle through them, as if looking to count aces and 10s. This worried Jeff in that the boss might take him for a card counter. Apparently the deck *was* abundant with aces and 10s. The pit boss hung like glue at the table and watched Jeff's every move with bulging eyes. However, those eyes did not shift in Dawn's direction, which meant it was only card-counting steam.

Jeff knew the only way to allay the boss's suspicions was to take on a carefree attitude and shoot the shit with him. Keep his eyes off the cards as much as possible. "How's it goin', Charlie?" Jeff asked, gleaning the guy's name from the nameplate above his breast.

Charlie's eyes moved off Jeff's cards to look him in the eye. "Okay, sir," he said a little stiffly. "Where you from?"

"L.A."

"Go to Vegas much?"

"Not really. I find the people in the casinos up here much nicer, know what I mean?"

"I hear you, sir." He started to relax.

Jeff proffered his hand. "Call me Jeff." He'd thought about giving a phony name but then decided it would serve no purpose.

"Good to have you at Bally's, Jeff. If there's anything I can do for you, just let me know."

"'Preciate that, Charlie."

During that exchange, Jeff had seen the green marking glint off the blue back of a top card. In midstride with Charlie, he bet $2,000 without bothering to look at the ace he knew was coming. He didn't look at his hand until he flipped both cards over and saw his blackjack. Charlie congratulated him. The scene did the trick and Charlie lost whatever suspicions he'd had. When Jeff got up, ahead $12,000 and change, Charlie offered dinner and tickets for the show on the house. Jeff thanked him graciously, but told him he already had plans to see a show at the Reno Hilton.

Their next big show took place a week later at the Las Vegas

Hilton. Flush from more than fifty grand in profits from the Reno trip, Jeff and Dawn hit the big time in the lavish Strip casinos. Their act had matured very quickly. The only problem Jeff saw on the horizon would be too much winning. He could not repeatedly play at the same casinos and keep winning, at least not too often. About the biggest crime in casinos, be it Vegas or anywhere else, was simply winning. Once you did too much of that, surveillance departments, already keen that you were probably cheating, would set out to figure out just how you were doing it.

They won $33,000 at the Hilton and attracted a shitload of attention. While Jeff played, spectators gathered behind him as though he were a celebrity. They oohed and aahed with his $2,000 and $3,000 blackjacks. When he doubled down a $5,000 bet and won, they gave him an applause. Even though this was not heat, it was not in any way beneficial to their operation. But there wasn't much Jeff could do about it. A Hilton security guard had stood behind him, but it still got a little out of control.

They went to Caesars Palace. To Jeff's surprise, there was only one handheld game in the entire casino, and a floorman and pit boss watched it hawkishly. Jeff decided to leave it alone, so they went next store to the Mirage.

Steve Wynn's Mirage had been the first casino in the world to install 24/7 video coverage on every square inch of gaming space. Every table was covered all the time. Not that this worried Jeff – Dawn's movements marking the cards would not be picked up by routine surveillance – but the Mirage's reputation of being bent in its efforts to deter and prosecute cheaters had to be reckoned with. Jeff decided he'd play to the max there, albeit very carefully.

So caught up in the planning and carrying out of their scam, they'd overlooked a basic detail and had a mini-emergency at the Mirage: Dawn ran out of solution!

Up to that point, they had used the same bottle of solution. Jeff had plenty more bottles at Dawn's apartment, but they had forgotten to bring a full one with them. They returned to the apartment, picked up a bottle and went back to the Mirage. They found another handheld double-deck game and got to work.

Their first hour on the game, they actually had a losing session. Four times Jeff bet $2,000 knowing his first card was an ace. He went zero-for-four on the blackjacks and unluckily proceeded to lose each of the hands. Of the seven times he bet $1,000, in the knowledge his first card would be a 10, he won only twice. In all, it was an $18,000 bath. The bosses were quick to offer complimentary dinners and show tickets, but it didn't take the sting out of the loss.

The first weekend in Vegas was still a huge success. They beat the casinos for twenty grand and picked up no steam. The following week, Jeff toyed with the idea of recruiting someone else into the scam. He recalled Dawn's having mentioned her friend Donna, who might want to help out marking the cards. But what Jeff was thinking was to add another big player, someone, be it male or female, who could substitute for him and play the hands. He felt that his constant exposure as a big player to the pit bosses would bring on the heat.

Jeff had a younger brother who lived in Hollywood. He was a great-looking guy who'd been waiting on tables and hoping to land a TV or film role that would catapult his acting career. An idea to jump-start his brother's career had come to Jeff, so he telephoned him from Dawn's apartment.

"Hey, Phil, it's me! How's it goin'?"

"Hey, big brother, what's up?"

"Guess what?"

"What?"

"I got a role for you!"

"An *acting* role?"

"You might call it that."

The next weekend Phil and his girlfriend Veronica were in Vegas. Jeff reserved them a deluxe room in the MGM. Since that casino had no handheld games, they wouldn't be working it. It turned out that Veronica was also a starving actress and, like Dawn, a knockout. The two women hit it off right away and there were no jealousies, something Jeff had worried might materialize and make working together impossible.

"I can't believe you're ripping off casinos," Phil said to his older brother in the hotel room. "I always thought you'd gone straight."

Phil hadn't. He'd dabbled in everything from running call girls to muling cocaine into the US from Colombia. A near conviction for the latter got him broke and very susceptible to illegal activities less dangerous. The first thing Jeff warned him about after detailing the scam was to not carry any drugs into the casino; he didn't care what Phil did in the privacy of his room.

"I did go straight," Jeff declared, "but then I lost a lot of money gambling on the square and fell into this scam."

"It's a beauty," Phil said. He'd already inserted a pair of contact lenses and been treated to a card-marking and solution-disappearing demonstration. Veronica, who'd been wearing shaded green lenses as part of her daily attire since arriving to Hollywood from Topeka three years earlier, was even more enthusiastic than Phil.

"I can't wait to get the part," she'd bubbled.

They spent a solid weak rehearsing without playing. Veronica learned how to mark the cards while Jeff taught Phil the fundamentals of playing blackjack. Little Brother had never even been to Las Vegas before. He didn't even know that blackjack paid 3-to-2. Jeff bought a little basic-strategy book from the

MGM gift shop and had Phil study it. Then he explained how Phil could utilize the marked cards to increase his bets and optimize his strategy. Being an adept street hustler, Phil picked up on the fine points of their scam as ably as memorizing his lines for an audition.

They spent two afternoons and evenings at the Nevada Landing in Jean and Whiskey Pete's at Stateline. As Dawn had before her, Veronica practiced marking the cards. She didn't feel comfortable storing the sponge in her pocketbook, so she kept it in garment pockets. She proved to be quite capable. No one seemed to notice her fingers' periodic forays into her pockets. Phil walked around the casinos with the lenses in his eyes, and couldn't believe it when he watched the markings disappear.

Two weeks after Phil and Veronica's arrival, the new two-man-two-woman team entered their first field of battle. They chose the Stardust casino to get the ball rolling. Jeff and Phil wore expensive casual threads to correspond with their roles as high-rolling gamblers. The women were clad in jeans and sweat shirts. As they were not betting considerably more than the table minimum, there was no reason to deck them out. Plus it was a reasonably cool autumn evening.

The plan of attack was a precise military operation, though at times would stray haphazardly in its logistics. The one iron rule of command was that Jeff and Phil would never play together on the same table. Jeff figured that two high rollers winning big at the same table would attract too much heat. It was better to spread the casino's wary eyes around the casino as much as possible.

The way they worked it was to have the women begin by marking cards on the same table. They'd wait until four spots opened up so that each woman could mark cards while playing two hands. Then after twenty minutes, Jeff would arrive and start firing away. Phil would wait in the wings at a casino bar.

After an hour on the first table, Dawn and Veronica would scatter to different tables and begin marking the cards. Then they would leave those tables to find others. The goal was to mark the cards on six different games. Each woman had a fresh bottle of solution; there'd be no running out.

As soon as one of the women left her second table, Phil would take her place or another vacant spot at that table and begin playing. Jeff would then play at the next table vacated by the other woman. They would continue in that fashion for four hours, staging a marking-cards version of casino musical chairs. During the escapade, Jeff would survey the entire operation to make sure none of the team members was attracting negative curiosity. If he noticed a problem, he'd immediately instruct each of his partners to leave the casino and head back to the hotel room at the MGM.

With both women playing two hands and marking cards at that first table, productivity was optimal. Coupled with a little luck, they reached the bonanza of marking every ace and 10-card in the double-deck, forty cards in all. When Jeff arrived at the table, Dawn signalled him this information by way of placing her chips in a certain formation that said "forty." Jeff, seeing that the dealer held the pack horizontally enough for him to discern the marking on the top card, wasted no time in getting lots of money in his betting circle. He started playing one hand at $1,000 and then spread to two as soon as the spot next to him opened. The 10s and aces came his way at the opportune times, and he was ahead ten grand in less than ten minutes. The Stardust, not being one of the top-notch classy Strip casinos, had a little difficulty swallowing Jeff's onslaught. The floorman hurried through the pit to tell the ranking pit boss what was happening on his blackjack table. When the pit boss got there, Jeff was laying $2,000 bets in both of his betting circles. He knew the first card of the round would be an ace and fall to his hand at first base.

Jeff snapped the blackjack on that first hand and made a hard twenty on his second. Under the pit boss's flaring eyes, the dealer paid Jeff $5,000. Again the green tinge of the top card shined in Jeff's eyes. This time it was a 10-card. He made the two monster bets and won them both, $4,000 more.

Phones started buzzing in the pit. Jeff placed $2,000 on each spot and was dealt a 3 and an 8 on his first hand, a 4 and a 7 on his second. The dealer's up card was a 6, his hole card a marked 10. There was a high probability the dealer would bust with sixteen.

Jeff saw the gleam of a 10-card on top of the dealer's pack. He smiled and slid four purple $500 chips next to the four already in his first betting circle. It was now a $4,000 double-down. The dealer slid the card under one set of Jeff's purple chips. Jeff already knew he'd made twenty-one, but the pit boss, still in the dark, was sweating bullets.

The new top card was again a 10! Another $4,000 double-down, and unless the dealer made a tying twenty-one, another winner. Jeff stood to make eight grand on the round.

He did!

The pit boss glared angrily at the dealer. Then he rushed to the podium and removed two new decks of cards from a drawer. He rushed back to the table and spread each deck into a horseshoe shape on the layout. Mumbling something unpleasant to the dealer, he snatched up the two marked decks from her discard rack and returned to the podium. He slammed the used decks into the same drawer. Then he took a ringing phone from its cradle.

It must have been a while since the Stardust took a hit like this, Jeff thought. But there would be no mercy. Inside that drawer, Jeff knew, the solution was already beginning to fade away. They could take the damn cards to a laboratory and shine a laser on it. By that time, they'd see nothing.

The assault continued according to plan. Dawn and Veronica were at two different tables. Veronica got up first. Phil slipped onto her vacated chair. Jeff took Dawn's a few minutes later. From where he sat, Jeff observed his brother and saw that he'd learned his job well. The dealer was cutting stacks of purple chips to pay his winning bets. Phil had split a pair 2s, then received another 2 and resplit that into a third hand. He ended up doubling down on two of the three hands, and won everything. The barrage against the Stardust was turning into a massacre.

And it went on. They didn't quite last the four hours, but after three their total profit was $65,000. Sixty-five grand! Jeff thought how just a few weeks ago he'd been a half-assed optometrist on the balls of his ass. Now, here he was, running what had to be the best card-marking scam ever!

It truly was. The foursome spent two years battering the Las Vegas Strip, the casinos in Reno, those in Lake Tahoe, where they got in plenty of delightful skiing at Heavenly Valley, and even made a few trips to Laughlin, the booming gambling town on the Colorado ninety miles south of Las Vegas. They would have embarked on trips to Atlantic City, Connecticut and Mississippi, but unfortunately there were no handheld games anywhere east of Nevada.

Soon there were no handheld games anywhere. As the gambling explosion of the late 1990s sprouted a half dozen new megaresorts out of the desert, casinos began moving more and more away from handheld games. The Bellagio, Venetian, Paris and Mandalay Bay all opted for 100 percent card shoes.

Jeff and Dawn and Phil and Veronica were saddened to see their beloved blackjack games dwindle away. But don't feel too sorry for them.

Over a two-year period they earned $7 million.

But Jeff never kept his promise to marry Dawn, the son of a bitch!

CHAPTER 4

THE FRENCH CIGARETTE SCAM

In May 1973, Pierre Fillion was dealing roulette in France's majestic Casino Deauville on the Atlantic coast. He'd been dealing there for fifteen years. Five days a week he spun the little ivory ball on one of the casino's English-style roulette wheels. Despite Casino Deauville's inordinately regal interior, with its high ceilings, red carpeting, Renaissance paintings and tapestries, many European gamblers shunned the fancy French roulette wheels whose croupiers used golden hand rakes to push plaques and chips back and forth across the large tables. They favored the unspectacular English version of roulette that shed the flair for swiftness and quicker action.

To Pierre, it was just a job. He looked at the handsome casino with its towering ceilings and lustrous chandeliers as nothing more than a workplace. The fabulously wealthy people who strolled amid the Old World ambience placing their wagers were nothing more than customers. That they were draped in tuxedos, silk evening gowns and diamond jewelry that glittered like the chandeliers did not impress him. His only reflection was that it was too bad none of it was his.

Pierre was unmarried, and his personal life was as drab as his roulette job, except for the one thing that gave him passion: He was a ham and short-wave radio buff. Every morning when he got off work a few hours before dawn, Pierre took to his radio shack outside his modest home and submerged himself in his joyous occupation of building radios and transmitters, testing frequencies, and picking up sounds of music and language, most of which he couldn't understand. But he loved identifying from which countries the broadcasts emanated. He even kept charts. Those coming from other continents thrilled him the most. So did the ones from communist-block countries.

One early morning he picked up a signal from Montréal. He had no problem understanding the Québecois brand of French even if the accents were at times funny. Two men with sophisticated knowledge of radios and transmitters were talking about building a new prototype for a remote-controlled model airplane. In describing the circuitry involved with the transmitter, one of the men used a French phrase for describing something that functioned like a well-oiled machine. The words were: *Fonctionner commes des roulettes*. Pierre was a listener more than a talker, so he did not partake in their conversation, but he was keenly interested in what they said. He'd loved model airplanes as a kid.

The following midnight, the Casino Deauville was exceptionally crowded with the influx of tourists and movie people who'd jetted across the country from the Côte d'Azur, where the Caanes Film Festival had just closed. Pierre dealt his roulette game to a full table of distinguished international clientele. They stacked their 100-and 500-franc chips all over the layout as if in a frenzy. In Europe, roulette was the game of choice.

Suddenly, Pierre got more interested in dealing roulette than he'd ever been in fifteen years. It had nothing to do with the well-heeled people or their bets. It was watching the little ivory ball that he'd just launched into motion with a powerful snap of his middle finger. His eyes had become transfixed on the spinning ball as it raced around the sloping groove in the opposite direction of the rotating inner cylinder of the wheel. He was mesmerized by the ball as if seeing it for the first time. His eyes followed revolution after revolution. When it finally slowed, Pierre called out, "Rien ne va plus," which meant "No more bets."

The ball dropped into the number 7 slot in the bowl. Pierre announced, "*Numero sept, rouge, impair*." He reached over the layout with both hands, picked away clumps of losing chips and deposited them into his working well. Then he swept the remaining losers, clearing the layout of all the chips except for the outside winners and a lone 1,000-franc chip straight up on number 7.

From the casino's reserves of neatly stacked chips against the base of the burnished wheel, he extracted a stack of 100-franc chips to pay winning bets on red and odd. Then he removed two stacks of 1,000-franc chips, peeled five off the bottom of one, and paid 35,000 francs to the gentleman who'd bet the number straight up. That payoff, around $7,000, would have exceeded the limit in most American casinos, but for Casino Deauville it was just another moderately large bet that marked the start of the summer season.

Pierre whipped the ivory ball into its next series of revolutions. He was still eerily entranced by it, but this time his brain was beginning to decipher why. As his eyes followed the ball, his mind heard the words from the short-wave transmission the night before. *Fonctionner commes des roulettes*. But now he was thinking not of remote-controlled model airplanes but rather the game of roulette. What if he somehow invented or constructed a remote-control roulette ball? Actually built a receiver into the ball that would receive a signal that controlled the ball's velocity. It would have to be tiny and virtually weightless, but the thought sent shivers down his spine.

He pictured himself as a child on the beach flying remote-controlled model aircraft with his father. On his thirteenth birthday, his parents had bought him a model of a Bloch MB 150, the

150, the premier World War Two French fighter plane. He would fly it every weather-permitting Sunday after church. It had become the great joy of his childhood, along with his fascination for radios. What he remembered now, some twenty-five years later, was the remote-control apparatus for the airplane. It was about the size of a cigarette pack and had a panel of buttons. He could see himself pushing the buttons as he looked into the sky and watched the plane dive and then nose-up again.

At four o'clock he clocked out of the casino and went home. But this time he did not surf the airwaves. It was the first such occasion since he'd been hospitalized for kidney stones in 1968. Pierre Fillion had too many brain waves passing through his head. For the moment, there was no room for radio waves.

The problem was twofold: the transmitter to send the signal to a receiver embedded in a roulette ball; and the roulette ball itself. Pierre knew he could find a tiny receiver for placement into the ball. But a transmitting device would not be as easy. Not the conductor carrying current to radiate a radio signal but the concealment of that device. He knew he could not activate a transmitter himself while dealing the game, thus he envisioned a co-conspirator who could carry out that function from a nearby position. But in the casino, it would have to be done in the dark. A transmitter would have to be concealed as effectively as a needle in a haystack.

First he turned his attention to the ball. Roulette balls were made of solid ivory and could not be tampered with in any way, let alone try to somehow insert an electronic receiver in one. The slightest imperfection in a ball would cause it to sail erratically around the cylinder. There would be an off-key note to its normal hissing sound as well. Any sharp casino person would pick up on it, personnel and patrons alike. Pierre knew right away that a ball would have to be made from scratch, actually fabricated around a tiny, weightless receiver.

There was only one person he knew in all of France who might be up to the task. His name was Guy Laurent and he was a very talented sculptor, but made a living that was very modest in comparison to his talent. He sold the statuettes he sculpted in his atelier to tourists passing by his stand on the promenade along the beach. Pierre figured that if Guy could sculpt the eyeballs of a Greek god, he'd have a pretty fair shot at sculpting a crooked roulette ball.

Guy was an early riser, albeit not before the crack of dawn. Pierre waited anxiously for the sun to come up, and when it did found himself tapping on the wooden door of his friend's clapboard house two blocks from the sea.

"*Bonjour, mon ami,*" Pierre said cheerfully in the bright early light. It promised to be a beautiful day along the French Atlantic coast.

"Good morning to you, my friend," Guy said with a glint of surprise in his eyes. "What are you doing here at such an hour?"

"Did I wake you up?"

"No, the knock on the door did." Guy had quite a sense of humor for a Frenchman.

"I have something important to discuss with you," Pierre said in a conspiratorial voice, as if the French Secret Service was in earshot.

"Let's go in my atelier."

Pierre followed his friend through a small foyer to a door that led down a staircase into the basement. Guy's atelier was as small as it was cramped. There was everything from small figurines to life-size statues, the most impressive being a beautifully chiselled stone statue of Charles de Gaulle. There was hardly room to make one's way between the packed shelves jutting from the walls and the bronze and clay busts lining the floor in no identifiable patterns. The worktable was squeezed in an aperture next to the shelving.

"How do you get anything done in here?" Pierre wondered.

"It's been a wet spring," Guy answered with a fatalistic shrug. "I've been stuck with a lot of my sculptures."

Pierre nodded sorrowfully. About the only business in Deauville not hurt by that spring's inclement weather was the casino. "Well, maybe I have an idea that will make it up to you."

Guy sat on his workbench, Pierre on an adjacent small stool. "I could sure as hell use a good idea," Guy said.

Pierre pulled a roulette ball out of his pocket. "You see this?"

"It looks like a roulette ball."

"Of course it's a roulette ball."

"Why did you bring it here?"

"Because I have a good idea." Pierre carefully set the ball on the worktable in front of Guy so it wouldn't roll off. "I want to make a remote-controlled roulette ball that I can sneak into my game when I'm dealing." He went back into his pocket and removed a small cellophane bag, from which he extracted a tiny electronic receiver. It was just a bit larger than a pinhead. He gently laid it on the worktable next to the roulette ball. "This is a radio receiver," he explained. "What I want to do is imbed this receiver into that roulette ball. Not this exact receiver but one of a similar size and nature."

Guy looked at the little roulette ball sitting next to the littler radio receiver. He certainly seemed confused. "How are you going to do that?" he asked. "You can't ply a hole in the ball and stick the receiver in it." He picked up the ball. "This is made of ivory. Impossible to crack and then mend the fissure."

Pierre gave a hearty laugh. His friend was so creative and talented but lacked much in common sense. "Do you think I'd be here to tell you I wanted to drill a hole in the ball and stick in the receiver? Come on, *mon vieux*, I am here to call on your talents and skills."

"Mine?"

Pierre nodded with a broad smile. "Yours, *mon vieux*. You haven't been my friend all these years for nothing." In fact, they'd met just after the War in preparatory school.

Guy's eyes narrowed. "What do you want me to do?"

"I don't want you to do anything to that ball. I want you to make me a new one. Right here in your atelier. But you have to make it with the receiver already inside it. You see? Can you do it?"

Guy's eyes brightened, but only for a second. "My wife would kill me if I got involved with this."

Pierre shrugged. "Don't tell her."

"*Putain!* That's easy for you to say. You're not married."

Pierre placed his hand affectionately on his old friend's shoulder. "Listen, *mon vieux*, the weather forecasts for the summer are not very promising. Your busts are going to suffocate in here. If you do this for me, I will give you percent20 percent of whatever the profits will be. And you won't give a shit if it rains until winter."

"How much would that be?"

Pierre spread his hands in a gesture a Gaullic futility. "How can I tell you that now? Let's start off by seeing if you can make the ball."

"Can you make the right receiver?"

"I'll get to work on it if you agree to make the ball."

Guy looked upward as though thinking of his wife upstairs in bed. "*D'accord*," he said.

Guy's younger sister Monique happened to be one of the sexiest women that side of France. She was a raven-haired temptress with a voluptuous body, but in spite of it never made professional use of her physical attributes. Instead of moving to Paris as a teenager in pursuit of some glamorous career, she married a local baker named Armand, who was naturally more thrilled to roll his hands around his young wife's body than around a mound of dough. There had been much of that, but none of it resulted in pregnancy. Monique had gone to her gynecologist and learned that there were no problems with her plumbing. She urged Armand to go to his doctor and get checked out. Perhaps he had a low sperm count or was infertile. But Armand was too proud and refused. He constantly told his wife they should keep trying.

Monique had since given up and worked various jobs in and around Deauville. She'd been a bank teller, substitute schoolteacher and worked in a clothing boutique. She'd done just about everything except work in Armand's bakery, which she steadfastly refused to do. During it all, and to her credit, she'd only once strayed into an extramarital affair. It had been with a policeman in the neighboring town of Trouville, who'd pulled her over and gave her a speeding ticket. It had only lasted the length of time it took to get the ticket fixed. Considering that every other male encountering her made a pass, Monique's infidelity could hardly be thought of as a blemish on her character.

When Pierre arrived at his sister's house later that morning, he did not yet know exactly how Monique would fit into his plans. But he knew her participation would be integral. Her stunning beauty would at least serve as some sort of distraction. Until he could figure out the means by which a transmitter could be smuggled and used in the casino, he would not be able to allocate individual functions for pulling off the scam.

Monique came to the door wearing a frumpy housedress. Even in that, Pierre noticed, she was tremendously sexy. No matter how much she tried to hide her sex appeal, it seeped through like oil on cloth. Her long raven hair was knotted into a bun, which did nothing to lessen the striking features of her face. Her high cheekbones, full lips and perfectly rounded chin looked like one of the sculptured busts in Guy Laurent's atelier.

As was customary, Pierre kissed his sister on both cheeks.

"*T'as faim*?" she asked her only sibling.

"That depends if you're preparing crêpes," he said.

"*Oui, bien sûr.* Would you like chocolate or cinnamon?"

"Both would be fine, Monique."

Like always, the crêpes were delicious. After Pierre had finished three with chocolate and three with cinnamon, he said, "Do you think Armand would get involved in a casino scam?" He knew that his sister would. In fact, he knew that she knew he knew, so there was no reason to ask it.

Monique sat across the table from him. From hooks on the ceiling hung pots, pans, kettles, and various cooking utensils. Monique was a good cook in her own right, a trait not unexpected in a beautiful woman in French society.

"Maybe," she said. "The bakery is doing all right, but I suppose he'd be interested in making some extra money. Especially if what you have in mind will take place after business hours. Armand will not leave his bakery when it's open for any reason."

Pierre smiled. "It would be taking place in the evening."

"Are you going to cheat your roulette table?"

"My dear sister, you catch on fast."

Monique got up from the table to retrieve her handbag from the counter. She opened it and removed a pack of Marlboros.

"You're smoking American cigarettes now?"

"I've been smoking them for years."

"I don't like the shape of American cigarette boxes." After Monique lit up, she laid the pack on the table. Pierre scooped it up and began looking at it – curiously. It was true that American cigarette boxes were narrower but thicker than French ones, but that's not what piqued him.

"What difference does the box make?" Monique said pointedly. "It's the flavor that counts."

Pierre didn't hear a word. His brain had just gotten rocked by a thunderbolt. He stared intently at the Marlboro box and nodded approvingly. Then he dumped the remaining cigarettes onto the kitchen table, put the empty box in his pocket and ran out of his sister's house.

"*Tu est fou*!" she called out after him. Her brother was one crazy son of a bitch.

Pierre spent the entirety of his two days off in his radio shack. He did not bother with sending and receiving radio transmissions. Instead, he got right to work on the components needed for the scam. First he delved through the hundreds of radio receivers he'd accumulated over the years. He found a tiny one that was a perfect fit for the innards of a roulette ball. Then he patiently sorted through dozens of vacuum tubes to find the ones he needed to fabricate an electronic transmitter. He twisted the maze of circuitry into a small coil the size of a dime and attached it to the inside of the Marlboro box, in the front. He then cut out the cardboard of the box to the approximate circumference of the coiled transmitter. The last step was the cosmetic work to overlay and conceal a button that made the contact to activate the transmitter. This he did with red touch-up dye. He could not completely obscure the abnormality of the box, but since the person holding it would have it securely in his grip, the part of the box containing the button would be sufficiently hidden.

By the end of his second day off, Pierre had applied the finishing touches to the Marlboro box. It was now a fully functioning transmitter that would emit the signal to the receiver inside the roulette ball. The signal was calibrated to send the ball into a controlled dive that would result in its landing in specific groups of six numbers. Pierre knew from experience that there was no way to overcome the crazy bounces roulette balls took. But by having the ball land in a specified field with a high degree of accuracy, the ball would stay put in that section of six numbers often enough. Surely he could obtain a frequency much more impressive than the 16 percent chance a ball would find any given group of six numbers at random. The big question was whether the receiver inside the ball would be able to pick up the signal if the cigarette pack were inside a pocket or handbag. Of course that would be the ideal situation. If such were not the case, then the cigarette pack would have to be held in the air when the remote button was pressed. This and other questions would be answered when they got to the testing stage.

Pierre found Guy in his atelier working on a bust of the American president, Richard Nixon. "Why are you sculpting him?" he asked, somewhat amazed.

"Why not?"

"I don't think there's ever been an American president more hated by us French than he. Why not sculpt Franklin D. Roosevelt? He liberated our damn country for Christ's sake."

"I've been selling FDR busts for the past three summers. Now with the Vietnam peace talks in Paris, I think that Nixon's bust will be a good seller."

"Well, maybe you won't need Nixon," Pierre said." He laid the Marlboro box and the receiver on Guy's worktable. Guy picked up the box and admired it.

"My sister smokes them," Pierre said.

"That's a fine job you did, *mon vieux*."

"You just press the button and the transmitter sends the signal. I just need you to make the ball with this transmitter inside it. The ball has to be the exact same size and weight as the real ball. The transmitter weighs almost nothing, so it doesn't affect either. So, can you do it, *mon vieux*?"

Guy tilted his head and pursed his lips. "Come back in two days."

"I will see you then." Pierre put the cigarette box back in his pocket and left Guy with ball.

Guy's wife often descended into the atelier to watch him work. So he waited until well after dinner to sneak down and work on Pierre's roulette ball. First he measured the diameter of the ball; it was five-eighths of an inch. Then he weighed it: 2.1 grams. He did not have any ivory at his disposal, but a synthetic plastic compound would do the trick.

From a bulk sheet of synthetic plastic, he molded a mass into the round shape of a roulette ball. Before it hardened, he inserted the receiver. He then smoothed out the surface with a sander and applied two coats of ivory-colored dye and let it dry. When it did, he took the diameter and weight measurements of the new ball. He had achieved near perfection! The diameter was exactly five-eighths of an inch, and it weighed a smidgeon over 2.1 grams.

While Guy was working on the ball, Pierre had telephoned a casino supply warehouse and inquired how much it would cost for their cheapest roulette wheel. When the manager told him 2,000 francs, Pierre clarified that he only wanted the wheel and not the entire table. When the manager said that he'd understood correctly, Pierre asked if he knew someone who sold secondhand wheels. The manager didn't, but advised Pierre that sometimes they turned up in heaps of bric-a-brac in a junkyard. He recommended going to Paris, where there were dozens of such places.

Pierre would have gone to Paris, but he found just what he needed in a pile of scraps fifty miles outside of Deauville. It was an old wheel abandoned by, of all places, the Casino Deauville. And it was in fine shape. Pierre knew roulette wheels inside and out, and he quickly determined that all the parts in the inner disk were in good working condition. He paid 200 francs and drove the wheel immediately to Guy's atelier.

Pierre marvelled at the little phony roulette ball Guy put in his hand.

"What do you think, *mon vieux*?"

"*Formidable!* It's perfect." After a second look, Pierre said, "You didn't forget to put the receiver in here, did you?"

Guy laughed heartily. "Do you take me for an idiot!"

Pierre rubbed the ball between his thumb and forefinger. "The feel and color are perfect."

"*Oui, monsieur*."

Pierre set the wheel on the worktable. He spun the inner disc counter-clockwise, then snapped Guy's ball into revolutions along the groove clockwise. Gripping the Marlboro pack in his pocket, he counted nine revolutions, then pressed the transmitter button with his thumb. They watched the ball's revolutions, but nothing happened.

"Did it receive the signal?" Guy asked.

"*Merde*!" Pierre snapped. "Let's try it again." He laid the ball on the track and let it whirl. After nine revolutions he pressed the button. The ball did not react.

"Are you sure your equipment is good?" Guy asked pessimistically.

Pierre spun the ball again. This time he held the cigarette pack outside his pocket. When he pressed the button, the ball decelerated slightly, barely noticeable to the eye. Pierre closely followed its revolutions, his lips mouthing the count for each one. Just before the ball began its dive into the bowl housing the number slots, he called out, "Eleven!"

The ball bounced and dribbled, then fell into the number 36 slot.

"You missed by twenty-five," Guy said astutely.

"Shut up, you idiot!" Pierre hissed. "I did not miss. Don't you see? The Thirty-six36 slot is right next to 11. The idea is to pinpoint what section of the wheel the ball will drop into, not the exact number. If I play 100 francs straight up on six numbers next to one another, my total wager is 600 francs. If one of them hits, I get paid 35-to-1 – 3,500 francs. So my profit is 3,000 francs. If I can predict into which six-number group the ball will land just one in five times, I'll get rich."

"Oh, excuse me," Guy said meekly. "I'm not very good with probabilities."

"You don't have to be. I just want you to make three more balls." Pierre reached into his pocket and laid three tiny receivers on the worktable. "They're identical to the one you put in this ball." He removed it from the wheel and spun it again. At the last possible instant before he would call "no more bets" on his live game, he yelled out, "Nine!" The ball dropped into the number 14 slot, two slots away from number 9.

Pierre ran a hundred more test spins, alternating by fractions of seconds the precise moment he pressed the button on the Marlboro pack. Five times he hit the number on the nose. Another thirty-five he was within the six-number field. Based on 100-franc bets, that hundred-spin experiment would have yielded 84,000 francs in a live casino.

That night he dined at his sister's house with Monique and her husband, Armand. After a delicious meal of broiled lemon sole in a rich butter sauce with Chablis, they got down to business. As Monique had said, Armand was quite willing as long as it didn't interfere with his bakery.

"So Monique is going to operate your gadget, and I will be the gambler," Armand said after the last bite of his crème brulée dessert.

"*Oui*. Since she's a natural smoker, she'll look very natural holding the cigarette pack. Plus her beauty will get all the attention, not what she's doing."

"How much can we win from the casino?"

"That depends on how much heat we take. You will also have to play on some other tables legitimately. If you're only playing on mine and winning all the time, they'll get on to us.

We mustn't be greedy. I think we can make a small fortune if we play it cool. The casino rakes in hundreds of millions of francs in high season, so maybe we can get a little of that for ourselves."

Armand looked at his gorgeous wife. "Are you sure you're up to this, *ma chère*?"

Monique smiled with a twinkle in her cat-green eyes. "I am sure, *mon amour*."

Armand looked at his brother-in-law. "And how shall we split the money?"

"Three ways, *mon cher*: percent40 percent for you and Monique together, percent40 percent for me, and percent20 percent for Guy Laurent, who made the ball. Does that sound fair to you?"

Armand would have preferred half the profits for him and his wife but did not complain.

They retired to the salon, where Pierre carefully went over all the details of his plan. Since no one at the Casino Deauville knew Armand and Monique Lavallier, Armand could pose as a high roller while Monique would just be another pretty woman floating around the casino. In summertime, there were flocks of them who passed their days on the beach and their nights at the casino, many of whom were on the make for rich international sugar daddies. Husband and wife would not know each other, and sometimes one would be in the casino without the other.

Their starting bankroll was 50,000 francs, all the spare cash they could muster between them, including a 10,000-franc loan from Guy. To start, Armand would bet the same series of six numbers, 500 francs straight up on each. He would occasionally make the same bet in a different fashion by employing the European *voisin* bet, which was to make a single wager that covered one number and its two neighboring numbers on either side on the wheel. This would give the appearance that Armand was mixing up his bets somewhat. In addition, he would make throwaway bets on inside numbers not part of the six-number field and on outside even money and 2-to-1 propositions, all to reinforce the camouflage. Once he started winning, the principal bets would steadily increase until they reached the table limits.

Pierre explained to Monique the importance of handling the cigarette pack as unobtrusively as possible. Although there was nothing unusual about someone holding a pack of cigarettes in a casino, there was when someone held one all the time. You could get away with ferrying a drink around, but not a pack of cigarettes. Monique assured her brother that she'd be able to carry the cigarettes in a way no one would notice, using her handbag as a shield. Only when it came time to push the button would she have to bring the pack in view, and even that she could do discreetly. In a crowded casino with the majority of people either smoking or drinking, she should be able to blend right in.

The final facet of the scam did not concern Pierre's sister or brother-in-law. This was the most important and dangerous part: how he would sneak the rigged roulette ball into play and then remove it each time he left the table. To accomplish that feat, Pierre constructed a trapping mechanism consisting of a spring wire and a rubber receptacle that he would fasten around his right forearm just above the wrist. The sleeve of both his frilled shirt and tuxedo jacket would help secure it.

At the beginning of his shift he would pick up the casino ball from the number slot it rested in, then clench it between his middle and index fingers and deftly guide it into his sleeve, where it would be caught by the trapping mechanism. Then he'd let the rigged ball in the fleshy part of his palm curl onto the same two fingers, ready to place it against the groove of the wheel and spin it. On his last spin before leaving the table, he would bump his wrist against the table surface while stacking chips, thereby triggering the mechanism to release the casino ball. Then he'd switch that ball back into play with the same movements he'd used to introduce the rigged ball, taking the rigged one with him off the game. He'd practiced the movements a thousand times, and had them mastered like a trained magician.

The scam began the Sunday evening of the day the Formula One grand prix raced through the streets of Monaco. Pierre would have thought nothing of it, but the legendary British race-car driver Graham Hill not only showed up that night at the Casino Deauville with a beautiful woman but decided to play English roulette on Pierre's table. Naturally everyone in the casino, French and non-French alike, made a big fuss over the Formula One star, who'd flown to Deauville just after the race.

As soon as Pierre arrived at his table, Hill and the woman were already there playing. The table was packed with jetsetters. A gaggle of celebrity gawkers stood around the perimeter watching. The best thing about it was that no one was paying much attention to the dealer, so when it came time to switch the balls, Pierre wouldn't have to worry about wandering eyes settling on his hands.

The dealer leaving the table bade everyone good luck. Pierre stepped into his slot behind the burnished wheel and looked in the bowl for the casino roulette ball. It happened to be in the number 13 slot. He hoped it wasn't a bad omen as he watched the players pour their bets onto the layout from every direction. Then he waved his arm in a arc over the layout and called out, *"Rien ne va plus."*

As he lifted the ball from the bowl, he shot a glance at the inspector sitting on the high chair in the pit above the table. The man stared absently down to the layout. Pierre glanced around the table at the players. Satisfied no one was watching, he flicked the ball with his two fingers up his sleeve and into the trapping device. He could not hear it, but he felt the ball spring right into the rubber receptacle clasped to his forearm. He breathed a sigh of relief. He'd successfully pulled off the first major coup of the scam.

Now he let the rigged ball in his palm fall to his fingers. He set it against the inner groove of the wheel and let it rip. The ball launched into a series of speeding revolutions and slowed at its normal rate. Then it dropped, trickled around the bowl and landed in the number 4 slot. Pierre placed the marker on top of the chips in the number 4 box on the layout, then swept away the losers and paid the winners.

Ten minutes later, a man who'd spent most of that day covered in flour but who was now draped in black evening dress with a red cummerbund arrived at the table. He sat in the lone empty chair next to Graham Hill. From his jacket pocket he removed a leather sheath filled with 500-franc notes and laid them on the table. Pierre tallied them to 25,000 francs, then exchanged them for fifty 500-franc chips. He said, "*Bon chance, monsieur,*" to the gentleman, who responded, "*Merci.*"

Pierre watched the players make their bets. From every direction chips rained onto the layout. It was as if a great race against time was taking place to get the bets down. Within seconds, each of the thirty-six numbers and zero had piles of chips on it straight up or on intersecting lines with neighboring boxes. Armand bet precisely how Pierre had instructed him: one 500-franc chip straight up on numbers 1, 5, 10, 16, 24 and 33. These six numbers were spread from the top of the betting layout to the bottom in no discernible order. But on the wheel they were a neat side-by-side group. The order of the six consecutive numbers on the inner disc was: 10, 5, 24, 16, 33, 1. If one of them won, Armand would be paid 17,500 francs. He would lose 500 francs on the other five numbers, a total loss of 2,500 francs. His total profit for the spin would therefore be 15,000 francs. If none of the numbers came in, Armand stood to lose a total of 3,000 francs.

Pierre called out, *"Rien ne va plus,"* in accompaniment to an elongated wave of his arm across the layout. Everyone finished betting. Then he gripped the rigged ball between his middle and index fingers, set it against the groove and snapped it loose with the exact force needed to generate the exact speed he had calculated. The ball took off, hissing around the cylinder.

At that moment, a raven-haired beauty in a soft pink evening gown and a pearl necklace stepped up to the table. Many sets of eyes darted upward from the table to take in the sight of this lovely creature, but not all of them. When gambling was at issue, some gentlemen and jealous ladies would not take their eyes off the layout. The woman removed a pack of Marlboros from her gold-trimmed handbag. Before she could place a cigarette between her lips, a stylish gentleman in a tux was at her side proffering a gold Dunhill lighter. He lit her cigarette, and she thanked him.

But she looked at him for only a fraction of a second. Her eyes darted back to the spinning ball on the roulette wheel. She concentrated deeply, remembering what Pierre had told her to do. She counted the revolutions each time the ball passed the precise three o'clock position on the wheel, the point at which it was most visible to her. When the ball reached that point on its ninth revolution, her thumb pressed the button on the cigarette pack.

"Are you American?" the gentleman who'd lit her Marlboro asked in English.

Monique spoke adequate English, having once taught it as a substitute teacher. "No, *monsieur,*" she responded in a charming accent. "I just like American cigarettes very much." It was not an oddity to see Frenchwomen smoking American cigarettes.

"I see," the gentleman said in French. "In any event, I wish you a profitable evening."

She thanked him, and he walked off. She hoped his wish came true.

Pierre had also been counting the ball's revolutions. When he reached the ninth, he could not fathom any disruption to the ball's movement. He wondered if the gadget had functioned properly. He'd tested it a thousand times in Guy's atelier, but maybe something in the casino interfered with the transmitter's signal. With all their surveillance and communications equipment, interference was possible. But then again, he'd hardly noticed the tiny modification of the ball's movement when it had received the signal during the testing process.

The ball slid off the track and dropped into the bowl. It rattled around briefly and then fell smack into the number 16 slot. Pierre for an instant could not remember if that number was one of Armand's. But when his eyes shot to the 16 box on the layout, he saw Armand's blue 500-franc chip lying on the bottom of an assortment of chips straight up on the number.

"Numero seize, rouge, pair," Pierre called out, briefly making eye contact with Armand. He swept the losers off the layout. Then paid the winners. He slid thirty-five 500-franc chips to Armand. They made 15,000 francs on the spin, minus incidental losses on the camouflage bets.

Monique did not put the Marlboro pack in her handbag, instead holding it in her right hand at her side, where the handbag hanging from her shoulder would keep it unnoticed. In her left hand she carried a glass of wine, which deflected attention from her right. As she'd told Pierre, she looked like the rest of the patrons with a drink or cigarette in hand.

On the roulette layout, the players began feverishly spreading their chips over their favorite numbers for the next spin. According to plan, Armand made the same six bets on the same numbers. Pierre spun the ball with the same force. It reached its ninth revolution within a half-second of the time it had taken to reach the same point on the previous spin. That was Pierre's function. If he could maintain the proper velocity every spin, and if Monique could time her pressing of the button with the same constant accuracy, they would succeed dramatically as long as the electronic equipment did not malfunction.

Ten feet from the table, Monique had found an unimpeded line of sight to the wheel. This was the perfect location as she was close enough to transmit the signal yet far enough away to be outside the scope of the fixed overhead surveillance camera. In the early 1970s, casino surveillance cameras were much less sophisticated, and rarely was there coverage on every table. Observers in the eye in the sky had to pan and tilt from table to table, thus they did not pan through open casino space to observe people away from the tables as often as they do today.

Monique's sharp eyes saw the orbiting ball pass the three o'clock spot on its eighth revolution. She eased her right hand away from the handbag. She didn't have to raise it much to get the Marlboro pack in line with the roulette wheel. When the ball made its ninth revolution past three o'clock, she pressed the button and gently let her hand fall back to her side.

The ball began its controlled dive as Pierre called out, "*Rien ne va plus.*" This time when it departed the groove, it fell dead into the number 33 slot without bouncing out. Pierre knew instantly that 33 was in their winning field. He called out, "*Numero trente-trois, noir, impair.*" Armand won another 15,000 francs.

The next two spins missed their six-number section, but not by much. The first was one slot away on the right, the second two slots away on the left. The following spin caught number 1, another winner. Each time, Monique handled the cigarette pack without hindrance.

Armand played until quarter of four in the morning. After the first hour, he was ahead 100,000 francs and raised his wagers to 1,000 francs on each number. After the second, when he was ahead 350,000 francs, Pierre made eye contact with him and then looked to his left. This was their signal telling Armand to switch his primary betting to a new group of six numbers: 0, 32, 15, 19, 4, 21. There was no need to make Monique aware of this. She would continue gauging the ball's revolutions around the wheel and press the remote button when it passed the spot at three o'clock on the ninth revolution. The key to controlling the outcome with the new numbers resided in Pierre's ability to make the subtle adjustment in the speed of his spins. The torque his finger-snap launching of the ball generated had to be slightly increased or decreased in order to govern the ball's landings in different sections of the bowl, in conjunction with its controlled dive activated by the receiver inside it.

The maximum straight-up bet at the Casino Deauville was 2,000 francs. The 70,000 francs it paid was equivalent to $14,000. The last two hours Armand played, he bet the 2,000-franc max on each of the six numbers. Pierre had signalled him once again to change the series of numbers he bet. By the time Armand was ahead a million francs, he drew the attention of the casino manager, who came up behind him at the table and introduced himself. In a display of typical French discretion, the manager did not ask Armand for his name. Unlike today's American casinos, pit personnel in Europe did not come running to take your name and rate your play. The French casino boss just wanted to inform his unknown high roller how much of a pleasure it was to have him gambling at the Casino Deauville.

During the spin he was there, Pierre had made eye contact with Monique and then looked to his right. This was the signal to temporarily halt her function. Until he again made eye contact with her and then looked to his left, she would not press the button on the Marlboro pack. If ever Pierre rubbed his nose distinctly after making eye contact with her, Monique would immediately leave the casino. He would only give that signal in the event he felt the casino was on to their scam and an immediate escape was necessary.

Once the casino boss left, they resumed. They hit eight of the last ten spins before calling it a night, winning another half-million francs. Fifteen minutes before closing time, Pierre signalled Armand and Monique that they were done. Monique slipped out of the casino while Armand steered stacks of 1,000-franc and 5,000-franc roulette chips across the layout. Pierre gathered them into his well, counted them out, then with the inspector's approval exchanged them for twenty 100,000-franc plaques, which Armand took to the cashier and exchanged for 2 million francs in cash. He also cashed a handful of 1,000-franc and 5,000-franc chips. In all, the crooked threesome had cleared more than 2 million francs that first night of the scam.

The last phase was to take the rigged ball out of play and switch the casino ball back in. A handful of players still remained at the table. While they pasted the layout with chips, Pierre glanced up at the inspector, then, as he mucked losing chips from the previous spin, let his wrist bump into the table. The one fear was that the spring would not kick the ball out of the receptacle. Even if that happened, it did not necessarily mean they would be discovered. But the risk would always be there. If the rigged ball was left behind and somehow discovered by the casino, they could be set up the next time they operated their scam.

The following weekend they started on Friday evening. Armand arrived in his splendidly tailored evening dress at nine o'clocknine . This time Monique was already in the casino. She'd been there gambling for an hour, but not on Pierre's table. They'd figured that she should at least show the casino some action when not operating the remote control.

The casino was jammed up as the French coastal resort was now in full summer swing. Pierre's table had a new assortment of beautifully tanned and elegantly dressed people. Armand arrived at the table with 200,000 francs in chips he had purchased at the casino cage. He immediately placed 2,000 francs straight up on six numbers that neighbored one another on the wheel. He also made a series of random bets that had nothing to do with their scam.

The first six spins they lost. This exceeded their previous longest losing streak by two. Pierre worried that something had gone wrong. One more losing spin and he would halt their operation for that night. He would return to Guy's atelier, where more tests on the equipment would be conducted.

But the seventh spin was a winner. So was the eighth. Then the ninth, tenth and eleventh. They went on a tear. When Armand was ahead a million francs, he again drew the casino manager to the table. But this time the boss only observed, did not approach the lucky gambler. And Pierre did not give Monique the signal to halt. The scam was rolling along perfectly, functioning *comme des roulettes*. Nothing was evident in the flight of the ball that would appear suspicious. Pierre decided to continue despite the heat.

When Armand was ahead 2 million francs, he drew the attention of the casino's principal owner. The dapper silver-haired gentleman had been in his office when he received a call from his manager that the same player from the week before was again winning at a highly unusual rate on the same English roulette table. The owner decided to take a closer look at his new high-stakes player. He was bothered because he knew who all his high rollers were. But this new one was a stranger.

Watching his action as he stood directly behind Armand, the owner could not put his finger on anything indicating cheating. He was an old-time sharpie himself and knew most of the scams. In his younger days patrolling Casino Deauville's carpeted floor, he'd spotted and busted up many a scam in progress, including the most skilled Italian pastposting teams.

So he made the rash decision that this unknown gambler was

just on a highly improbable winning streak that would soon, like the rest he'd seen over the years, end up how his favorite singer, Frank Sinatra, sang: "Riding high in April, shot down in May..."

Leaving the table on his way back to his office, his eyes fell on someone else he'd never before noticed in his casino: a beautiful woman with full breasts in a beige evening gown. As he was well acquainted with his big gamblers, he was equally well acquainted with the beautiful women frequenting his casino, whether they were companions of his high rollers or high-class hookers on the make. But who was this one?

He was told an hour later that the mysterious gambler kept on winning. At three-thirty in the morning, the head cashier buzzed his office to say that the gambler had cashed out for 2.5 million francs at the cage. The next night, Saturday, he was notified that the same gambler had returned to the English roulette table. Bugged again, he immediately descended on the casino for a close-up view of the guy's action. In utter amazement, he watched the gambler amass a whopping 4 million francs in chips while nothing seemed amiss with the dealing of the game. He still opted not to approach the gambler, but went up to the beautiful woman who'd been standing off to the side of the roulette table and piquing his curiosity.

"*Bonsoir, madame,*" he said graciously.

"*Bonsoir, monsieur.*" Monique knew exactly who he was. She had made no attempt to hide the cigarette pack.

"I don't believe we've met," he said. "Are you enjoying the evening without the company of a gentleman?" His tone was chivalrous, just as her brother had told her it would be.

"*Oui*. I like to come to the casino alone. Sometimes I gamble, sometimes I don't."

"May I present myself." It was not a question. "My name is Yves Vashon. I am the proprietor of Casino Deauville."

"*Enchanté*." She transferred the Marlboro pack to her left hand and offered him her right. Vashon grasped it delicately and kissed it.

"The pleasure is for me," he said nobly. Then suddenly he thrust his hand in his inside jacket pocket. He pulled it back out, having withdrawn nothing. Then he delved inside his trousers pockets with both hands. They came out empty. "Hmmm, seems I've left my cigarettes in my office. May I intrude for one of yours? I do like Marlboros as well."

Monique had realized this could happen the moment before it did, so she was not caught off guard. Holding the pack outward with the front part housing the button facing her, she flipped open the cover with her forefinger and exposed the cigarettes to Vashon. Though she felt awkward handling the pack in that fashion, Vashon did not seem to notice a peculiarity. The cigarettes were loose, so he easily slipped two ringed fingers in the pack and extracted a cigarette.

"*Merci beaucoup, madame*," he said, and turned to leave. But then stopped. "*Excusez-moi*, you didn't present yourself."

"Ah, *Oui*, of course." She feigned embarrassment. "I am *Madame* Pouget."

He waited for more.

"Chantal Pouget."

He smiled at the coup. "May I call you Chantal?"

"You may."

"Then I wish you a pleasant and very lucky evening, Chantal. I hope to see you again." He flashed another charming smile and walked off.

During the encounter, Monique had missed a spin. This was the first time it happened. She didn't know whether that spin had lost or won, but she did know she'd passed a crucial test. She'd been cool enough under pressure and was able to resume operating the gadget as soon as Vashon had left her alone.

But the next night, it became obvious that Vashon wanted to make her his mistress. Pierre had decided that Armand would not show up at the casino. They would simply have Monique float around the casino and play roulette to give the impression she was also a gambler. She played on several of the larger French roulette tables and bet 100-franc chips. She always had a Marlboro pack lying on the table in front of her, but of course it was not the one housing the transmitter.

A legitimate roulette ball was coursing the track when Monique felt a hand rest on her shoulder. She looked up from her chair at the table and saw Vashon standing over her.

"*Bonsoir,* Chantal."

"*Bonsoir,* Monsieur Vashon."

"Please call me Honoré."

"*Bonsoir,* Honoré."

"How is my casino treating you this evening?"

Monique smiled but not too flirtatiously: "*Comme ci comme ça.*"

"Well, don't you worry, Chantal. If the croupiers do not take care of you, I will. Would you like to join me for a cup of champagne and caviar later this evening?"

"Oh, that's very nice of you, Honoré, but I really must be going soon."

"Very well. Perhaps another time." His hand went inside his jacket pocket, and then he frowned. "I can't believe I've again been so absentminded." He indicated the pack of Marlboros on the layout. "Do you mind?"

She smiled. "Go right ahead." She watched him lift the pack, exactly what she wanted. He would see it was nothing more than a normal pack of Marlboro cigarettes.

"You're going to have me smoking these American cigarettes regularly," he said with debonair charm, then finally walked off.

Pierre, Monique and Armand discussed the Vashon situation

midweek over dinner. Armand thought it was great that the casino owner was taking an interest in her. He was convinced that the more time he spent ogling his wife, the less time he'd spend watching their crooked roulette game. "Vashon's libido can only help us," he figured.

Pierre agreed, but worried nonetheless that Vashon would stumble onto their scam by being too close to Monique and the Marlboro pack.

It was Monique who quelled her brother's worries. "Don't worry, Pierre. I can handle him. He just wants to get in my pants. He is not suspicious in the least." She told them of his having seen the "clean" cigarette pack at the roulette table.

Armand laughed. "Imagine if it had been the rigged pack and he picked it up and pressed the button! He would be helping us rob his own casino!"

They all shared in the humor, then after some more discussion decided they'd continue their attack the following weekend. At that point, they had scammed the Casino Deauville out of 9 million francs, nearly 2 million American dollars. The sky appeared to be the limit.

On Friday night, Vashon was all over Monique like a bee on honey. She couldn't get rid of him. He was becoming a nuisance to the point of interfering with the scam. She tried every which way to give him the message, at first subtly and politely, but then with a little more assertiveness.

"My husband will be returning from England shortly," she said at one point while Vashon stood next to her smoking.

"How come your husband never accompanies you to the casino, Chantal?"

The only reply she could think of was "Because he doesn't gamble."

"Then why don't you and I take a gamble together and board my yacht right now and sail to Bora Bora?"

Monique made herself gush. "That's very generous of you, Honoré, but I'm afraid that wouldn't be possible."

He took the rejection gracefully, but only because he'd be back for another attempt.

Due to Vashon's repetitive harassment of Monique, their earnings suffered that weekend. Armand only won a million francs. The last thing Pierre would have imagined was that their scam would be slowed because his sister was so goddamned sexy.

Unbeknownst to Pierre, Monique and Armand, Honoré Vashon was not a man to be trifled with. He did not take well to being rejected by women; it was his self-proclaimed God-given right to have any woman he wanted for his mistress. During the week, Vashon had two things on his mind: the woman he knew as Chantal Pouget and the unknown gambler who was winning chunks of money at roulette. When he was told by his casino manager that the gambler's winnings had accumulated to 10 million francs in three weeks at his casino, Vashon decided it was time to find out who this lucky bastard was. Perhaps something was going down at that roulette table.

On his way to the table, Vashon saw Monique but did not acknowledge her. He strode right up to Armand, stood rigidly above him and said, "*Bonsoir, monsieur*. My name is Honoré Vashon. I am the proprietor of the casino."

Armand, not nearly as cool as his wife under pressure, was taken aback. But he still managed to say without wavering, "*Bonsoir, Monsieur* Vashon."

Vashon did not advise Armand to call him Honoré. "I see that you've become a frequent patron of our establishment, and I like to get to know those who play here at the Casino Deauville. If only for the reason that I may do whatever is necessary to accommodate them, *Monsieur*...?"

Armand blurted the first phony name that came to him:

"Cartier…Alain Cartier."

"Ah," Vashon gushed. "You're a Cartier!"

"Oui – mais non, *monsieur!* My name is Cartier, but I am not one of *the* Cartiers."

"Oh, excuse me. It's just by the significance of your wagers that I came to that errant conclusion."

"I understand," Armand said.

Pierre watched and listened to the discourse. He couldn't be sure if Vashon was suspicious, but did notice that the casino owner never looked in his direction. Pierre did, however, flash the signal to Monique to halt operating the Marlboro pack.

Vashon looked at Armand's mounting chips on the table and said, "You've been enjoying quite a run of good luck here, *Monsieur* Cartier."

"I must say I have." Armand gave a smile that seemed to annoy Vashon, and Pierre caught it.

"Well then, I wish you continued success, *Monsieur* Cartier. *Bonne chance*." Vashon strode off, passed by Monique without as much as a nod, and went up to his office.

Vashon was now sure that this Cartier character was a hustler. But how was he hitting that roulette table like this? The one blatant thing about it was that Cartier always played at the same table. There had to be a reason. Could the wheel itself be defective? Maybe Cartier had picked up on an imperfection with its inner workings and exploited it.

He summoned the casino manager to his office.

"Get some experts in here and have them take apart that wheel. Something must be wrong with it."

On Monday morning when the casino was closed, those experts came. They took apart the wheel and examined every working piece integral to the ball's spinning around the disk and the wheel's revolutions in the opposite direction. But all they found was that the wheel was in perfect balance. There was not even the slightest imperfection that could produce biased outcomes.

Vashon was astonished to hear this. His next step Tuesday morning was a telephone call to the chief of Deauville's police department. "His name is Alain Cartier," he told the chief. "See if you can find out who the hell he is." On Wednesday, Chief Delaitre called back and told Vashon that there were no Alain Cartiers with a criminal record as far as both he and the French National Police were concerned.

Finally, Vashon's suspicion fell on the dealer. It was on Pierre Fillion's shifts that the casino's money was being lost. Maybe there was some sophisticated scam in which Fillion and Cartier were partners. He'd seen dealer–player partnerships before.

On Friday night, while Armand gambled and won at the table, Vashon, the casino manager, and their surveillance head secretly watched Pierre deal the game from above. They paid close attention to his every movement, but his motion was the same every spin. They noticed nothing out of the ordinary, nothing indicating an attempt to control the velocity of the ball. It made the same number of revolutions before going into its descent every time. Vashon couldn't believe it. Under their very eyes, Cartier had won another 3 million francs. As Monique had not been impeded by Vashon's advances, she'd been able to operate the device freely without pause.

On Saturday morning, the chain-smoking casino owner lit up a French cigarette at his desk. He hadn't gone home nor had he slept a wink on his office sofa. He'd grown totally obsessed by the scam he was sure must be taking place in his casino. As he harped on it, his thoughts meandered toward Chantal Pouget. He realized he was going nowhere fast with the raven-haired temptress. And it pissed him off. What woman would refuse a trip on his yacht, married or unmarried?

That night he began watching her with a different eye. Why

was she so often in the casino, apparently alone? Why did she always stand by the English roulette table without making a bet on it? He'd seen her play roulette, but only on the French tables. Another strange thing he'd noticed was that she always carried a pack of cigarettes yet never smoked. He observed her now on his video monitor; she was standing by the same English roulette wheel and had the Marlboro pack in her hand. But she was not smoking. Had he ever seen her with a cigarette in her mouth?

All this boiled down to a final perplexing question: Was there a connection between her presence near that English table and its losing so much money whenever Cartier played there?

Agonizingly watching Cartier raking in pile after pile of chips on his screen, Vashon grabbed the phone off its cradle and called a private security firm he'd used only once since becoming the owner of the casino. It was a wild hunch, but as well the only possibility he'd not yet exhausted. "Get a debugging crew in here and sweep the goddamn casino!"

"Now?" the surprised security man on the other end of the line asked.

"Now!" Vashon barked into the receiver and hung up.

It happened very discreetly with the debugging crew posing as waiters. No one seemed to notice their detection equipment.

Two hours later, with Armand winning two million more francs, the principal casino owner approached Monique with the most inviting smile she'd yet seen on his face. "Bonjour, Chantal. It's so nice to see you again."

"Bonjour, Honoré."

Then Vashon reached inside his jacket pocket. And then his trousers pockets.

Monique thought, *Not again*!

Vashon clucked his tongue as if annoyed at himself. "With all my apologies, Chantal, can I please put you out one more time for a cigarette? I promise it will be the last time."

Monique smiled. "Of course." She held the Marlboro pack out to him with her thumb securely over the button. She flicked open the cover with her forefinger.

Suddenly she felt a hand rudely grab the pack out of her hand. It was not Vashon's. It belonged to a man with a moustache she'd never before seen in the casino. He flipped over the pack, immediately saw the button, then passed it to a second man Monique had also never seen in the casino. The second man opened the cover, reached inside the pack and pulled out the transmitter.

"You're under arrest, *madame,*" he said coldly.

When Armand had lost eight spins in a row, breaking their record for consecutive losses, Pierre finally looked across the table for Monique. But she wasn't there. He scanned the casino. Perhaps she'd moved to another spot to gain better access to the wheel.

But she was gone.

He got Armand's attention and rubbed his nose emphatically, the signal to cash out the chips he had left on the table and get the hell out. Armand jumped out of the chair as if his butt had caught fire. He bolted from the table, forgetting his chips, and was intercepted by Vashon's security men as he descended the stairs leading to the exit. Finally, when Pierre bumped his wrist against the table to release the casino ball and put it back into play, he felt something cold and hard clasp around it. It was a handcuff that a second later was joined to another handcuff around his other wrist.

The scam had truly been a marvel. Were Monique not such a sexy and beautiful woman, perhaps it would have gone on much longer. As it was, Pierre, Monique and Armand beat the Casino Deauville for more than 15 million francs ($3 million) during its month of operation. Unfortunately, they had to surrender all of it before beginning their prison sentences. Even

Guy Laurent, who'd received only a half-share of the profits for making the rigged roulette ball, received a full share of the prison sentence: four years.

The French cigarette scam was the basis for the well-known 1984 French film *Les Tricheurs* (The cheatersCheaters).

Chapter 5

The Titanic Scam

One of the world's greatest gambling scams did not take place in a casino or racetrack but rather onboard the most famous ocean liner in history. Believe it or not, it happened onboard the *Titanic,* two days before the great ship hit the iceberg. The guy who pulled it off went down with the vessel, but before dying he recounted the scam to a young stowaway while they lay clinging to a life raft in the icy waters of the North Atlantic. The first thing the bowled over lad did on his rescue was to tell anyone else who'd listen. The recounting of it passed from generation to generation of British hustlers, and to this very day you can walk into an English pub and overhear people talking about Piers Mason.

Piers was a good old Anglo Saxon con artist. He was as dashing and charming as they came, but like all scammers did not start out in the major leagues. He started off as an orphaned waif picking the pockets of Europe's elite in the fashionable districts of London. He did rather well, but on his seventeenth birthday picked the wrong pocket belonging to a very irate Dutchman who snatched the lad's hand coming out of his pocket and broke two of his fingers. While his fingers mended, Piers enlisted his childhood chum, Simon, to help him along with his next devious adventure.

They stood across the street from a Soho teahouse. Simon wore the rags in which he normally traipsed about London. Piers was dressed in his Sunday best, his two broken fingers coiled in tape.

Piers removed a £10 note and tore a quarter-inch strip off the top right corner. "Order a cup of tea and pay for it with this," he said to Simon. "Drink the tea and then come back here with the change."

Simon took the note and found an outdoor table in front of the teahouse. He order his tea, paid the waitress with the £10 note Piers had given him, drank the tea and returned to Piers with the change.

"Wait here," Piers said. "You may hear a little brouhaha, but don't panic. It's par for the course." He went to the teahouse, took the table Simon had just vacated and ordered a tea. When the waitress delivered it, he paid with a £1 note, which she stuffed haphazardly in her little purse. While he sipped his tea, she fumbled through the purse to gather the coins for his change, 85 pence.

The instant the coins hit the table, Piers exclaimed, "Hey! I gave you a £10 note! Where's the rest of my change?"

The Irish hussy at once became indignant. "Go on!" she said. "You gave me a £1 note. You think I'm gonna fall for a dumb-ass trick like that?"

"Dumb-ass, my ass!" Piers shot back. "I gave you a £10 note. You're trying to screw me."

"Go screw yourself, bloke! You gave me a £1 note."

"I demand my proper change."

"Well, I'll go get the manager. We'll let him settle this."

She turned on her heel and went inside the teahouse. Turning heads and exclamations of surprise converged on Piers's table. Moments later, the waitress was back with a staid-looking man who seemed the type unappreciative of nonsense. Piers went on the offensive before he could open his mouth.

"I gave the bitch a £10 note for this crummy tea, and she's tried to rip me off," he yelled belligerently.

The manager was taken aback. "There's no reason for a temper tantrum like that, young man!"

"He gave me £1!" the waitress shrieked. "It's right here." She opened her purse and removed the £1 note Piers had given her. "See!"

Piers reached into the pocket of his stylish but secondhand trousers. He extracted a leather wallet he'd lifted from Marks & Spencer. "All I had in my wallet was two £10 notes." He pulled one out, and as he laid it on the table, the torn piece from the £10 note he'd handed Simon landed next to it. The "10" on it was intact.

"There!" Piers shouted in excitement, as if he had not perfectly timed the flick of his finger to coordinate the magic appearance of the torn strip. "I must have torn that note when I pulled it out of my wallet to pay you," he said to the waitress. "I bet you have a £10 note with its corner missing in your purse."

The waitress stared blankly at Piers.

"Go ahead and look," he said.

She looked at the manager, who seemed to be waiting for her to look inside her purse. She scowled at Piers, then reluctantly fished out a handful of crumpled bank notes. Two of them were tenners. One had its corner missing, which blatantly struck the eye as if the note had been brutally mutilated.

"You see!" Piers cried. "You tried to rip me off!"

The waitress flushed red. "I didn't try to rip..."

"I think you owe this young man an apology with his change," the manager said gravely with a frown.

The waitress was still not satisfied, but the evidence was overwhelming. She bit her tongue and laid £9 on the table. "I'm...I'm sorry, sir."

"Yes, we're very sorry, sir," the manager said. "Please enjoy your tea."

"Did it work?" Simon said anxiously when Piers rejoined him down the block. "It sounded like cats and dogs over there."

Piers laughed and slapped his mate on the shoulder. "Of course it worked, mate. Now let's just go have another cup of tea somewhere."

The ripped-bank-note scam worked two times in three. The odd time out, Piers would be rudely chased out of the establishment, nothing worse than that. The next scam they worked with British currency dropped from £10 notes to lowly pence. However, their profits were considerably higher. The first time they tried it was early in the morning at a kiosk outside Victoria Station. For this occasion, it was Piers wearing the rags and Simon the suit they'd bought at Marks & Spencer with the proceeds from their teahouse scam.

"All right, you know the script?" Piers asked.

"Yeah, I think I got it."

"Okay, then go. I'll be waiting inside the station at the information booth."

Simon approached the kiosk and selected the morning edition of *The Times* and a couple of candy bars. He laid the paper and candy on the counter under the eyes of the proprietor inside the kiosk. Removing a handful of coins from his pocket to pay, he dropped them. He screamed, "Shit!" as they hit the pavement and scattered in every direction. Then he hit bent over and grabbed up the rolling coins while the man inside the kiosk watched. When five minutes and a dozen customers later Simon was still on his hands and knees searching the area around the kiosk and cursing, the man finally asked, "How much did you lose, mate? Couldn't be worth you soiling your fine threads like that."

"It's worth a helluva lot more than that!" Simon said in a frantic voice. "You see, I just bought a rare penny from a busted-out coin dealer in a poker game. It's dated 1818 and there were only a few thousand minted that year. Plus it's in brilliant condition, shines like a freshly minted penny. I'm a collector myself, and it's the only piece missing in my penny collection."

The man got a little interested. "How much is it worth?"

"Two hundred quid."

"Two hundred quid for a penny!"

"The guy sold it to me for a hundred and fifty because he needed fast cash to get back in the poker game."

"That's a shame, mate."

Simon, following the script, looked at his wristwatch. "Look, I gotta go," he said between pants. "My train leaves in five minutes. But I'll tell you what: If you happen to find that penny around here, hold it for me. I'll be back at the end of the day. I'll pay you the full two hundred quid for it. I don't mind the loss, seeing it's the only date I don't have in my collection. Okay?"

"Sounds fair enough to me, mate."

Simon hurried off inside the station, purposely leaving behind the paper and candy bars he'd put on the counter. He found Piers reading *The Times* on a bench. "Okay, mate, he's all yours."

But Piers decided to wait two hours before heading to the kiosk. He knew that returning too soon would evoke the proprietor's suspicion and waiting too long risked his not being interested, if only because of the passage of time. One of the main arts of the con was timing. When you made your move at the right time, it paid. When your timing was off, you lost.

They spied the kiosk from the opposite side of a busy London thoroughfare. After the two hours passed, Piers crossed the street as soon as a cluster of customers had paid for their newspapers and left. He greeted the proprietor as he picked up the afternoon edition of the *Daily Mail* and laid it on the counter. Then he suddenly bent down to the pavement. When he straightened up there was a shiny penny in his open hand.

"Wow! Look at his," he said to the proprietor. "Pretty luster for a coin this old." As if to aid his cause, the rays of the midday sun bounced off the coin into the man's eyes.

"What's the date on it?" he asked very curiously.

"1818. I wonder how it could still be so shiny. I don't know anything about coins, but I guess this one's been out of circulation for a while."

"Let me see that, mate," the man said, thrusting his hand through the space over the counter.

Piers gladly handed him the penny. The man looked at it closely, admiring its luster, even more so the date. When he saw the 1818, he knew he had the valuable lost penny in his hand, and his head started calculating figures.

"You think it might be worth something?" Piers said, sounding as dumb as he could.

The proprietor gave a dismissive wave. "Nay, mate. It may be as bright as the cliffs of Dover, but a penny ain't nothin' but a penny."

"Gotta be worth something," Piers disagreed. Then he threw in the hook: "I bet I could sell it somewhere. Gotta be a coin dealer in central London somewhere." He put his hand out to retrieve the penny from the man, who suddenly didn't want to part with it.

"Tell you what, mate," the man said. "1818's the year my great-grandfather was born. The old bastard is still alive and kickin'. Maybe he'd like this shiny penny as a good luck charm, so I'll give you a quid for it. Whaddaya say?"

"A quid?" Piers knew he had him sucked in. Greed was working its way through his victim's brain. Preying on it was how good con artists made their living. "Something this old this shiny's gotta be worth a helluva lot more than one quid," he wised up.

"Look, mate, I'll give you five quid. How's that sound?"

Piers shook his head. "I got a better idea. How 'bout we go find a coin dealer. Whatever he says its worth, I'll give it to you for half."

"I can't leave my kiosk," the man said. "I get customers here every minute." This was not only the proprietor's out but also exactly what Piers knew he would say. In fact, the whole scam was based on that. There was no way the man would be able to take the time necessary to have the penny appraised. It was actually worth a bit less than £2, the price at which Piers had bought a hundred of them from coin merchants scattered all over London. Each one was as shiny as a freshly minted penny.

"Then forget it," Piers said with rehearsed impatience. "I'll go find a dealer my self. I ain't got no great-grandfather and I could use the money for whatever this coin is worth. It must be my lucky day." He stuck his hand out for the coin.

But the proprietor was really hooked. He was thinking of the well-dressed gentleman who had said he'd be back that afternoon to inquire if his missing penny had turned up. He would pay two hundred quid! "Well, how much you want for it, mate?"

Piers went into the dangling-the-carrot routine. "Well, I don't know. I guess I'd take fifty quid for it."

The man's eyes popped out of his head. "Fifty quid! What's in the ale you been drinkin', mate?"

"All right. Forty. And that's only because I'm in a rush."

Piers's insides warmed when the man responded, "Twenty, not a penny more."

"Thirty."

"Why you're a greedy little prick!" the man said indignantly. "I'll give you twenty-five quid, and consider that a gift."

"I will," Piers said, laying his hand flat on the counter, awaiting bank notes in payment.

The man made a grimace as he removed two tenners and a five from his cash drawer. He slapped them into Piers's hand.

"Thank you, sir," Piers said, smiling widely "And tell your great-grandfather 'happy birthday.'" He noticed the look of confusion on the proprietor's face when he walked away. He'd probably forgotten his own lie about the great-grandfather.

"How much did you get?" Simon asked inside Victoria Station. He was visibly atwitter with speculation.

"Twenty-five quid." One thing Piers never did was con his own partners. He was a strict adherent to honor among thieves.

"Not bad," Simon said. "That's more than twice the take of the ripped-bank-note scam."

Piers had already done the math. "Come on, you want to have some fun?"

"What?"

"Let's find another sucker, then we'll come back here at five o'clock and watch the greedy prick looking over every bloke passing by his kiosk, hoping it's you."

They laughed and headed out a different door leading to a sidestreet.

Their shiny-penny scam was almost a no-miss provided the victim had the money. It was the epitome of capitalizing on human greed. They worked it in kiosks all over London, then expanded it to carriage stands and various shops, conning drivers and shopkeepers looking to make an extra quid. They overlapped the victims so that there would be no down time between Simon's losing the penny and Piers's finding it at each location. They worked it in shifts, the morning given to losing rare pence all over London, the afternoon to finding them. To prove to Simon how powerful the scam was, Piers dared him to help fleece a London bobby on his beat. Simon was at first appalled that Piers was crazy enough to try out a con on a copper, but was nevertheless awed enough to go along.

The first cop fell for it. So did the second. And the third. The fourth hit Piers over the head with his nightstick and advised him to stick with the village idiots.

Piers did.

When the maturing con man entered his twenties, he distanced himself from his numerous street cons and began hustling poker and chess. In poker games usually housed in the back rooms of East London pubs, he teamed up with a pair of cardsharps to hustle drunken Brits and Irishmen. They either played in collusion, bumping up pots when one of them had the goods, or outright cheated by dealing seconds and marking cards. This means of earning a living proved moderately sufficient, but often took a physical toll on the body. A good barometer of that was when a newcomer asking the barkeep when the poker game would break up received the response "When the next fistfight breaks out." Piers and his fellow cheats did get roughed up occasionally, the worst of which for Piers was a broken nose.

But it was playing chess that marked the evolution of Piers Mason into a world-class confidence artist. He'd first learned the game growing up in the orphanage. He'd become a very good player, but his progress toward becoming a great one had been sidetracked by his wayward activities in the street. Despite that, he gained entry into London's prestigious chess clubs, where a lot of backgammon was also played for considerable amounts of money.

Piers often played chess against the clubs' international masters who were just a rung below grandmasters. From time to time he managed a draw when playing white. He didn't mind losing money to these superior chess players because he truly enjoyed the experience, considering it an honor to play with them. Besides, whatever money he lost, he usually made up playing backgammon against hot-headed Middle Eastern gamblers whom Piers manipulated terribly with the doubling cube. Piers had a natural talent for gambling that was related to his skills as a con artist preying on people's greed. He was expert on making losing gamblers steam and lose even more.

In the Mayfair Club, Piers became very friendly with a very attractive waitress named Isabel who came from a well-heeled family. Her grandfather had been one of the founders of the club. Being a waitress there was not like being a waitress in a typical English pub. The job actually held some prestige.

Isabel became excited by the suave young gambler she served at the club's tables. She sensed in him a flair for the adventurous, and wanted to be part of it. She knew he was through and through a hustler. She also for some reason resented the upper crust of society and liked when she saw Piers beat its elegant members out of money. In violation of the club's rules, they became lovers.

By early 1912, much of the talk around the Mayfair's chess and backgammon tables was about the upcoming maiden voyage of the *Titanic,* billed as the greatest ship ever to be put to sea, a floating, unsinkable palace. A handful of the club's members were slated to be aboard for the monumental event. Piers got to thinking that he'd like to be aboard as well. Not out of a fondness for behemoth ships or the sea, or that he desired to go to New York, but rather he figured there would be an ocean of money-making opportunities aboard a vessel filled to the gills with all that high-society money.

Isabel pledged her allegiance to join him. She'd been tiring of waitressing, and with Piers gone the boredom of her job would be insufferable. Before falling for him, she had planned to study at the Sorbonne in Paris, but then decided the French could wait a while. Her family naturally objected to this rash decision.

Studying at the leading French university would round out her cultured background. She would become one of Britain's most sought-after debutantes. She told them she didn't care. She'd already met her Prince Charming, and he was ready to take her on the wonderful voyage. She left out the part that he'd be aiming to swindle the same men her parents envisioned fancying their daughter's hand at London's society balls.

Piers was quite aware of the roster of *Titanic* fortune holders making that historical crossing and wasn't about to blow the opportunity to get into their wallets. The first order of business was to have as much ammunition as possible for his regal attack. He called in all the debts from slow-paying Egyptians and Persians who owed him money from the backgammon tables. Then he begged, borrowed and stole every penny of front money he could, without knowing exactly how he'd use it on the ship. The one part of his plan he was sure of was that removing those rich pigeons from their money had to be done through some form of gambling.

Like the riverboats steaming down the Mississippi, the principal form of gambling on the gigantic ocean liner was poker. The nightly high-stakes game onboard was filled with Barons, Earls and varied aristocrats who fawned on each other in several languages, most of which Piers had made it his business to learn. He had a tremendous affinity for foreign languages, and knew that speaking them impressed people in the highest social circles.

His first idea to break the ice (no pun intended) was to slip a marked deck of cards into play and thieve his noble opponents by reading their hole cards. But the main problem with that was that some of these people were sharp (after all, most people who'd made fortunes were not idiots) and might notice the markings. In those days, specially made eyeglasses or contact lenses for card scams did not exist. Then he thought about teaching Isabel to mark cards by subtly scratching their backs with her fingernails. But he nixed that idea as well, realizing that she had absolutely no familiarity with poker and wouldn't be able to properly handle the cards, let alone mark them.

Isabel and Piers were in their stateroom dressing into formal evening attire when Piers told her of his decision not to cheat the poker game.

"But how else are you going to get their money, honey?" Isabel asked with comic but great concern.

"I don't know, but I'll figure something out while I'm playing."

"Playing?"

"That's right." Piers's confidence, like that of all con men, was unshakeable.

"But darling," Isabel said with a seductive rub embracing his shoulders. "How can you play honestly with them? Our bankroll is only fifty thousand quid."

"I will play conservatively," Piers assured her. "It's only my presence in the game that is important. While sitting there among all that blue blood, I will figure something out. Trust me."

She did, and he did – figure something out.

Stuck nearly £10,000 that first night at the gilded poker table, Piers picked up an interesting tidbit in the lofty chatter flowing across the table. Aboard the ship were two chess grandmasters on their way to a prestigious chess tournament in New York. One was Russian, the other German. Both had been invited to take part in the poker game, but both professed to be too busy studying their chess strategies and declined.

Piers had witnessed many matches involving grandmasters who occasionally showed up at the Mayfair Club. Often one of them would play several matches simultaneously. There would be as many as a dozen chessboards lined up next to one another on a long table. The grandmaster would walk down the line on one side of the table, his dozen opponents seated on the other. He would make his move on each board, usually within seconds, then without waiting for the opponent's riposte proceed to the next one. The end result was always the same: The grandmaster won all the matches when playing white and two thirds of them when playing black. Those he did not win resulted in draws. A loss happened only on rare occasion.

It was recalling these simultaneous matches that gave Piers the idea for what would become one of the world's greatest gambling scams.

At a well-chosen moment in the poker game, Piers, who had by that time ingratiated himself into their crisscrossing conversations, made a statement that none of the regal gentlemen could believe.

"My fiancée can play and hold her own with either grandmaster," he declared like a bellicose general who knew his troops would recapture the hill.

None of the poker players at first believed his ears. Finally one of them asked Piers to clarify what he meant. When Piers repeated it, another of the players said in amazement, "You think your…fiancée can play chess with Borzov and Heilmann?" Borzov was the Russian, Heilmann the German.

"I'm sure of it," Piers said in a steely voice, all the while knowing that Isabel had never touched a chess piece in her life.

After a hearty round of chuckling, one of the nobility said to Piers, "Would you care to wager on that? I'm sure I can convince Messieurs Borzov and Heilmann to accept an invitation for a match."

"I will tell you what," Piers said boldly. "I will have my fiancée play both grandmasters. I will stake £40,000 (all he had left) that she attains a stalemate with at least one of them."

They all laughed again. Uproariously. Finally one asked,

"Well, then, which of the two grandmasters would your fiancée play first?" He looked around the table seeking mock assurance it was a good question.

Piers shrugged grandly. "She will play both simultaneously."

Again the laughter roared.

"Simultaneously?" It was a chorus.

"Yes, simultaneously," Piers repeated for effect.

The majestic group thought the emboldened con man was off his rocker, but the last thing they thought was that he was a con man. After a few more rounds of belly laughter, a wealthy retired British admiral hushed his high-society fellows and stood up at the table facing Piers. He gave the con artist a lookover and then smiled.

"You're quite a dapper young man," he said, "but I think you've lost your marbles. Do you really want to wager forty thousand quid that your girlfr…fiancée can earn a stalemate against either Borzov or Heilmann, two of the greatest grandmasters in the world?"

Piers stood up and met the admiral's gaze. "Yes, I do."

The admiral's eyes scanned the men seated below him at the table. Then to Piers: "Mind if I ask how much money you brought along on this journey?"

"My life savings," Piers answered proudly.

After a collective exhalation of shock, the admiral asked, "And how much would that be?"

"Fifty thousand quid." But Piers did not let it be known that the totality of that sum had been made up of hustles, loans and stolen booty.

"And you want to wager forty thousand of it?"

"I've already lost the other ten." Piers indicated the poker table, which drew a guffaw from the men seated around it.

The admiral smiled broadly. "If there's one thing I admire within His Majesty's realm it's one of his subjects with big brass balls. And those, young man, you seem to have. So I'll tell you what I'm going to do. I'm going to arrange simultaneous matches between your fiancée...What's her name?"

"Isabel."

"...Isabel...and both chess masters, and if Isabel achieves a stalemate with either I will give you £100,000 sterling. You don't need to put up one penny. If she *wins* one of the matches, I will pay you £1 million sterling. I won't bother mentioning the possibility of her winning both matches because I can't even believe I had the audacity to suggest that her winning one is somehow possible."

Piers nodded politely, not believing his ears. These pigeons were not going to make him put up his money! "And if she loses both matches I owe you nothing?" Piers asked just to be certain.

The admiral looked around the table as if for concurrence. He seemed to get it. He nodded graciously. "Yes, though I would expect you'd buy us all a glass of champagne and cognac."

"Make it two!" one of them bellowed.

So the admiral and his regal mates set out to organize the matches. Naturally Borzov and Heilmann, who each had the large ego typical of any chess grandmaster, were loath to lower themselves to a match with "some unknown woman." But the admiral promised to sweeten their pies should they indulge him. It seemed he was a man who knew no bounds when it came to entertaining himself. He assured his mates and himself that there'd be plenty of uproarious laughter over bubbling champagne and caviar once the matches were over.

Meanwhile, sitting on the bed in their stateroom, Piers burbled his enthusiasm for the scam to Isabel. When she understood that he intended for her to play two of the greatest chess players in the world, simultaneously or one at a time, she thought he was stone-cold nuts and that maybe she should have listened to her parents and considered enrollment at the Sorbonne.

"Have you forgotten one small thing?" she asked in a tone of voice so filled with disbelief it was comical.

"What's that?"

"I don't even know how to move one single chess piece. In fact, I don't know the difference between a pawn and a horse."

"Well, let's start off on the right foot, sweetheart. In proper chess terminology, it's a knight, not a horse."

Isabel jumped off the bed. "What the hell difference does it make whether it's a knight or a horse! I don't know how to move it! Piers, have you gone nuts!"

"No, I have not. You, my darling, are not only going to shock the world, but you are going to make us a £100,000 richer. All you have to do is obtain a draw with one of the grandmasters. You don't have to checkmate either."

"And just how the hell do you think I will arrive at accomplishing that?"

Piers smiled lasciviously at his girlfriend. "Come sit back down on the bed, sweetheart, and I'll tell you."

She reluctantly sat on the bed. Piers immediately began kissing and fondling her, and mumbled, "Later."

At dinner the evening of the match, the atmosphere aboard the *Titanic* buzzed with anticipation of the event. Nobody took the match itself seriously, with the exception of Piers, but nearly everyone was just dying of curiosity to see who this mysterious if not talented woman could be. Piers had already paid off stewards working the cruise to spread the word that she was extremely beautiful, which was only a slight exaggeration.

The tables were set up in the ship's grand ballroom. A partition separated them. It was agreed that one-minute intervals would be the maximum between moves. The only request Piers had made of the admiral was that spectators be prohibited from viewing both matches. He explained that Isabel's concentration would be thrown if the same people were watching and commenting on her play in two different matches. The admiral, after discussing the request briefly with his peers, consented. The grandmasters as well saw no reason for objection, though they expressed their consent with derisive chuckles.

So chairs for the spectators were set up in such a way that allowed them to view only one of the two matches.

When Isabel made her grand entrance wearing a beautifully tailored, exquisite white evening gown, the audience buzzed first with sighs of delightful approval and then in hushed banter about whether or not this striking woman could play chess. At the time, women had not made significant inroads or contributions to the chess world, and according to Borzov and Heilmann never would.

Neither Borzov nor Heilmann would enter the arena before their opponent. That she was a woman made no difference. They were the grandmasters, the champions, and thus demanded the same respect given a modern-day heavyweight champion stepping into the boxing ring.

Borzov was a diminutive man, but with a lion's mane of silver hair that made his physical stature appear every bit as elevated as his standing in chess circles. He had a full matching beard that gave him both a scholarly and religious overtone. In all, he cut an impressive figure, who if nothing else had to inspire a degree of trepidation in a nineteen-year-old lassie who'd never played chess in her life.

Heilmann was a taller man with substantial girth and typical Teutonic bearing. He had thinning hair, still dark, and a slight reddish tint to his face. It was rumored that his sexy Czechoslovakian wife had turned him into a beer guzzling alcoholic, although no one had seen him overindulging himself in drink in the ship's ballroom.

The admiral made the presentations in front of the mesmerized gathering on each side of the partition. Before that moment,

Isabel had seen neither grandmaster aboard the ship. Each one, however, seemed mightily impressed with her looks, which seemed to put them even more at ease for the upcoming matches. After all, how could a woman this attractive be a quality chess player? they reasoned. In general, they were right.

The match with Borzov started first. The Russian played white, so in all fairness Isabel would play white against Heilmann. Borzov opened by advancing a white pawn. Isabel studied the board with a seemingly practiced eye, then suddenly stood up and gracefully skirted the partition to stand across the board from the German. She made her opening move, waited for Heilmann's countermove and then returned to her match with Borzov.

Piers sat in the front row of spectators on the Heilmann side of the partition. He watched with approval as Isabel passed by on her way back to Borzov's side. She did not look at him, nor did she have to. No signals needed to be exchanged; Isabel had been thoroughly prepped and was now on her own.

Back on Borzov's side, Isabel did not sit down. She made her move, watched Borzov make his, then returned to Heilmann and made her next move against him with one of her white pawns. Then she crossed back around the partition to Borzov, under the eyes of the audience's growing curiosity, which was slowly turning to fascination.

Isabel never sat down again. She moved with poise from table to table, never coming close to the one-minute limit on the clock. It seemed to the audience on both sides of the partition that she knew her chess moves inside and out. After ten minutes, it was obvious to everyone that Isabel was holding her own and would be no pushover for either opponent. The admiral, sitting on the Borzov side, appeared astounded. His royal poker mates, split on both sides of the partition, were also in varying states of disbelief. The only person not looking amazed by the events unfolding was Piers Mason. He was also the only spectator aboard the *Titanic* who knew that before this grand evening of chess, his graceful protégée had never seen a chessboard that was not on display in some fancy store's vitrine.

Thirty minutes into the matches, Heilmann began to show visible signs of distress. Beads of perspiration began seeping out on his forehead. Not being able to put away an unknown chess opponent was bad enough, but not being able to win out over a woman was a sheer blow to his Teutonic pride. He would not be able to face his friends in the beer halls of Munich, let alone his wife, who happened to be sitting right next to Piers in the front row. Piers couldn't be sure that she was coming on to him, but the saucy Czech woman with the round face and big tits had a funny habit of letting her shoes collide softly with Piers's calves. Meanwhile, her husband the grandmaster was wondering how on heaven's earth this woman was able to stay in the match with him.

Back on the other side, the admiral, although he'd seemed amused by the idea of shelling out a barrel of cash should this woman reach a stalemate or better with one of her opponents, still seemed to be in the grips of stupefaction.

After an hour, the Russian began coming apart as well. He knew he was playing white, which afforded him the advantage against any player in the world, even those who might be slightly better than he. But in spite of that, each and every offensive move he made was countered perfectly by this beautiful woman. How was this possible? He could count on the fingers of a single hand the number of opponents who had parried so well with him. Every thrust he made at her on the chessboard was beaten back with the skill of a Crusades swordsman on the battlefield. How could he show his face to the genteel New Yorkers at the chess tournament? If news got out he couldn't beat some woman on a boat, no matter how goddamn big the

Titanic was, he might as well just walk outside to the deck, peer into the darkness of the ocean and...

On the other side, Heilmann was now beside himself. He'd played against the world's best. He'd seen every schematic opening, knew the histories and subtleties of each. They were all vulnerable once the slightest miscalculation was made by the player with white. Virtually every opponent he'd played black against made the slight error Heilmann needed to turn his defending black chessmen into an offensive onslaught.

But not against this woman! Not...what was her name again? Her offensive attack was relentless. All he could do was ward off her thrusts and hang on. And that was only to attain the stalemate. He was leaps and bounds away from thinking about winning. *Leaps and bounds!* This was madness!

Piers, who had the option of crossing the partition at any time during the matches, remained calm in his chair on Heilmann's side. He'd been smiling discreetly since the start of the matches, but now his smile broadened in step with the German's visual frustration. Heilmann's wife's advances became more aggressive as she watched her husband fall apart. She had moved her butt to the edge of the seat on Piers's side while sexily arching her feet and wiggling her toes inside her gold-laced sandals. Perhaps Piers would find a way to celebrate in private with the hot Czech woman before the ship reached port in New York. He'd always thought about bedding down with a horny Eastern European.

Nearing the end, both grandmasters knew they were helplessly deadlocked with their opponent. It was unthinkable but it was happening. However, the Russian playing white still knew he couldn't lose the match, therefore would never accept a stalemate. The German, on the other hand, was beginning to believe he could not win the match, and if he lost it (unaware that an iceberg would soon end his embarrassment) would actually contemplate suicide. He suspected his wife wouldn't care that much, anyway.

In the most humbling moment of his life, the grandmaster Heilmann offered his lovely opponent a draw.

None of the three chess players survived the catastrophic accident to live in the aftermath of that unforgettable night of chess. Neither did Piers Mason. He froze to death clinging onto the raft in icy waters. Only the stowaway Piers confided in before dying would live to tell how Piers and Isabel did it. Piers had told the kid only because he wanted him to brag about it so that everyone in England would remember Piers Mason for having pulled off the greatest scam in maritime history.

Personally, I think he did.

Like any fantastic hustle, its beauty was in its simplicity. The fact that Isabel didn't even know how to move the knight had no bearing on the outcome. Piers's brainstorm was in recognizing that by having the two matches partitioned off from each other, he could effectively pit Borzov against Heilmann, with Isabel's role in the challenge being nothing more than a mere messenger between the two. And they managed to keep the audience in the dark as to what was going down.

The key to making the scam work was threefold: having Isabel play white against one opponent and black against the other; having whichever opponent playing white make his move before Isabel opened with white against the second opponent; and allowing a sufficient interval between moves. In that fashion, Isabel was able to get up and prance between the two tables for a full minute before having to make a move.

But she hardly needed the full minute. All Isabel did was take each move Borzov made against her and copy it to the adjoining chessboard against Heilmann. Then when Heilmann countered, she simply took his move and copied it to the chessboard between her and Borzov. The result of this chicanery was that Borzov and Heilmann were engaged in a chess match against each other, and neither knew it. To further enhance the scam, Piers came up with the idea to disallow the viewing of both matches by anyone, thus no one could spill the beans that Isabel was plagiarizing both players' moves.

The scam was truly ingenious. In my twenty-five years of developing fundamentally sound casino-cheating moves, I strove to come up with those that were simple because simplicity always worked best. It may seem astonishing that two great minds such as Borzov's and Heilmann's were unable to reason how Isabel had managed the stalemates, even more so when the odds of that miracle were in the neighborhood of infinity. But since the grandmasters were so obsessed by their chess-playing and their egos, the thought that the matches might have been a scam never occurred to either one. I'm sure that if somehow they could read this passage, they'd roll over in their graves.

Chapter 6

The Kowloon Baccarat Scam

In the mid-1990s, the Asian gambling mecca of Macao on the southern coast of China was in a state of disarray. This because in 1999, administrative power was slated to revert to the People's Republic of China. Since the inception of legalized gambling casinos on the small peninsula adjacent to Hong Kong, it had been a Portuguese colony. For nearly forty years, one man, the Chinese billionaire Stanley Ho, had maintained virtual monopolistic control over Macao's casinos. He ruled them with an iron fist and thrived alongside the brutal Chinese Triads, criminal organizations that rivalled the Japanese Yakuza and Italian Mafia when it came to spreading fear and corruption.

But along with the end of the century's historic shift in power, came the winds of drastic change in Macao's casino industry. That longtime dominance Stanley Ho had so ruthlessly enjoyed was about to blow off the peninsula and forever be lost at sea. Las Vegas opportunists such as Steve Wynn and Sheldon Adelson would acquire property on the island and build Vegas-style megaresort casinos that would give true meaning to Macao's moniker "The Las Vegas of Asia."

Those Vegas casino operators invading Macao would be joined by casino companies from Australia and Europe. Everyone wanted a piece of what promised to be a casino explosion with the magnitude of the one that had reshaped Vegas in the late 1990s. And it would not only be Macao. Singapore was also in the process of changing its laws to allow gambling casinos. So was Vietnam. By the end of the new millennium's first decade, revenue from Asian casinos might reach numbers that would make even Las Vegas envious.

But in 1997, Stanley Ho was still firmly in control. His flagship Macao casino was the Lisboa, the biggest and grandest on the peninsula. When he had first established his stronghold on Asian gambling, his casinos offered only Asian games. Western favorites such as blackjack and roulette did not interest inveterate Chinese gamblers who craved fast and furious action more than any race on the planet. Pai gow and fan-tan dominated Macao's casino tables. But then baccarat slowly began to make inroads into the Far East. Something about the elegance and mystique of the game preferred by European royalty appealed to the Chinese. Big baccarat tables began appearing in Ho's casinos in the late 1950s. The Chinese loved handling the card shoe and dealing the cards as the "banker." They took immense pleasure in their drawn-out process of peeking at their cards while the rest of the table awaited their fate. Whenever their first card was an 8 or 9, they'd ever so slowly bend and shift the second card, hoping to spot the linings of a picture card that would give them a natural winner. They did the same thing when drawing a third card after no natural had been made. In all, they created the dramatic tension seen today on televised poker events.

In the mid-19'60s, baccarat gained acceptance as a principal gambling game among Asian high rollers. Their newfound passion was in evidence by those Chinese gamblers coming to Las Vegas. By the early 1970s, every major Strip casino's baccarat salon was filled with 90 percent Asian players, virtually all of them Chinese. In Macao, Stanley Ho followed Las Vegas's lead with the installation of the mini-baccarat tables that simplified the mechanics of dealing the game to that of blackjack, where a single dealer handled all the action.

In June 1997, a young Chinese named Jing Lu dealt on the big baccarat table in Stanley Ho's Lisboa. So did Hong Lu and Huan Lu. The three young men were not related, but they were good friends who'd been reared in Kowloon, on the peninsula opposite Hong Kong. Although the Lus were part of no criminal Triad, they were loosely associated with one, as it was difficult not to be unless you were a devout religious monk or something of the sort. Each had been dealing baccarat at the Lisboa for close to a decade, and they were all somewhat nervous about what their future held with the imminent political change coming to Macao. Would they still have jobs once the Chinese took administrative control of the Portuguese colony? What would become of their boss, Stanley Ho, when the government granted licenses to other casino operators? Would foreign casino companies stay with the local workforce, or would they launch a massive wave of immigration to man the thousands of new gaming tables spread over the floors of yet unbuilt casino megaresorts.

Three Chinese men known to the Lus, who all had the last name Ma and *were* related, were also members of Kowloon's most feared Triad, the Sun Yee On. One of their businesses, which actually was not illegal, was conducted in Stanley Ho's Lisboa, with the absolute trust and compliance of the Asian casino king himself. The practice was called *bate-ficha,* the circulation to gamblers of "dead" casino chips. These were special chips redeemable only to the chip "rollers" who circulated them. The Mas bought them from the Lisboa and distributed them to certain high rollers who in turn benefited by enlisting the Mas' services for the procurement of everything from free jetfoil and show tickets to paid prostitutes and drugs. Though these side activities were often illegal, the usage of these dead chips was not legislated by the colony's administrators and was controlled by organized gangs of criminals.

But even this long established business might be threatened at the turn of the century by the new administration. The Triads worried about losing their lucrative profits from it, and those worries filtered down to the Mas.

So with clouding uncertainties blowing off the South China Sea into Macao, the climate was soon ripe for big-time scams as hustlers wanted to take advantage of the confusion to pad their bankrolls for an indefinite future.

All three Lus lived in Macao but jetfoiled back to Kowloon on their days off, a practice common with casino employees. It was just an hour ride by the high-speed turbojet whipping through the waters surrounding the peninsula. There, the Lus had their families, their hangouts and their crossings with the Mas and other Chinese gangsters. Triad members usually did not approach casino dealers with scams to rip off the casinos. After all, Stanley Ho himself wielded tremendous power with the Triads. To rip off one of his casinos and incur his wrath was to cut off one's nose to spite his face. Better was to leave the casinos alone and draw illicit monies from prostitution and drugs, which is what the Mas had been doing. Thus the three Lus were quite surprised when the three leather-clad Mas found them eating in their favorite local restaurant shack and began dangerous talk of how they might join forces to rip off Stanley Ho's Lisboa.

The leader of the Mas was Yoyo Ma, whose given name had nothing to do with a yo-yo on a string. In fact, in contrast to the joy the yo-yo brought to countless Chinese children, Yoyo Ma was a ruthless son of a bitch who didn't much go in for soft or subtle cons. But that was until his second youngest brother, Fa, let him in on a baccarat scam he'd been dreaming up as they made the rounds of the Lisboa casino circulating dead chips. Fa had actually gotten the idea from the youngest Ma brother, Bo, a degenerate baccarat player constantly blowing his cut of the profits from their dead chips business.

Over scattered vegetable dishes, soda cans and ashtrays, Yoyo Ma said in Cantonese, directing his talk mostly to Jing, the eldest Lu who sat between Hong and Huan on their side of the rectangular table, "You guys are gonna be out on the balls of your asses when the communists take back Macao. It's not even sure that Stanley Ho will maintain his power there. So maybe we can help you rob the Lisboa of a little baccarat money."

On hearing this, the first thing Jing Lu thought was that the Mas desired to heist their baccarat table brandishing machine guns. For what they needed the Lus in the commission of such an attack eluded him.

Sensing that Jing was formulating the wrong idea, Yoyo said quickly, "It's not a *robbery* robbery. The plan is to rob Ho's casino with a little finesse."

The three Lus all looked at Bo Ma. They had seen him go down the drain for vast amounts of money on their baccarat table, and a temper to go with it. Many of the Lisboa's pit personnel were familiar with Bo's reckless gambling and predisposition to rude behavior at the table. But none had ever challenged him on it because he was well connected to the dead chip trade, which meant he was well connected to the Sun Yee On.

"What did you have in mind?" Jing asked, taking a puff on the cigarette clenched between his lips.

"If this is about switching in a cooler, forget it," Hong Lu advised swiftly. That scam of switching one eight-deck shoe for another with prearranged cards had already been tried, and failed.

"Same thing if you're planning to have us fix up crooked hands while shuffling the cards," said Huan Lu just as swiftly.

Yoyo Ma laughed and looked from side to side at his brothers, who were laughing as well. "Do you think we're stupid?" he chided Jing Lu through a burst of cigarette smoke he'd blown squarely in his face, as if in a rebuke.

"Then what is it?" Jing shot back.

Fa Ma spoke: "What you just said about fixing up crooked hands while you're shuffling" – he shook his head – "forget it. What I'm talking about is doing absolutely nothing at all with the shuffle."

A look of consternation came to Jing's face. He looked side to side at his two comrade-Lus and noted they wore similar expressions. When Jing verbalized their doubts, Bo Ma clarified it. "What you guys have to do is *not* shuffle. In other words, after the entire shoe of cards is played out on your table, pretend to shuffle up for the new shoe without disturbing the order of the cards. Every card must remain in the order that it came out of the shoe. Not one can be disturbed. Understand?"

"What is that going to do?" Jing wondered.

"It's going to make us as much cash as there is tea in China," Yoyo said flamboyantly. "And we're going to split it fifty-fifty. Half for you three and half for us three."

"You didn't answer my question," Jing said impatiently. "How is not shuffling the baccarat cards going to rip off the game?"

Fa took over since he'd thought the whole thing out. "All we'd have to do is record the order of the cards played for one entire shoe, then play the next shoe perfectly because we'd know the order of the cards coming out. It's simple. We would know the result of each hand in advance, thus we bet "player" and "banker" or "tie" accordingly." Bo had told him it was the nuts, which meant it was foolproof if pulled off right.

The three Lus' eyebrows arched simultaneously; they'd understood within a fraction of a second of one another. What the Mas had said held all the water in the South China Sea. In spite of their crass dealings in both Hong Kong and Macao, their idea reeked of subtle ingenuity because it was so simple in theory. If, for example, a baccarat player knew the first seven cards to be dealt from a new shoe were 2-K-6-Q-J-9-3, he would know that the 2 was the "burn" card, dictating that the next two cards, the king and the 6, would be burned along with the 2 and placed through the table's discard slot before the first hand was dealt. Then following the dealing sequence of the game, the player's cards would be the queen and the 9, forming the highest winning hand of "natural nine" (10s counting as zero). The banker would receive the jack and the 3, a total of three and a loser. Thus the gambler at the table would know in advance to wager on the player's hand as it was predetermined to be the sure winner. If an entire shoe were recorded in that fashion, the outcome of every hand in it would be known prior to the deal. A fortune of money could be made at a high-limit table.

Baccarat was a unique casino game. Not only in its mystique but also in the way it was dealt and the rules of the game. Unlike blackjack, the other major Western card game offered in Macao's casinos, baccarat followed a specific set of rules by which the players made no decisions that affected the order of the cards. There were two sides in baccarat: player and banker. Each gambler bet on one of those sides to attain the hand closest to nine, or that both player and banker would finish with the same total, resulting in a tie hand. Once the gambler placed his bet, there was nothing further for him to do except await the outcome. There was no decision-making, no hitting or standing. The person holding the bank dealt two cards out of the shoe to the player and the banker. The head dealer standing in a slot at the middle of the long oval table received the cards for each side and placed them in the appropriate boxes corresponding to player and banker. If no natural winning hand of seven, eight or nine was realized on the initial deal, then a third card was drawn by one or both sides depending on specific rules governing each situation. There were no deviations. This meant that once a new baccarat shoe was loaded, the cards would follow a predetermined sequence, regardless of how the people at the table wagered.

"Are you guys up to it?" Yoyo asked, snubbing out his cigarette in an already overflowing ashtray, immediately lighting another.

Jing did not have to confer with his buddies to know they were up to it. "I don't know if we can do it," he said. "None of us has the kind of skills that are necessary."

"There's a fourth dealer in our crew," Hong said dubiously. "We all work an hour on and twenty minutes off. Even if we could handle the cards, we might not be able to keep him in the dark."

"Can you get him?" Yoyo asked ominously.

Huan shrugged. "Maybe if we convinced him the whole thing is possible."

"It is," Bo said. "You've got to practice some cheating moves. I will show you how it's done."

Jing's eyes narrowed. "How would you know how it's done? You're a gambler; you've never been a baccarat dealer."

The three Mas laughed. "That's not entirely true, as you'll soon see," Bo said. "Manipulating the cards while shuffling at baccarat is not as hard as you may think. It's not magic. It just takes some deceptive moves that have to be mastered."

"So are you guys in?" Yoyo asked with diminishing patience, glaring at Jing. "If not, I'm sure there are plenty of baccarat crews in Ho's casinos who'd take us up on our offer."

This time Jing glanced at Hong and Huan. They both mirrored his own appearance: medium-length black hair, dark eyes and sharp cheekbones. Their angular features were more distinct than classic oriental. Hong's head tilted slightly as if to say the Triad's proposition was worth looking into. Huan stared wordlessly at Jing, deferring the decision to him. Jing turned back to the Mas and scanned their faces, then his eyes fell on Bo.

"We're ready for the first lesson."

"Good," Fa said with a final blow of smoke from his cigarette. "It begins right now. Follow us."

They ended up at an old warehouse on the docks whose façade had Chinese characters and English words depicting the "Hai Cheng Trading Company." Most of the space inside was covered with various assortments of home and office furniture. Heading toward the rear through aisles of desks, swivel chairs and file cabinets, they came on a door leading to a closed-off area of the warehouse. Yoyo pushed it open. They stepped into a small casino. There were two oblong regulation-size baccarat tables, a roulette wheel and a half dozen pai gow tables. The only thing missing was a surveillance camera.

"It opens at six o'clock," Yoyo said, looking at his watch. "So we have plenty of time to practice."

The Lus understood. Chinese undesirables who'd been banned from Macao's casinos regularly gambled in illegal joints in and around Hong Kong. This place was one of them. They were all controlled by the Triads, who used the profits to finance diverse activities such as their dead chip investments in Macao.

The Mas led the Lus to the first baccarat table. It was fully equipped and ready to go. There was a clear, plastic card shoe, eight boxes of unopened playing cards, and filled tubes of gambling chips in the wide metal rack built into the table.

They all took seats around the table. Bo sat in the slot that would be occupied by the head dealer who called the game. In front of him on the layout were the player and banker boxes on which the head dealer placed the cards dealt from the shoe. In the center of the table was a round wooden plate with a slot in the middle, through which the head dealer dropped the played cards after each hand. The cards fell into a receptacle in the belly of the table and were retrieved when it came time to shuffle them for a new shoe.

Bo opened the eight boxes and removed the cards, placing each deck next to one another on the layout. He picked up a single deck and began shuffling and bridging the cards. The Lus were quite impressed by the way Bo handled them. His hands were graceful, his fingers dancing around the edges of the cards. They realized what Bo had meant when he'd said at the restaurant that it wasn't entirely true that he'd never been a baccarat dealer. Obviously, he'd dealt many hours of baccarat at the very table they sat at. No doubt he was skillful at cheating the players.

Bo continued shuffling and bridging the cards as he spoke, interlacing them with a series of fancy one-handed cuts. "The first step of the setup is to be sure that when you drop the played cards into the discard slot, you do it carefully so that they do not get out of order when they fall through. If one card gets out of sequence, then the whole thing is fucked up. The distance they travel to the surface of the tray is minimal, so this should not be a problem." Bo peeled six cards off the deck in his grip, the maximum number of cards that would be used in a single hand of baccarat, and gently slid them through the slot.

"So let's start from the beginning," he said. "The shoe has been played out and now it's time to shuffle up. You take the cards out of the discard tray and you stack them up. Every detail about your phony shuffling procedure right up until you load the cards in the shoe has to look as legitimate as possible…"

Procedure for shuffling in baccarat differed greatly from that in blackjack. First, the cards were spread facedown and washed in swirls around the layout. Then they were gathered and stacked facedown into one tall pack, which was then divided into several small packs that were shuffled repeatedly until a new eight-deck pack was formed. At that point, one of the two seated dealers "laced" the cards. Holding the long pack horizontally down on the table with one hand, he used his other to remove a two-deck clump of cards from the bottom that he spliced loosely into the top of the remaining six-deck pack. Then he ran the clump down the length of the pack in a slicing motion reminiscent of sawing through a block of wood, creating a fan of cards arching uniformly over the pack. The dealer's final touch was to gently push the fanned cards downward to complete their integration into the pack. Then he would insert the red plastic cut card approximately fifteen cards from the bottom of the eight-deck stack. When that cut card came out of the shoe during the deal of the game, it signalled that the last hand was being played. At its conclusion, the dealers would settle up whatever commissions players had accumulated in their commission boxes and then begin the shuffle process for the next shoe.

If each of these dealing procedures were enforced rigorously at the Lisboa, the scam the Mas had envisioned would be impossible. It certainly was not possible to avoid disturbing the order of the cards when thoroughly washing them and performing a correct "lace." But nearly all Macao dealers cut corners when making up new shoes at the baccarat tables. They not only got away with it, but the casinos actually encouraged this procedural dereliction. That because a full baccarat shuffle completely adhering to regulations took as much as fifteen minutes, a lot of valuable time during which casino coffers would not be filling with cash. So the Lisboa baccarat bosses, as did their counterparts at the other Macao casinos, looked the other way as dealers performed speedy, abridged shuffles that sometimes bordered on outright sloppiness.

Although Jing was the leader of the Lus, Huan had the best hands and was doubtlessly the most skilled baccarat dealer of the three, thus he was chosen to be the one to perform the fake lace. The scam would go down at the point in their dealing rotation where Huan was one of the two seated dealers. Each seated dealer took part in the washing and shuffling of the cards, while the head dealer standing in the slot opposite his peers either helped or just watched. The head dealer, however, never performed the lace. To keep things as simple as possible, they decided that the head dealer would not get involved in the shuffle. It would be hard enough to keep the cards in order with two dealers handling them, let alone three.

Bo took a clump of cards off the eight-deck stack sitting in front of him. He laid them on the table and with both hands began swirling them in circular motions, carefully making sure that none escaped from the undulating pack. "The key is to keep the pressure of your hands equally distributed over the cards, making sure that none of them gets loose. If any does, just slip it back in place. Make sure you watch what you're doing very closely, so that you see the exact spot from which a card slid out. Then when you're finished, pay close attention while restacking them into one stack. It's very easy to lose your concentration and forget which stack goes on top of which."

Jing, Hong, and Huan each took a clump of cards and began swirling them to the rhythm of Bo's lead. Yoyo and Fa Ma watched approvingly. The very fact that three Lisboa baccarat dealers were at that moment seated at their illicit baccarat table emulating their baby brother's cheating moves gave promise to a very profitable scam. None of the Lus appeared to have difficulty keeping the order of the cards intact during the swirling wash. After an hour of practicing it, Bo moved on to the next step.

"Now, the false shuffling of the cards is actually the easiest part. Take around a deck and a half of the cards from the wash." Bo scooped up the cards he'd been whirling around the table. He brought them together to form an even pack. "When you're ready to shuffle, separate the cards into two packs, but make sure one pack is smaller than the other. Since you're all righthanded, use your left hand to hold the smaller pack." In his left hand Bo held a third of the cards; his right held two-thirds. He moved them into each other and began slowly riffling with the larger pack in his right hand. "Now you begin shuffling. You do a real shuffle, but only on the very inner corners of the cards. You end with the bulk of cards from the smaller pack on top." Bo finished riffling the cards into a whole pack with those from his left hand falling on top. "Now, as you're bringing your fingers together when finishing your shuffle, you press down slightly with your right hand holding the larger pack." Bo did this, and the corners of the shuffled cards came completely undone, without making a telling noise. "You do this while moving your hands together as if finishing the shuffle. Then just quickly slide the smaller pack guided by your left hand on top."

The three Lus followed in sync while Bo observed.

"You have to practice these moves over and over again to be convincing. Once you've mastered the moves, no one will notice them even when watching closely. When you no longer hear the sound of the corners of the cards coming undone, then you'll know you're doing it right. Practice this for an hour, then I'll show you the lace."

As Jing practiced false shuffling, he wondered why such a skilled card mechanic like Bo Ma was also one of Macao's most degenerate gamblers. At first he'd been surprised that members of the Sun Yee On Triad went in for becoming professional cardsharps, but then it hit him that the Mas' casino didn't have Stanley Ho's bankroll and thus would have no tolerance for lucky gamblers and winning streaks. Jing figured that this whole warehouse casino had to be rigged. That Bo was a degenerate gambler to boot was a testimonial to how deeply gambling was ingrained in Chinese culture. Whatever money Bo made from their scam, Jing figured, he would blow it right back legitimately on the Lisboa's green-felt baccarat tables.

After an hour, the back-room casino was hazy with smoke. None of the Lus had been able to practice without a cigarette in his mouth. Bo watched their progress with a keen eye while

Yoyo and Fa played fan-tan at the end of the baccarat table. Finally Bo halted the Lus' false shuffling.

"Okay," he said, "the lace is the most difficult part. Obviously, you cannot do a complete lace where you push the two decks of fanned cards squarely into the pack. There would be no way to retrieve them in order and bring them back to the bottom. So what you have to do is lace with only one deck instead of two, and only saw halfway through the pack so that it's not too hard to retrieve the fanned cards. When you do that, use your left hand that's holding the main pack to shield what your right hand is doing. Make it look like you're pressing the fanned cards into the pack, but what you do is pull them out of the pack, keeping their precise order, and return them to the back of the pack. Since no one really cares about the performance of the lace, the bosses in the pit won't think anything of it even if they notice a cockeyed lace. The last thing they would think, anyway, is that you're trying to preserve the order of the cards. Believe me, they have never imagined a scam like this because it's too simple."

The Lus knew that Bo was right. They had often been sloppy on their baccarat table. On a few occasions they had not even bothered with the lace. There was no risk of being written up for lackadaisical dealing procedure. This was, after all, Macao, not Las Vegas. There was no Gaming Control Board of any significance. The casino regulatory authority was controlled by Stanley Ho. As long as he was satisfied how his baccarat dealers dealt the game, nothing else mattered.

Lisboa pit bosses suspecting a scam was another story. A barometer of their real risk could not be read from Bo Ma's word. True, the inherent workings of the scam were as easy as they were sound. Having "recorders" track the cards coming out of one shoe and then passing that information to different gamblers playing the following shoe was as simple as it got. Then once the Lus succeeded in performing the false shuffle and got the cards into the shoe without mixing their order, nothing could stop them from breaking the bank at the baccarat table. Unless, of course, Stanley Ho's men somehow caught on while the scam was in progress and crashed the table right in the middle of it.

Could that happen? Jing Lu wondered. Of course it could. But that was the chance they'd have to take. The more likely scenario of their getting caught would be surveillance running back videotape after the fact and seeing plain evidence of false shuffling and lacing. But in that case, as long as the Mas got out of the casino with the cash, the Lus would have the chance to get off Macao with their shares and then go into hiding in Kowloon.

How much cash would that be? Jing thought as he and his comrades practiced lacing the cards. Hopefully enough that he'd never again have to work in a casino.

At five o'clock, Bo snaked up his sleeve to look at his watch. Jing noticed a stark black tattoo of a dragon just above his wrist, no doubt the mark distinguishing Bo as a member of the Sun Yee On. "All right," he said. "You guys have two weeks to practice this. The scam must take place two weeks from tonight." Bo did not elaborate on why, nor did the Lus feel compelled to satisfy their urge to ask. Perhaps, Jing Lu thought, other people besides dealers had been recruited for their scam. Maybe someone in surveillance, which would be fine with them as long as their cuts came from the Mas' half of the spoils.

"This is how it's going to go down," Fa said while Bo put the cards back in their boxes. "There will be four recorders playing on your baccarat table. They will be there long before you begin your shift, in order to guarantee they have seats when you deal your first shoe. They will record the first shoe during which Huan is one of the two seated dealers. After the cards are played out, take as long as possible to complete the fake shuffling process. This will give the recorders time to compare their trackings. If three of the four show the exact same order of cards, it's a go. If not, then we do it on the next shoe. You will know it's a go when the three of us take three of the seats abandoned by the recorders, whom you will not know until they're no longer there. The fourth abandoned seat will also be taken by one of our associates. We will each bet the maximum 60,000 patacas (nearly $7,500) every hand, but we will not win every hand. To make it look believable, a certain percentage of the hands have to be lost, though we will capitalize on every player and bank streak in the shoe. We will also occasionally bet on tie hands when we know they're coming."

"Why don't you have your people fill all the empty chairs at the table?" Jing asked. Doing so would substantially increase the profits.

"That is not your worry," Yoyo snapped.

Jing wondered if the Mas planned to do exactly that and keep the Lus in the dark, thereby getting a higher percentage of the profits. But the move would be obvious in that players seldom bet the 60,000-Macau-pataca maximum, and those who did would stick out. In any event, Jing knew that the Lus would have to keep their mouths shut. If the Mas ended up with a bigger share, so be it. The only real worry was that they might be screwed by the Mas and never see their end of the money. However, the Triads were known for not ripping off people they recruited for their Macao casino ventures.

As if sensing their concern, Yoyo said, "You will receive your cut of the money the morning after the scam, right here at this table. There will be no questioning of it. We will deal with you as we've dealt with our dead chip customers in Ho's casinos. Understood?"

The Lus understood that there had never been any problems with the Triads dealing dead chips. They paid whoever they had to pay off, and their customers never got cheated for even the slightest amount when they exchanged chips for cash.

"We should clear in the neighborhood of 15 to 20 million patacas ($2 million to $2.5 million), based on seventy-five hands in the shoe," Fa said.

"So, are you in?" Yoyo asked with finality.

The three Lus considered each other for a few seconds. Jing spoke for each when he said, "We're in."

"What about the fourth dealer?"

Jing had been thinking that maybe that fourth dealer wasn't needed. The rotation of dealers shifted every twenty minutes. The dealer returning from break would replace the head dealer, who'd leave the table to go on break. Twenty minutes later, the head dealer on the game would rotate to the first seated dealer's position behind the table's chip rack. The dealer who'd occupied that position would shift to the second seated dealer's position behind the chip rack. The dealer abandoning that position would become the new head dealer and be the next to go on break. In this fashion, the fourth dealer would be absent from the table for a duration of twenty minutes. During that time, the false shuffle and lace could be performed. That the fourth dealer would return while the fixed shoe was in play would not matter because he'd be unaware of the fix. By doing it that way, the Lus would avoid having to cut up their half of the profits four ways. They'd each make a third instead of a quarter.

"We don't need the fourth dealer," Jing said succinctly. "The fix must go in while he's on break. Anytime the three of us are on the game, it can go down."

Yoyo looked at Bo as if needing his concurrence that the Lus did not need the fourth dealer's collaboration. Bo and Fa both nodded without hesitation.

"Very well," Yoyo said. "We do it with just you three. Do the false shuffle on your second full shoe. That means your first shuffle will be legit. If the fourth dealer is on the table during your second shoe, then revert to the next shoe he is not." He spread his palms in conclusion. "Okay?"

The three Lus nodded.

"All right," Fa said. "We meet here every day at noon until the day of the scam."

"Practice makes perfect," Bo said.

"You guys had better be perfect," Yoyo said. There was a foreboding note of menace in his tone.

Within the fortnight, Bo Ma was satisfied that the Lus had indeed made perfect. They had mastered the false washing and shuffling techniques he had taught them. Huan Lu repeatedly demonstrated that he could perform the fake lace to the highest degree possible. The day of the scam, a final meeting was held at the warehouse.

They sat around the baccarat table, the Mas on one side, the Lus on the other. The shoe and unopened boxes of cards sat in the middle of the table, though they were not touched as the practice sessions were over. All six smoked while the Mas did most of the talking, rehashing each and every fine point of the scam. Jing Lu had one question: .

"How are your recorders going to keep track of the played cards? I imagine they're going to write them down on the scorecards, but exactly how?"

Jing was referring to the scorecards that baccarat salons freely supplied to players at the table who wanted to keep track of the hands. They contained three columns delineating each possible outcome: player- win; bank- win and tie hand. People scoring the hands usually put a check mark or an X in the appropriate column after they were played. The majority of baccarat players used these scorecards to follow a vast array of patterns that led them to bet one way or another. The casinos loved this because gamblers foolishly believed that winning patterns could be deciphered by examining sequences on their scorecards. The key to the Mas' recorders being able to track the cards was that they would not appear to be doing anything suspicious when taking notes by writing, whereas in blackjack that would bring instant card counting heat. However, Jing was concerned that the recorders could bring attention to themselves by writing down the actual card values on the scorecards.

"Do not worry," Fa answered. "They will be using check marks and Xs like everyone else. By slightly altering the way they make their marks and Xs, they'll be able to record all ten card values without anyone taking notice."

That explanation was good enough for the Lus.

"Okay, it goes down tonight," Yoyo Ma said. "We meet here tomorrow at noon to divvy up the money. And don't be late," he added. "If you're late, you don't get any money."

The Lus tensed up. They didn't know how serious Yoyo was, but they knew not to be late.

The Lus' shift began at o'clockseven o'clock. When they entered the Lisboa's plush baccarat salon, all fourteen velvet chairs around the oblong table were taken. Each player was Chinese, and five were women. As Fa Ma had said, they had no idea which four players were the recorders. For the moment, there was no extraordinary action on the game. Most of the players were betting a few thousand patacas per hand, the bets equally distributed between player and banker. The largest bet was 5,000 patacas.

On reporting to the baccarat boss, Huan Lu was told to go on break. Jing, Hong and the fourth dealer, Dai Wu, replaced the day-shift dealers. Jing was assigned to begin as head dealer, Dai the first seated dealer behind the chip rack and Hong the second seated dealer. Huan would relieve Jing in twenty minutes, as the swing-shift rotation began. This meant that it would be a full hour before Dai went on break. They would not be able to prepare the cards for the scam until then, and they'd have to hope that a shoe was played out while Dai was on break. If not, they'd have to wait another hour before getting a second chance. There was always the unlikely chance that there'd be no shuffles during Dai's six breaks, in which case they would have to try again the following evening. However, the Lus would be able to lessen the probability of that occurrence by exercizing subtle control over the speed of the game. In any event, they'd have to be patient.

It turned out that the patience required was even more exasperating than they'd imagined. When Dai took his first break, the shoe was half full. The Lus tried desperately to speed up the game in order to reach a shuffle before he returned, but could not exhaust the cards in time. On Dai's second break, the pit boss for some reason decided to sit at the table and bullshit with the Lus while they shuffled. On his third, the cards were again still in play. Finally on his fourth, they got their chance.

During their first four tours of duty on the baccarat table, only one of the original fourteen players had given up his seat. Even though this was not highly unusual, it sparked suspicion on the Lus' part that the Mas had employed more than the four recorders they'd said would already be at the table before their shift began.

It worked out that Hong relieved Dai as the head dealer. Jing was the first seated dealer, Huan the second seated dealer. Jing would handle the bets on the left side of the layout in the slots marked 1 through 7. Huan would manage those on the right side in the slots marked 8 through 15. In conformity to the universal omen of bad luck, there was no number 13 player slot at the table.

Just a few hands had to be played out before the red plastic cut card slid out of the shoe, signifying the last hand. After Jing and Huan paid the last winning bets and settled the debts in the players' commission boxes, Hong opened up the table's discard tray and very carefully removed the cards and spread them on the center of the layout. Ten of the fourteen players got up and either stretched out near the table or left the baccarat salon. None surrendered their chairs, leaving their chips and scorecards on the layout.

Jing and Huan strained to see all the scorecards on their respective halves of the table. Neither saw any markings on them out of the ordinary. Fa's explanation of the check marks and Xs had been correct. The markings on the scorecards gave no clue as to who the recorders might be.

Hong took a sweeping glance around the baccarat salon. Four other tables were in action. As at their table, the bosses standing over the others appeared to be relaxed. There hadn't been any scams or unreasonably big winners of late, no reason for the casino to be on alert. Each oval table was watched on either end by a boss. Then there were the two baccarat head bosses who roved among the tables, both watching the action and catering to the needs of high rollers. During shuffles, the table bosses usually grabbed a cup of coffee or smoked a cigarette. They were not prone to watch over their dealers preparing a new shoe.

Hong looked down at the four players who remained seated at their table. Two men sat to his right in chairs 4 and 5, a man and woman to his left in chairs 12 and 14. None of them appeared to be together, and none appeared interested in what would go on during the shuffle process. They all smoked, drank and regarded their scorecards aimlessly.

Satisfied that everything was cool, Hong gently pushed the eight decks of cards in a tight pack toward Jing and Huan. The two seated dealers divided the pack in half and began whirling the cards in the circular motion that Bo Ma had taught them. Ever so careful not to allow the cards to fall out of order, they completed the undulating waves and collected the cards into two four-deck stacks. Then they each moved into the fake shuffling stage, dividing their stacks of cards into single decks and performing the weighted false rippling techniques they'd been practicing twelve hours a day for two weeks. Hong closely observed them, his sharply focused eyes on guard for a card losing its place that Jing and Huan might miss, so deep was their concentration on the task at hand. In the event he spotted a dislodged card, Hong would have to notify them verbally, which was not dangerous as baccarat dealers customarily spoke during the fifteen-minute process of preparing a new shoe.

They all perspired profusely in the heat of the moment, but were not deterred. They knew that they were taking a tremendous risk and were unsure what the punishment would be should they get caught. But they had made their commitment to the scam, and it was not in Chinese culture to go back on one's decision, whether or not the Triads were involved.

After five minutes of false shuffling, they each built their cards into one stack. Jing passed his stack to Huan, who placed it on top of the stack in front of him. As was required before lacing the cards, Huan called out, "Lacing," to the bosses, letting them know he was about to embark on that procedure. One of the bosses in the distance muttered back, "Okay." Neither boss turned to watch. They were still having their coffee and chit-chatting. They would not resume their positions at each end of the table until the action resumed.

Huan glanced at Hong, who gave a subtle nod to let his co-conspirator know that everything was clear; no one was behind stealing a glance at his actions on the table. Huan's right hand removed a single-deck clump of cards from the bottom of the eight-deck stack his left hand held horizontally in place on the layout. He very delicately began splicing the cards in his right hand into the top of the stack. When he was finished, he quickly withdrew those cards from the stack, shading the move with the extended palm of his left hand, and placed them back on the bottom of the stack, effectively nullifying the lace. Then he stuck the red cut card fifteen cards from the bottom and loaded the stack into the shoe. Finally, he extracted the first card from the shoe, a 7, then burned seven more cards and slipped them through the discard slot. He passed the fixed shoe across the table to Hong.

The players who'd left the table before the shuffle filtered back into the baccarat salon and took their seats. The four who'd sat there during the interim suddenly scooped up their chips from the layout and exited. They were immediately replaced by four new players. But none of them were the Mas. Fa had said that all three Mas would play high rollers, and would be joined by a fourth unknown accomplice. But here were four more strangers, a man and woman who took chairs 4 and 5 and another couple who sat in chairs 12 and 14. Each couple was intimate, though they gave no sign of knowing the other.

What was going on? the Lus wondered. Had something gone wrong? Or had these two couples just wandered by chance into the baccarat salon and beat the Mas to their seats at the precise moment of truth?

No, Jing thought, that wasn't possible. No way the Mas would go through all that planning and preparation only to lose their seats and have to regroup later on. These must be the players they recruited to take the money off the table. They had chosen to keep the Lus in the dark for whatever reason, most likely to protect their identities in case the Lus reneged or went as far as to alert the authorities that they had been solicited for a giant scam. Although the Mas knew such a turncoat move was nearly impossible, they had nevertheless prepared for it. Whatever, Jing was now certain these were the Mas' players.

Their first bets confirmed it. All four new players bet 60,000 patacas, the table maximum, on the banker. They all used dead chips, obviously supplied by the Mas' Sun Yee On Triad. By chance, the shoe had been in possession of the gentleman banker who'd occupied chair 5 before the shuffle. Since the banker had won the last hand prior to the shuffle, the new shoe was returned to that position on the table. The woman now occupying chair 5, an extremely attractive Eurasian with jet black hair and feline eyes who belonged to the Mas, took the shoe with long, graceful hands, her slender fingers glittering with diamonds and painted red nails. She knuckled the shoe for luck, a gesture that testified to her experience playing baccarat.

Hong, standing tall in his slot at the center of the table, surveyed the layout and saw everyone's bet in place. Besides the four maximum bets placed by their cohorts, the next largest was 10,000 patacas. He focused on the woman whose slender hand was draped over the sloping shoe. "Cards please," he prompted her with oriental flair.

The woman effortlessly slid the first card from the shoe to Hong's waiting hand, then the second card to herself, which she tucked underneath the front corner of the shoe. She slid the third card to Hong and tucked the fourth under the shoe. Hong's eyes swept the layout for the largest bet on the players' side. A gentleman in chair 9 had 8,000 patacas wagered on player. Hong said, "Players' cards for the gentleman in chair 9," as he tossed him the cards facedown. The man picked them off the felt and began the long, drawn-out process of peeking at them, as if he could somehow will the cards into a natural nine. Finally he flipped them faceup on the table. They were a king and a 6.

"The players show a 6," Hong sang out, then gathered them in and placed them squarely in the players' card box at the center of the layout. "Banker's cards please."

The elegant woman did not bother with the drawn-out peeking. She flipped her cards right over as if she knew the outcome. They were a queen and a 7, an automatic winner.

"Bank wins, 7 over six6," Hong called as he laid the cards in the banker's card box just below the players' one. "Pay the bank."

Jing, on the low side of the table, removed the losing bets from the player slots, then paid the couple in chairs 4 and 5 a handsome 60,000 patacas each. Huan, on the high side, swept the losers and paid the couple in chairs 12 and 14 the same 60,000 patacas each.

So far so good, thought the three Lus.

The woman in chair 5 seemed anxious to recommence, but Hong held his palm high in the air to halt her dealing. "Place your bets," he said to the entire table, then watched as they all did so. Again the two couples wagered the table maximum. This time the whole table switched to the bank side in support of the stunning woman banker.

Hong's palm fell to a beckoning hand. "The cards please."

The woman dealt them rapidly, one to Hong, one to herself. Then another to Hong and another to herself. Since no one had bet on player, Hong flipped over the player cards himself. They were both jacks.

"The players show baccarat, nothing," he announced. "Banker's cards please."

The woman turned them right over, looked at them and smiled when she saw the pair of 9s.

"Bank wins with natural eight," Hong called. "Pay the bank."

Jing's and Huan's hands carried stacks of winning chips to their respective sides of the table. They paid off another 240,000 patacas to their unknown partners. Jing noticed that no eye contact was being made between the two couples. His own eyes locked on the woman's as he paid her, but there was not the slightest hint of affiliation in her eyes. She was a stone-cold beauty, there only to take off the casino.

On the third hand, both couples maintained their 60,000-

pataca bets. And lost. The shoe passed to the man in chair 6. The couple in chairs 4 and 5 continued betting 60,000 patacas, while the couple across the table reduced their wagers to 40,000. The Mas had intelligently mixed up the betting patterns, as it would be glaringly obvious if both couples bet identically on every hand.

The player won three hands in a row. Both couples won each time. It was now apparent that the recorders had done their jobs well. They had succeeded in passing off the order of the cards for the entire shoe to the four people now seated at the table making large bets. With wonderment, Jing Lu came to understand exactly how they'd accomplished that. The four players who'd previously occupied their places had of course taken their chips with them, but they had left behind their scorecards, which most players usually did. Then when the high-rolling scammers hit the table, they simply used those cards to make believe they were keeping track of which side was winning the hands during the current shoe. But all they really did was read the perfect order of the cards in the patterns of check marks and Xs. Jing realized that they were still pressed to quickly calculate which side would win. The scorecards only gave them the value and order of the cards about to come out of the shoe, not which side would win. Therefore, each player in the take-off phase of the scam had to have an agile mind. So, thought Jing, there was more to this Eurasian beauty than met the eye.

By the time the shoe crossed to the other side of the table and reached their gentleman cohort in chair 12, the foursome was ahead two million patacas. The bosses at either end of the table had begun sweating their action. One of them had gone to the telephone on a bureau off to the side of the table. He made a series of calls, probably to higher-ups in the casino and surveillance observers upstairs. In either case, the Lus were not overly concerned. If surveillance began looking closer at the action, they would find nothing along the lines of cheating. It would not occur to them that the shoe had been fixed until much later. Besides, high-rolling baccarat players had often made fabulous scores at the Lisboa, women among them.

The man in chair 12 dealt a pair of winning bank hands, then lost and passed the shoe to his female partner in chair 14. She was also a pretty woman, though not quite as striking as her counterpart in chair 5. Her low-cut dress and sparkling jewelry, however, matched the other woman's stride for stride. She gave the shoe the same knuckling to bring luck, and, to the pit personnel and other players not privy to the scam, it apparently did.

She dealt out nine consecutive bank winners, playing the part of a fiery woman gambler on a hot streak. She erupted in bursts of joy each time her bank won, despite the fact she knew the outcome was preordained. She slammed the shoe and rapped the table each time Hong called out "bank wins." The rest of the table was swept away in her energy and enthusiasm. It was contagious. During the streak, not one person at the table bet on player. The Lisboa was not only getting cheated, it was getting beat by a consortium of legitimate gamblers who were whipped into a frenzy by the fired-up woman.

Jing realized that this was all scripted by the Mas. Creating such a charged-up atmosphere burned away heat and suspicion. A quiet winning table inversely made the bosses suspect something was not aboveboard. The Mas had astutely waited until the second woman got the shoe before invoking the histrionics needed to accompany the mechanical functions of the scam.

Dai Wu returned from his break. "Wow!" he exclaimed to Hong as he came in behind to replace him. "What's going on here?"

"Some very lucky players," Hong said coolly, then edged around the table to take Jing's place as the first seated dealer. Jing slid over to the second spot, and Huan went on break.

When Dai asked the man banking in chair 15 for the cards, the shoe was halfway through. The two couples were ahead 10 million patacas, right on pace with Fa Ma's forecast as to how much they might bilk from the Lisboa. As Fa had said, each of their four players had purposely lost several hands, sometimes two in a row. To further mix it up, they even bet on opposing sides. On some hands, one couple bet a total of 120,000 patacas on bank while the other bet half that much on player. On a few, the man and woman of each couple bet against each other. The Mas had employed every conceivable betting tactic to mask the scam from the Lisboa's baccarat bosses. But the one thing they could not conceal was that they were winning extraordinary sums at a phenomenal rate. Two security guards arriving at the table with cases of chips to refill the dealers' depleted rack was evidence of that.

Which is what drew the attention of Macao's most important person. From out of nowhere, a thinly dapper Chinese man with a gracefully receding hairline appeared in the baccarat salon. He wore a dark suit and tie, and approached the boss at the elegant woman's side of the table. Jing Lu had seen him on two previous occasions and knew who he was. None other than Stanley Ho.

The baccarat boss's head immediately slanted in the direction of the couple occupying chairs 4 and 5. A second gesture indicated the couple across the long table in chairs 12 and 14. Ho was visibly perplexed because he did not know who these high rollers were. He seemed to take a special interest in the exotic woman in chair 5. The woman at one point turned around and looked Ho dead in the eye, giving him a kind of beguiling smile that Ho appeared to find both enchanting and challenging. He smiled back at her with a soft, almost imperceptible nod.

The action continued. In a bizarre twist, Dai Wu, standing at the head dealer's slot, became nervous under Ho's scrutiny while Jing and Hong Lu, the scammers, maintained their calm. Dai's voice grew unsteady as he made the calls and demanded the cards. His hands shook. Perhaps he felt as though Stanley Ho might hold him personally accountable for whatever money was lost on that baccarat table. The foursome winning that money showed Dai no mercy. They continued betting the max, demonstrating an uncanny ability to "follow" the shoe. When the shoe went player, so did they. When it went bank, their bets had magically jumped to the bank slots on the layout in front of them. Their dead chips became more and more alive, and kept piling high.

Ho appeared bothered, but the disposition of his facial expression hardly changed. He walked to the opposite end of the table and stood next to the boss. Again he made eye contact with the woman in chair 5, this time from the greater distance. He did not refrain from smiling. Neither did she. Ho also exchanged an outwardly pleasant glance with the couple below him in chairs 12 and 14. When the shoe was three-quarters through, Huan returned from break and replaced Dai as head dealer. Dai shifted to the first seated dealer's position on the low side; Hong slid over to the high side, and Jing went on break.

By this time, three other players on the table, whom the Lus assumed held no affiliation with the Mas or their scam, had reached the 60,000-pataca betting limit. Not only had they decided to bet the maximum but they'd also begun betting in accordance with the lucky pair of high-rolling couples who seemed able to do no wrong. They waited for the couples to make their bets, then placed identical bets. At this point, Yoyo Ma's players were no longer implementing camouflage tactics, no more betting on losers. It would be a straight bust-out operation from then until the last hand came out of the shoe. Stanley Ho was suffering a casino beating of the likes he rarely, if ever, saw.

When the red plastic cut card finally popped out of the shoe,

Jing figured nearly 30 million patacas had been won by the foursome. Another 15 million patacas in Lisboa gaming chips had flown out of the table's chip rack and scattered in every direction over the layout to form piles and stacks in front of the other players around the table. In all, there had been three separate chip refills on that baccarat game, something the Lus and Dai Wu had never seen over the course of a single shoe.

Two men suddenly appeared at the table. Stanley Ho was not the least bit surprised to see them, but Hong and Huan Lu were stunned.

They were none other than Yoyo and Fa Ma. To the utter amazement of the Lus, Yoyo went right up to Stanley Ho and shook his hand. They exchanged some whispered conversation during which gestures toward the two couples were clearly made. The Lus had no clue as to what was going on, nor would they ever, they each knew. They even wondered whether Stanley Ho himself was somehow implicated in the scam. Perhaps the whole thing was nothing more than a test of the Lisboa's internal security controls ordered by Ho himself, using the Mas to conduct it. But all that was mere speculation.

Yoyo went to a podium behind the baccarat table and extracted several plastic chip racks from a drawer. He handed half of them to Fa, who delivered those to the couple at the far side of the table. Yoyo laid down the remaining racks in front of the couple occupying chairs 4 and 5. In unison, the two couples stacked their chips into the racks. Yoyo and Fa promptly removed the filled racks from the layout, carried them out of the baccarat enclosure and disappeared.

Both Lus on the game thought of only one thing: their hope that the Mas would show up at the Kowloon warehouse at noon the next day.

Before Jing returned from break, Stanley Ho quietly exited the baccarat salon. The Lus dealt out their shift, leaving the casino at three in the morning. At three-twenty they were aboard the speeding jetfoil to Kowloon.

"What does it mean?" Huan Lu said nervously to Jing, staring over the railing at the ocean spray toward the lights of Macao behind them.

"Did those Ma bastards double-cross us?" asked Hong anxiously.

All Jing could think to say was "We'll find out tomorrow."

"Maybe Ho was in it, too," Huan said.

Jing shook his head. "What for? The man owns the whole peninsula. Besides that, he's one of the richest men in the world. What would he have to gain from ripping off a lousy thirty million from his own casino?"

Neither had a response.

They arrived in Kowloon at four-thirty then spent the next seven hours playing backgammon in the basement of Hong Lu's girlfriend's house. They were all highly agitated and began contemplating dreary futures in the event the Mas didn't show up with their money. The worst case scenario made for vivid imagery in their brains: not receiving their shares of the booty and being punished for their roles in the scam, both by legal authorities and whatever else the wrath of Stanley Ho might bring on them.

At ten minutes to twelve they arrived at the Hai Cheng Trading Company. There was no sign of life. At five minutes to, there was still no sign of the Mas. It appeared more and more likely that they had been tricked. Their tremendous risk had resulted in nothing more than to fatten the bankrolls of the Sun Yee On Triad.

At twelve o'clock sharp, a flashy four-door red jaguar turned into the grassy lot in front of the warehouse. All of its glass was shaded black. For a moment, the Lus didn't know if this was going to be a gangland hit or the assigned rendezvous with the

Mas, or both. Would their bodies be found in a swamp? Or would their pockets be lined with cash?

Yoyo Ma was first out of the car, swiftly popping out the front passenger door before the car had completely stopped. "You guys are early," he said briskly.

"You told us not to be late," Jing snapped back.

"I didn't tell you to be early." He dropped his cigarette butt to the ground and stomped it out. "Follow us."

Like they'd been doing every day for two weeks, the Lus followed the Mas inside the empty warehouse, not knowing if they were being led to their graves or their payday. Once inside, they went directly to the closed-off area housing the underground casino. On the baccarat table were neatly piled stacks of Macanese bank notes. Next to them were three Nike gym bags.

Suddenly Yoyo Ma pulled out a handgun with a silencer attached. The Lus froze and said their prayers for the afterlife. The three Mas grinned wickedly at them. Yoyo pointed the gun directly at Jing's head. "Listen carefully," he said in his most menacing voice. "If you ever breathe a word of our participation in this scam to anyone, be it to your girlfriends or to the police, I will cut off your balls before putting bullets in your well-groomed heads. Any questions?"

"Just one," Jing dared. "Was Stanley Ho in on this?"

"That is none of your business." Yoyo waved the gun at the cash on the table. "There's 14 million patacas on the table. Take it and get out of here. If you ever see any of us again, you don't approach us. You don't know us. Understand?"

Without answering, each Lu took a gym bag and filled it with cash. Ideally, it fit perfectly in all three.

The total take of the Kowloon baccarat scam was approximately 28 million patacas, roughly $3.5 million. The Lus fled Kowloon with their cash and now live happily in the United Kingdom.

CHAPTER 7

THE RITZ ROULETTE SCAM

Another of the world's great roulette scams took place in March 2004 at one of the great Edwardian gilded casinos of Europe, the Ritz Club, situated in the former ballroom of the famous Ritz Hotel in the heart of London's Piccadilly. Much like the French Cigarette Scam that preceded it by three decades, the Ritz caper involved targeting sectors on the spinning roulette wheel where the ball might land. Unlike the French scam, however, the Ritz scammers did not seek to manufacture a rigged roulette ball or any other equipment essential to the game. Nor did they attempt to influence the legitimate ball as it spun around the cylinder on its way to dropping into a number slot. The Ritz trio, as they became known, simply set out in quest of the perfect way to track the ball's revolutions and determine with a fair degree of accuracy where it would land.

The trio consisted of a chic and beautiful Hungarian woman and two suave James Bond type men, all in their thirties. Katarina Fekete, known to those close to her as Kata, had soft blond hair, deep blue eyes and a willowy figure that one might say could stop a roulette ball dead in mid-spin. She grew up in Budapest, studied economics and English at the city's Corvinus University. She obtained a degree in both, then worked for a Hungarian bank in its international department, where each day she bore witness to large sums of money being transferred around the globe, and pined for some of the wealth that a mere fraction of it would bring her.

Kata was very hip to Budapest's thriving nightlife and loved partying. She had never married, though she'd been involved with several men, practically none of whom spoke the same mother tongue. There had been Roland from Germany, Didier from France and Terrence from America. They were all businessman who had money. Each in his own way had shown Kata a good time in several European capitals and in American hot spots. Her first trip to London had been with Terrence, who'd first taken her to Miami. Terrence had been a bad gambler who maintained memberships in two of London's happening casinos: the Victoria Club and Crockfords. He'd taken Kata to both and given her chips to play roulette. Kata had been to Budapest's casinos and fancied playing roulette. Her favorite number was 4, and by betting on it she did a lot better than poor Terrence did at the blackjack table. In fact, Terrence's luck was so bad that he ended up asking Kata to lend him back some of the chips he had given her for roulette. Not surprisingly, Kata dumped Terrence when his gambling losses were such that he could no longer afford to take her jet-setting around the world's glamor cities.

One night cruising the Danube on the A 38, a lively dance club on a ship that attracted both Budapest's chic crowd and well-to-do Western tourists, Kata met up with a curious duo from Serbia. Vlad Markov and Goran Horvat were both stylish and handsome. As was often the case among strangers who later bonded in the formation of an illegal enterprise, the trio who would become the new millennium's most renowned roulette scammers became familiar by way of political discussion. It turned out that the two Serbs had met just hours before they crossed paths with the intoxicating Kata. Vlad had heard Goran speaking in Serbian on his cellphone while waiting for a bartender to fix his drink. Cellphones had special significance for Vlad, but of course Goran did not yet know that. When Vlad saw Goran end the call and replace the cell in his jacket pocket, he said to him in Serbian, "What do you think of the women on this dancing ship?"

Goran laughed. "I saw one blond who could stop this shit bucket faster than the iceberg did the *Titanic*."

Vlad laughed, and then they fell into an amicable conversation. When Goran inquired what Vlad was doing in Budapest besides eyeing beautiful women, his compatriot explained that he was there testing communications equipment, which was not at all a lie. Goran, on the other hand, claimed to be in Budapest scoping out possible investments for a new wave of flourishing Yugoslavian businessmen. When Vlad practically guffawed, Goran asked what was so funny.

"You're full of shit," Vlad said, both amusingly and accusingly. "You're no more an investment counselor than I am a homosexual."

Goran couldn't help but laugh and admit he was indeed full of shit.

Barely a minute later, the blond who'd caught Goran's eye crossed in front of them at the bar. "That's her," Goran said admiringly. "Is she not a beauty?"

"Definitely not a Serb," Vlad responded and drew another laugh from his newfound chum.

Evidently, the beauty in her cocktail dress now standing in front of them also thought it was funny. "No, I'm not Serbian," she said to them in their language, stunning them.

"Are you Hungarian?" Goran asked.

"Yes," she answered in Serbian.

"How is it that you speak Serbian?"

"I don't," she said. "I'm just pretending."

They all laughed, then began a night of drinking, dancing and conversation. Kata spoke only the basic Serbian she'd learned in school and from a close childhood friend whose family had fled to Budapest when Milosevic came to power in Belgrade. She'd also become quite informed about the atrocities committed by that regime, which finally led to Milosevic's arrest and detention at the Hague, where he'd been standing trial for war crimes.

It turned out that Goran spoke some Hungarian, but since Vlad did not, their conversation shifted to the one common language each of them spoke fluently: English. After a flirtatious opening filled with the usual jokes and compliments, they took a table together, where their talk shifted to backgrounds and politics. At first, Kata believed the two Serbs were involved in the business of human trafficking. Many young Hungarian girls seeking the better life elsewhere became ensnared in the filthy nets of sex-slave traders. As Serbs and Albanians were known to be major players in the trade and often in Hungary luring girls with false promises of well-paying, respectable jobs on the continent, Kata was hard pressed to believe they were anything but what she'd assumed them to be. To finally convince her otherwise, Vlad, as much to Goran's surprise as to Kata's, admitted that he was "an unlawful person often in violation of the law but not a nefarious being turning dreams of young girls into nightmares of forcible rape and slavery."

Vlad of course did not get into any details of his declaration, but it was enough to keep Kata from getting up to leave their table. They spoke of the farce that Milosevic's trial was becoming more and more of every day. It was the fall of 2003, and at the snail's pace of the proceedings, Milosevic would surely die before anything close to a verdict was realized. Both Vlad and Goran stated their opposition to Milosevic's regime. They did not believe in ethnic cleansing or in any other of Milosevic's policies. Each expressed his opinion that it was a tragedy of sorts that the ex-Yugoslavian president had not been killed. The trial itself was a huge waste of money and time.

Kata spoke of the many changes in her country since the collapse of the Soviet Bloc. She enthused how Hungarians delighted in their new brand of freedom. When she'd been a child, travel and pleasure were both restricted. Now there was a vibrant nightlife in Budapest, attested to by their very surroundings at that moment. There were even casinos, and when she mentioned them she noticed a twinkle in Vlad's eyes. So did Goran. They'd all smiled numerous times. Both men had been enraptured by the lovely woman's conversation.

The night floated by and drifted into a *ménage à trois* in a cozy Budapest hotel room. After the wee hours of sex and champagne, they parted ways. Kata threw on her clothing and went home to change for work at the bank. Goran had no specific plans for that day. He decided on a whim to stealthily follow Vlad.

First Vlad entered the Café Eklektika in the heart of Budapest. Goran bought a hot chocolate from a street vendor and waited until Vlad came out. When he did and hopped into a taxi, Goran grabbed the next cab and fell in behind. Vlad's taxi pulled into the Budapest Hilton. Strange, Goran thought, his countryman never mentioned anything about staying at the fashionable and expensive hotel.

But Vlad did not go to the front desk or toward the bank of elevators leading to the rooms. Instead, he walked through the lobby to the reception area of the Casino Budapest.

So he's a gambler, thought, Goran. Which was quite the coincidence because so was he; however, he was a professional. Goran was what had become known in the casino industry as an advantage player. He counted cards and tracked aces at blackjack. He peeked at hole cards in American casinos that used handheld decks, and had once belonged to a team that clocked biased wheels to gain an advantage at roulette. He did whatever it took to win money in casinos, sometimes taking him to the fringes of legality. At present, he was in Budapest checking out the city's casinos. He'd heard on the card counters' grapevine that there were some beatable blackjack games. There had been no reason to mention his profession to Vlad or Kata the night before. But maybe now there would be. Who knew?

Goran watched Vlad show his passport to a young woman behind the counter, then enter the casino. He pondered it momentarily and decided to follow. He showed the woman his Serbian passport and walked inside the rather small but well-appointed gaming salon.

It was more crowded than he would have thought. When the woman at reception mentioned the casino was open twenty-four hours, Goran had wondered why, but evidently gambling fever had caught fire in Budapest just as it had in Moscow.

He hung back near the threshold and watched Vlad take the last empty seat at a roulette table and buy chips. The table was full and noisy with action. After a few spins, Goran approached. He tapped his countryman on the shoulder. Vlad was quite surprised to see him.

"She was something else," he said with a warm smile, referring to the female object of their mutual conquest.

"Topping it off with a little roulette, I see," Goran said cheerfully.

"Do you play?" Vlad's eyes were trained on the layout, following his hands as they spread his chips around the layout. Goran observed that he was betting with minimum $1 chips. The main currency in Hungarian casinos was US dollars. Euros and British pounds were also accepted.

"I do, but prefer blackjack. Unless, of course, I run into a biased wheel I can win with."

Vlad turned around sharply as if very interested in Goran's last statement. "You like to play with an edge then?"

Goran laughed. "Did you ever hear the term 'advantage player?'"

"You're one of them?"

"I try to be."

"Maybe you ought to try to be one at roulette." He gave Goran a provocative smile with arched eyebrows. There was certainly a live wire between the two Serbs. They were naturally receptive to each other, as if a warm current passed between them. The sexual encounter with Kata surely had not hurt.

"Mind if I play a little with you?" Goran asked.

"Go right ahead. Even bet with me if you like." The way Vlad said it conveyed that betting with him would be a prudent approach to roulette.

In fact, it was. What Goran didn't know was that Vlad had come to Budapest on a mission to test the most sophisticated cheating equipment yet to be used at roulette. It had been constructed by a German electronics whiz Vlad knew in Frankfurt, who was at that moment in an American prison for tampering with bank's ATM machines. The device consisted of a laser scanner linked to a micro-computer inside a tiny cellphone. It had been Vlad's idea. His theory was that a scanner could measure the speed of the ball at the point of the dealer's release and then at a second point around the cylinder. Those computations could then be beamed to the micro-computer, which by calculating the declining orbit of the wheel could determine in which six-number section of the bowl the ball would land. That information would be flashed onto the screen of the cellphone several seconds before the dealer halted the betting, ample time to get the corresponding wagers down on the layout.

It was really quite simple in theory. All that remained to see was if the equipment would function properly in casinos. Vlad's plan was to attack the private gambling clubs in London. His first choice would have been Las Vegas, but he was well aware that Nevada gaming statutes considered the use of computerized equipment in casinos a serious felony. The penalty on getting caught was hard prison time. In the United Kingdom, laws governing the use of equipment to aid gamblers in casinos were much less defined, possibly not even considered a crime. Vlad much preferred to take his chances with the Brits.

He'd chosen Hungary to be the testing ground because its casinos were not as sophisticated as those on the continent. Whatever malfunctions occurred could be corrected before Vlad went for the serious cash in London. As well, the casino personnel in Budapest were less likely to stumble on a faulty gadget than those in more established gambling venues. Vlad knew all too well that if his magical cellphone were discovered anywhere, news of it would circulate around the world faster than a phone call.

Sitting at the middle of the table, the tiny cell was securely palmed in his large right hand, which was covered loosely by his left. It was completely hidden from not only the dealer on the game but also everyone around the table. Not even Goran, who stood right over Vlad's shoulder, could see it. When Vlad's left hand went to the layout to make his bets, his right still concealed the cell.

As the dealer set the ball on the wheel's inner groove, Vlad subtly aimed the cell in its direction, the point of the cell's antenna just a few millimeters inward from the edge of his outstretched middle finger, completely concealed. When the ball launched into its revolutions, Vlad held the cell steady. The ball sped in one direction while the wheel spun much slower in the other. Two seconds before the wheel made its third turn, Vlad faintly split his index and middle fingers a half centimeter apart over the cell to see its screen. It flashed the coordinates for the neighboring numbers 11 and 30. Vlad quickly bet those numbers as well as the two numbers positioned on either side of them on the wheel. The ball dropped into number 13, two slots from number 11, a winner.

On the next spin, Vlad again peeked at the cell's screen before the wheel completed its third turn. It flashed "0, 32." Vlad made the six corresponding bets. The ball landed on number 15, directly next to 0. On the third spin, the ball missed the targeted section by one number, but on the fourth hit one of the numbers displayed on the screen head-on.

Vlad ended the test session after twenty spins. Each spin he'd bet $5 straight up on each of the six numbers. Had he done that without the laser, the odds of him winning one of those bets would have been 5.17-to-1, just a fraction less than one win every six spins. He should have lost approximately $18 over the course of the twenty spins. But with the aid of the laser and micro-computer, one of Vlad's numbers had won fifteen of twenty times. He had won $2,100, which meant that the gadgetry had given him an advantage of 350 percent during the trial, a phenomenal result. Goran, who'd been betting as well, made $1,500.

"I've never seen anyone hit like that," Goran said with wonderment in the back of their taxi. They were headed to the Casino Las Vegas in the nearby Sofitel Hotel.

"I know," Vlad said simply.

"How did you do it?"

Vlad smiled crookedly at his new friend. "You're interested, aren't you?"

"Wouldn't you be if you were sitting where I am?"

Vlad laughed from the gut. "Let's give it another shot, then maybe I'll tell you the secret." At this stage, Vlad was already thinking of including Goran in the scam. Another trusted person betting the numbers would mean double the profits, and Vlad would surely take a piece of whatever Goran made.

The Casino Las Vegas was not as refined as the Casino Budapest, but it was busier inside. Late afternoon had jammed up four roulette tables with action. This time Goran's curiosity was such that he only watched. He knew by then Vlad was somehow cheating, but still had not suspected a device cupped inside his hand. He figured that his friend had devised a means to very accurately clock the wheel. Somewhere along his casino travels he'd heard the term "oglers" used to describe roulette players with the unique talent of being able to follow the spinning ball with their eyes and determine with accuracy on what section it would land, thereby greatly reducing the odds against them. He'd even heard about certain exercises oglers did to train their eyes for the task. Perhaps Vlad was an ogler.

In a café a short distance from the casino, where they sat sipping espressos after Vlad's second winning roulette session, Goran learned just how far off he'd been in his estimation that Vlad was an ogler.

"That's fantastic!" he said in a hushed voice, in spite of the fact they were speaking Serbian. "That little cellphone you got could bust the bank in the world's grandest casinos."

"That's the idea, my friend."

"But how illegal is it?"

"Very, in American casinos. However, in the United Kingdom it might not even be a misdemeanor. I've done some research on British gambling law. It happens to be quite antiquated. Whereas American gambling statutes clearly define possession of any device in a casino used to gain an advantage as a felony, British law makes no mention of such devices. So if one is ever discovered in play, I guess that it would be handled as a precedent."

"Just what are the chances of yours being discovered in play?" Goran asked doubtfully.

Vlad's radiated confidence. "The scanner inside the cellphone does not interfere with casinos' electronic and communications equipment. If it did, we would have seen evidence of it in the casinos we played at."

"How?"

"There would have been panic in the pits."

Goran nodded. He knew how casino personnel behaved when something bugged them. Discretion was not the order of their reactions.

A waiter came by asking if they'd like another espresso. Both said yes.

"So, would you like to be part of this?" Vlad asked.

Goran's answer left no room for ambiguousness. "I've already forgotten how to play blackjack."

"And you will give me a third of your profits in London," Vlad said conclusively.

"That's better than half."

"So it's agreed."

They shook hands.

In the next two months, they travelled together through casinos in RumaniaRomania, Austria, and Germany, testing the scanner and micro-computer in the cellphone. Along the way, there was a streak where the device did not function at an optimum level. It never deteriorated to a point where its use was unprofitable, but Vlad decided that improvements had to be made. He operated under the premise that the scanner's life expectancy in casinos would be short, so they had to go in with equipment that functioned as close to perfect as possible.

Vlad left Goran in Vienna and flew to Frankfurt to meet up with a Russian associate of the imprisoned German who'd built the device. The Russian, for whom the German vouched, swore that the scanner and micro-computer were working perfectly. Any deviations from the cellphone's previous accurate performances had to be due to imperfections associated with the revolutions of the roulette ball, either in identifying the dealer's starting point or something being amiss with certain casinos' roulette wheels. Vlad was not altogether comfortable with the explanation, but with the device's inventor imprisoned had to accept it.

By New Year's Eve, Vlad and Goran had returned to Budapest. To ring in the new year, they celebrated aboard the A 38. The floating dance ship was packed to the gills with champagne-toting revellers. Neither was surprised to run into Kata, who was there with several people she worked with at the bank. They immediately got to talking and reminiscing, and that intimate connection between the three rekindled in no time.

There had not been any conscious discussion between the two Serbs to either mention or involve Kata in the pending roulette scam. But as ideas come into being through the natural course of events, so did the hatching of their audacious scam. Talk of it started when Goran casually mentioned that he and Vlad had met by chance at the Casino Budapest two months earlier. Kata commented that she'd been there on several occasions and just adored playing roulette. Along the route of conversation, she shared her experiences of London and her forays into its private gambling clubs with her ex-American boyfriend. She said that he'd been a member of several of them and joined another while in her company. She spoke of the required twenty-four-hour "cooling off period" that required new members of British gambling clubs to wait that amount of time before actually gambling in the club. It was an old English law akin to the American version that governed the purchase of firearms, where after purchasing a gun you had to wait a period of time before taking possession of it. The supposed theory applied to gambling was that the wait allowed people to contemplate whether or not they really wanted to invest in gambling.

Vlad had been concerned about this private facet of British

gaming establishments. He knew London's casinos did background checks on all prospective members. Although he was clean as far as criminal convictions went, he was still a Serbian, and Serbians were not generally cast in favorable light when it came to gaining membership in places boasting an international clientele consisting of sheiks, barons and earls. Vlad had worried that he might even be refused membership and would then have to concoct another scheme to gain entry.

But a beautiful woman of Hungarian descent? No casino this or that side of a roulette wheel would refuse her. If she posed as his wife and they joined a London casino together, then brought along Goran as a guest, which members were permitted to do, it might just go off without a hitch.

"I'd love to go with you to London," Kata said jubilantly at their nightclub table, underneath strobe lights and rocking music. They were drinking champagne and laughing intimately, the evening drifting once again toward wee hours of shared sensual pleasures. "When are we going?"

"Within the month," Vlad replied. "I will of course let you know a week in advance."

They didn't arrive in London until mid-March 2004. The fact that Kata was already casino-wise was a great asset; she wouldn't have to be taught how to play roulette or anything else about casino etiquette. Vlad had selected the Ritz casino for the scam. He planned to beat other casinos as well, but London's most elite private gaming club would be hit first. They passed by the elegant hotel in London's Piccadilly in the afternoon. At the casino's reception, they filled out basic applications and presented their passports, whose primary pages were photocopied. Then a digital photograph of each new member was taken, after which they were told by the gentleman at the counter that they could enter the casino in exactly twenty-four hours.

It was thirty hours later when Mr. Vladimir Markov and his

wife Katarina, with their guest Goran Horvat, entered the Ritz casino. At the reception desk, the couple and their guest showed their passports and signed the casino register. A photograph was taken of Goran, as one was taken of all members' guests entering British casinos. In the inside pocket of his sports jacket, Vlad had £10,000 sterling. In the pockets of his trousers he had another £10,000. Goran carried £15,000 on his person that was part of Vlad's £35,000 bankroll. Kata carried no cash but didn't need any. She would use her "husband's" chips to make her bets.

Inside, the Ritz casino lived up to its gilded reputation. There were golden chandeliers hanging from ornate ceilings above plush red carpeting and draperies. The walls sported handsome murals depicting nineteenth-century life. There was a beautiful mahogany bar where immaculately dressed Arab princes and international playboys with gorgeous women toasted one another for luck. Most of the roulette tables were going full blast. They found one that had two available chairs. Vlad and Goran sat down. Kata stood off to the side of Vlad – for a reason. Her presence would certainly draw a lot more attention from casino personnel and patrons than either man's. Her being there thus served a double purpose: to bet and to draw lustful eyes on her. She had entered the casino's reception wearing a red fox coat that her American ex-lover had bought her after a rare gambling win. Now she looked splendid in her flowing black satin dress with its generous bodice.

The maximum bet straight up on numbers was £200. They were not interested in lesser bets. They would attack full-scale right away. There would be no camouflage bets to offset the fallout. They would quickly take heat but continue playing in what they knew would become a furnace, albeit an unseen one.

Vlad and Goran each threw £5,000 in £100 notes onto the layout, drawing a few glances from neighboring players. The dealer, a young woman with a lissom figure wearing a long, frilly dress, pushed two stacks of £100 chips capped with two £500 chips to each of them. She advised that it would be up to them to keep track of their individual bets as they'd be playing with casino chips, not the roulette chips that were assigned to specific players. They nodded and verbally affirmed their understanding.

The dealer wished them good luck, cased her layout, which was already filled up with piles of chips on every number, and spun the ball. Vlad's right hand shifted subtly toward the wheel. The cellphone was palmed in it with ease, the antenna's head pointed at the ball's take-off point. The ball whizzed around the wheel in its revolutions as the cylinder orbited in the opposing direction. Vlad's eyes fixed on it like glue. At the precise instant clocked in his mind, his fingers over the cell split and the screen came into view. It flashed "14, 31." He knew they had but seconds to get their bets down onto the layout before the betting would be closed. But Vlad had memorized the entire sequence of numbers on the wheel. He knew them better than the alphabet. He knew the corresponding positions of the numbers on the layout just as well. His cohorts had also put this crucial information to memory, but he was still the lead.

Vlad had his stack of £100 chips in his left hand. The split second his eyes saw 14 and 31 on the screen, his loaded hand moved to the layout and dropped two chips on both numbers, then two chips on numbers 1, 9, 20 and 22. He could have utilized a verbal "neighbors" bet, where he would call out to the dealer his single bet on all those numbers and toss her his chips, which she would place in the neighbors box accordingly, but there was no time to do that. Certainly not for all three bettors.

Kata and Goran did not simply wait to follow Vlad's lead with their chips. They would only use his lead when needed, in instances where they couldn't recall the juxtaposition of the numbers involved. By the time Vlad had finished making his bets, Kata and Goran had two of their £100 chips on four of the six numbers. They got their last two bets down just half a second after Vlad had.

"Finish betting," the dealer called out, then waved her hand across the table to close the wagering. Two seconds later the ball dropped off the groove, dribbled briefly and settled into a pocket.

Bull's-eye! Number 31.

The dealer swept the losers, then paid the winners. There was an assortment of colored roulette chips belonging to other players beneath the marker over the winning number. The dealer paid those first, the highest payoff among them amounting to £700. Then she paid Vlad, Kata and Goran £7,000 each for their bets of £200 straight up on number 31. They'd each had five losing bets of the same amount, totalling £1,000, which meant their individual profit for the spin was £6,000. As a threesome they took £18,000 off the table. Beforehand, Vlad had made the same arrangement with Kata that he'd made with Goran back in Budapest: he'd take a third of her winnings when it was over.

As the ball took flight for the next spin, Vlad's cellphone told him it should land in the section centered by the numbers 10 and 23. Again his left hand led their betting parade onto the layout. In seeming chaos but in reality absolute precision, their hands covered the numbers 5, 8, 10, 23, 24 and 30 with six £100 chips. They accomplished that feat just as the dealer urged the table to finish betting. The ball fell smack in the pocket for number 30, earning them another £18,000.

Vlad's doubts about the Russian's explanation for the cellphone's periodic subpar performance had completely obliterated after the first five spins on the wheel. They'd won all five and were ahead £90,000. It was going so smoothly that it seemed the roulette ball itself was in cahoots with the cellphone. Not one of those five spins produced a wildly bouncing ball, but rather direct drops and small dribbles into the number slots. Of course that was just coincidental, though Vlad was extremely grateful to get out of the box with a bang. A poor performance by the device at the outset combined with bad luck could have put their entire bankroll in jeopardy after a dozen spins. One thing for sure, Vlad was not going to decrease their bets after consecutive losers. Either the device would work or it wouldn't.

"Work" soon became the understatement of the year. In the first hour and a half, they hit sixteen of twenty spins. That was four times greater than the smallest winning percentage when choosing six-number sections at random. They had won an astonishing £270,000. Despite this highly irregular win in such a small period of time, the Ritz casino personnel were not too concerned. British casinos operated with a much higher degree of on-floor surveillance of gaming tables than their American counterparts. The inspectors in the pit noticed nothing suspicious in the play of the three Eastern Europeans. For the moment, neither did the surveillance observers hidden in dark rooms watching them on video screens.

On their roulette table itself, discretion reigned. The pit inspector watching their action remained silent. The dealer was extremely professional, albeit stoic. She handled their action as though she'd often seen its likes. Tipping was not permitted in British casinos, and neither gentleman nor the dashing blond made the mistake of offering to do so. There was no reason to forestall the continuation of their assault, except for a very elemental one: the cellphone's screen began to struggle with its display and then lost it altogether.

Vlad felt like swallowing the roulette ball when he realized why – the goddamn battery! He'd forgotten to recharge it before they left their West London hotel. Due to the scanner and microcomputer working inside the cellphone, the battery drained at a pace much quicker than when powering an idle one.

They cashed out £300,000 and called it a night. After departing the Ritz, they went directly to their hotel. This time there was no partying into the early morning hours. They each retired to their separate rooms. Vlad immediately hooked up the cellphone to the charger. As he lay in bed, he reflected on the first night's events at the Ritz.

It had gone exceedingly well. There had been no heat at the roulette table and no questioning on cashing out their chips. Of course the casino had offered to pay by check, and of course the lucky gamblers insisted on cash. Vlad estimated that the Ritz could handle one more night of their action, then they'd bring their gig somewhere else.

The next morning, they met downstairs for coffee. "How did you sleep?" Vlad asked his partners as if it were a funny question.

"Not a wink," replied Goran. "My body was as charged up as your cellphone."

Laughing, Kata said, "The current reached my bed, too."

A waitress delivered hot croissants to the table. Their delicious aroma suspended their conversation for a moment.

"So are we going to play the Ritz tonight?" Goran asked.

Vlad finished a sip of hot coffee and nodded. "Yes, one more night."

"What after that?" asked Kata, her eyes big with the promise of more roulette cash.

"Depends," Vlad said. "We might start up right away in another casino, or maybe cool it for a while."

"Why cool it?" Goran asked. "Isn't it better to go for as much as we can as fast as possible?"

Vlad hitched his shoulders. "Maybe. The problem here in London is that the casinos communicate with each other better than anywhere in the world."

"I thought they were all private clubs," Kata said.

"More the reason their intercasino communication is impeccable," Vlad explained. "They have no active gaming control agents like Las Vegas does, so they have to worry about their casinos for themselves. There is a police vice squad that investigates gaming incidents, but they only get involved if they're called by a casino looking to file a complaint."

They arrived by cab at the Ritz at eight o'clock in the evening. A uniformed valet wearing a tall hat held the door for them as they entered. The casino was not yet full, but there were enough patrons floating around the roulette tables to enable their play. Obviously, they couldn't be the only players at a table, in which case detection of the device would be more likely. So they chose the busiest wheel and took the same positions alongside the table they'd occupied the night before. Only Vlad sat. Goran and Kata huddled over him, effectively providing him cover.

As they had the previous night, they got off to a fast start. The device hit four of the first five spins. Their bets did not vary, still £200 straight up on each of the six numbers in the targeted section. The dealer and inspector on the game were not the same employees from the night before, but conducted themselves in the same manner. Nothing but utter professionalism. Neither one's demeanor changed as the trio won spin after spin. They watched the trio's stacks of chips pile up on the table. Their expressions did not waver each time security brought more chips to reinforce the table's reserves.

By the second hour, they were so good that on a few occasions Kata and Goran actually beat Vlad to the last of the bets. They could not see the cellphone's screen, thus they had to wait for Vlad to place the initial two bets. Then they could call on their memory for the two neighboring bets on either side. That they could ever accomplish that before Vlad was truly remarkable.

After the third hour, they were ahead £500,000.

After the fourth, there was a sudden intrusion.

A debonair fellow in a tuxedo stepped between Goran and Kata, said hello to them but offered his hand to Vlad as he spoke. "My name is Lloyd Davies; I'm the president of the Ritz Club."

The first problem was that the phone was in Vlad's right hand, the shaking hand. The second problem was that if he didn't shake Mr. Davies' hand, it would look terribly discourteous if not altogether suspicious. So Vlad did the only thing he could think to do. He suddenly raised the cellphone and pressed it against his jaw. He said, "Excuse me," to the Ritz president, then spoke Serbian into the phone. Although the phone hadn't rung, it could have been in the vibration mode. Vlad said goodbye and stuffed it in his jacket pocket. Then he turned his attention to Davies, who'd seen nothing out of the ordinary: just another international patron speaking his native language on his cellphone.

"Pleasure, Mr. Davies," Vlad said and shook his hand.

"Can I offer all of you dinner tonight on the Ritz?" He spoke to all three, but directed his gaze to Vlad, because Vlad was the male member while Goran was only the guest.

"That's very nice of you, but it won't be necessary. We're leaving London in the morning, so after we've finished playing we're going to head back to our hotel."

"What a shame," Davies said, as if it were. "But if there's anything I can do for you, all of you, just give a call."

"Thank you, that's kind," Vlad said, and was echoed by Goran and Kata.

Davies walked off and disappeared, but Vlad was bugged. What spooked him was that the president of the casino had made no reference to their winning streak. Not even a "continued good luck" on leaving. It was as if Davies by design avoided mentioning their good fortune at the table. Vlad also knew that it was unusual for legitimate high rollers to decline comps from casino presidents.

He waited a full hour before slipping the cellphone back into his hand. During that time, they did not alter their betting patterns. To do so would be noticeable and might invite suspicion. They were lucky enough not to get hurt while playing aboveboard. Vlad just chose six numbers at random, and one of them came in often enough to limit their losses to £10,000. At one point Kata made a mistake by betting her favorite number 4 when Vlad had not bet on it. She'd figured that since they were not operating the scanner, she might make it look good by betting on different numbers. But that was a mistake because there was no reason to do *anything* different in the interim. Casino bosses might wonder why all of a sudden she was not betting the same numbers as her husband.

No harm was done as Vlad just smooched her, whispering in her ear to keep betting as he did.

When Vlad slipped the cell back into his hand, they picked up right where they'd left off. Their £100 chips rained over the numbers on the layout, then grew into mountains on the table in front of them. They repeatedly exchanged stacks of chips into £10,000 plaques that were only used in dealing with super high rollers. At one-thirty in the morning, the table began to thin out. By two o'clock, the casino had emptied to the point where they could no longer play. It was time to cash out, and now they could celebrate. They had won £1 million! In two days, they had beaten the Ritz for £1.3 million! A smashing score.

Before they received their funds, Davies showed up at the cashier. "Congratulations," he said, shaking the two Serbs' hands. "I've never seen anyone win at roulette like that."

So now he's congratulating us, thought Vlad. He wondered to what point Davies suspected a scam. "Thank you," he replied graciously. "It was a pleasure."

Vlad, Kata and Goran had wanted their stunning success at the Ritz to be kept a private pleasure, but the whole world found out about it a week later when they were arrested by London's Metropolitan vice squad and Scotland Yard officers. The Ritz casino's security experts had examined their closed-circuit television footage, over and over again. Though it was not made public exactly how they came to suspect that the trio had cheated their roulette tables, one tipoff was surely their exorbitant win rate, which simply defied the odds for too long. The experts had followed every bet they'd made and calculated they'd played with a 400 percent advantage. How was this possible over two days, they wondered. The one thing they knew, it wasn't possible without cheating. Therefore, if no visible cheating techniques appeared on their videotapes, it had to be something invisible that involved tracking the roulette ball and accurately predicting where it would land. The only device capable of that was some kind of computer.

An ensuing search of the three hotel rooms occupied by the trio turned up the cellphone and bundles of cash. All was confiscated as evidence. Their bank accounts were frozen during a nine-month investigation by Scotland Yard that not only looked into "winning by deception" in a casino but also money laundering. But in the end, Vlad, Goran, and Kata were all exonerated. As Vlad had predicted, British gaming law was too murky to allow for a successful prosecution of the sort. The 1845 law governing cheating at gambling did not take into account new advances in computer technology that aid or constitute cheating. In view of that, and in light of the fact that Vlad's scanner only provided information as to where the roulette ball would land without manipulating the ball or any other equipment on the wheel, Scotland Yard determined in December 2004 that no charges would be filed.

The cellphone and cash winnings were returned to the threesome. Their celebratory threesome in the penthouse of a luxury hotel other than the Ritz lasted an entire week.

CHAPTER 8

THE ATLANTIC CITY KENO CAPER

Were it not for the negligence and plain stupidity of perhaps the most brilliant casino scammer of all-time, Ron Harris's talents may have made him even more money than mine had made me. Harris, a lanky forty-year-old with green eyes and long hair pulled back in a ponytail, had been working without incident for the Nevada Gaming Control Board (NGCB) for twelve years when in 1995 he made news that stunned the gaming industry. His duties consisted of testing slot machines at casinos throughout the state, making sure they functioned properly and that their integrity could not be compromised. He and his co-workers would go into casinos and randomly test machines to make sure they contained only computer chips that were previously approved by the Board's Enforcement Division. These chips were called EPROMs (erasable programmable read-only memories) and controlled the payback percentages on slot machines.

Ron was a whiz of computer whizzes, so immensely talented that the NGCB entrusted his expertise almost single-handedly to safeguard the state's computerized slot machines. As a kid, he was a profound tinkerer. While his peers flipped baseball cards and played dodge ball, Ron dived headfirst into the world of electronics. At the age of two, he took apart his grandmother's antique watch. At ten, he rigged a makeshift alarm system of wires and a 9-volt battery to alert him whenever someone entered his bedroom. In his teens, a day hardly went by that Ron's head was not buried in some gadgetry with wires sprouting in every direction.

After high school, Ron joined the engineering firm of EG&G, Inc. at the Nevada Test Site as an electronics technician. He enjoyed the job and was thrilled to get paid for something he loved doing. But he soon found himself sacked from the job when a background check revealed that he had failed to disclose he had smoked marijuana as a student.

But Ron did not let that derail him. Through an advertisement, he landed his job with the Electronic Services Division of the NGCB. The Board was pleased to have someone with his solid background in math and engineering. He worked in a protected area where he and his co-workers oversaw the testing of the state's 200,000 slot machines. The main facet of his job was to ensure that all slot machines, particularly the newer models that were constantly upgraded, offered gamblers a fair share of winning.

Ron showed an affinity for his work and did his job well. One of his functions was to investigate scams designed to bilk money from slot machines. His investigations branched out into other casino games, most notably keno. Ron worked diligently and quickly developed a reputation as someone who wouldn't rest until a scam was busted.

In 1989, Ron worked long and hard to learn how a crooked slot-route operator, American Coin Company, and its chief computer programmer, Larry Volk, rigged video poker machines to prevent them from hitting royal flushes. Largely due to Ron's work, the company lost its gaming license and was fined $1 million. But before the owners of American Coin could be successfully prosecuted, Volk, who had agreed to testify against them, was shot to death in the driveway of his home.

This turn of events deeply upset Ron Harris, who believed those owners were the guiltiest parties in the scam.

In 1993 Ron, still dedicated to his post, busted a retired scientist who'd made an illicit fortune when he programmed a homemade, palm-size computer to predict when International Game Technology's Fortune 1 video poker machine would pay jackpots. But the scientist received a sentence of only 200 hours of community service, no jail time. Ron was appalled and disillusioned by this. He later said, "I spent weeks and months on this, and he won money and got probation. It was frustrating." Convicted cheats were receiving mere slaps on the wrist.

In addition to the frustrations of his professional life, Ron was also going through personal trauma. He'd been having disagreements with his wife, Vicki Berliner, that escalated into ugly domestic disputes. This had a terrible effect on their young son. Finally, they divorced and Vicki moved from Las Vegas to Southern California. But she was hurting for money and Ron had fallen way behind in child support payments. Things were looking very bleak in Ron's life by the time 1994 rolled around.

Desperately needing a large cash infusion, Ron decided to do something about it. But for that he would have to cross the line. He'd long been envious of slot manufacturers and casino operators making hundreds of millions of dollars from naïve gamblers, and he no longer feared his vast knowledge of how to rig slot machines. Thus, without inhibitions, Ron set out to put his knowledge to work.

In early February 1994, he telephoned his ex-wife. "Vicki," he said as persuasively as he could. "I know you need money, so meet me at the airport in Reno."

"What for?" she asked, not really sure what to make of it.

"Because you are going to win a slot jackpot, and I know you won't tell anyone how we did it."

"How are we going to do it?"

"Don't worry about it," Ron said impatiently. "I just have a way of setting something up for you. It's a guarantee to win the jackpot. Leave it at that."

What Ron had figured out was a way to rig Universal slot machines. His technique became known as gaffing, and he could apply it best to computer chips that controlled Universal's three-coin, three-reel slot machines. By secretly modifying these chips under the guise of verifying their defense against tampering, he programmed them to activate 200-coin credits after a prearranged sequence of inserting coins was followed for a series of successive pulls. At that point, Ron had the option of either cashing out the credits or pulling the slots' handles an additional 240 times with varying coin sequences to trigger the top jackpots. For instance, on one particular machine he devised a sequence of pulls whereby he'd insert three coins, followed by two coins, then another two coins, then one coin, then three coins, then two final coins that would rig the machine to automatically pay out the top jackpot. He did this by erasing the memory on the EPROM chips and substituting his own programming that activated the jackpots. He knew his gaffs were foolproof and that he could operate the entire scam himself. The problem was, however, that he could not be the person to collect the jackpots because identification had to be shown. It would stink to high heaven to see someone in his position with the NGCB win large jackpots. Not only that, but employees of the NGCB were sworn not to engage in any gambling in Nevada casinos.

In spite of that, Ron had been entering casinos in various disguises and serving himself to the 200 credits he made available on the machines. In fact, he was using these machines as one used bank ATMs to withdraw cash. At his liking, he simply toured casinos and made his withdrawals. But this was chump change. He knew that his talents deserved bigger paydays, which was the reason to get his ex-wife involved in his scams.

Ron flew up to Reno. He rented a car and visited various casinos in both Reno and Lake Tahoe, gaffing selected slot machines. A week later he met Vicki at the airport. They drove up to the Crystal Bay Club in beautiful Lake Tahoe. In their rented car in the parking lot, Ron said, "Okay, wait here for twenty minutes. Then come inside the casino and find me at the bank of nickel slot machines. I'll indicate the machine that you're to play on. But you don't play on that one first. Play on the one next to it, or a few machines away from it. Then after a full pulls, go play on the one I indicated. Be wary of someone else trying to grab that machine from you; there will be 200 free credits on it. If someone goes for it, just beat them to it."

"Okay," Vicki said nervously. But she urgently needed the money.

Ron found the machine he'd already gaffed. He played it for fifteen minutes, accumulating the 200 credits by activating the rigged computer chip. Right on time, Vicki appeared in the aisle between the banks of slot machines. Ron got up; Vicki sat at a machine a few seats away. She inserted her nickels, made a few aimless pulls, then scooted over to the machine Ron had vacated. She played that machine for half an hour, drawing against the credits Ron had left on it.

Suddenly lights flashed and bells rang!

She'd hit the jackpot!: $5,000.

Vicki Berliner was amazed. She told the attendant who came over how she couldn't believe she'd been so lucky. When the slot manager joined them and asked for identification, she gladly obliged while Ron, wearing a ball cap with his long hair rolled up underneath, watched in the distance.

"That was unbelievable!" Vicki beamed in the car as they left the Crystal Bay Club and pulled onto the mountain road back toward Reno.

"Don't forget that I get half," Ron said without amusement.

"I'm the one fixing this all up."

"But I'm the one taking the risk collecting the jackpot."

"All right, I'll give you 60 percent, only because of our boy."

"Agreed."

They went on to hit jackpots at several Reno casinos, starting with Fitzgeralds. After five jackpots on nickel machines, they upgraded to quarter machines. The jackpots increased, but so did Vicki's apprehension. Ron took her back to Vegas, where she won several more jackpots. But then she burned out and returned to California. She'd made a nice little bundle to help out with her bills. Maybe, she told Ron, she'd come back at a later date and do it again.

Ron didn't feel like waiting. He contacted a friend, Lynda Doane, and convinced her to take Vicki's place. She did but didn't last long. Ron turned to various friends and acquaintances who claimed jackpots over the next year. Finally, he got in touch with an old high school buddy, Reid McNeal, now an underwater photographer who Ron believed had a larcenous heart and would stick with him once he got a taste of some easy money.

"Reid," Ron said enthusiastically over the phone, "I want you to come out to Vegas."

"What have you got up your sleeve?" Reid wondered.

"A gaff," Ron replied. "Get on the next plane and I'll show it to you when you're here."

Reid arrived, and that very night found himself in a Vegas casino collecting a slot jackpot.

The next day, he collected another, then three days later, still another. In the course of two weeks, Reid won six jackpots for more than $30,000. He was ready to stay a while, but was quite surprised when Ron told him they were heading out of town together.

"Where to?" he asked his computer-whiz buddy.

"Atlantic City."

"I've been there. They've got thousands of those slot babies along the boardwalk."

Ron chuckled. "You can forget them, good buddy," he quipped. "I have something else in mind."

"Let me guess," Reid said, knowing Ron's affinity for numbers crunching. "We're gonna count cards at blackjack."

"Wrong game."

"Something at craps?" When Ron didn't answer, Reid added, "You figured out how to control the dice?"

"What would that have to do with computers?"

"I heard about using computers in roulette." He smiled. "That's your gig, ain't it?"

Ron noticed that Reid seemed hip to whatever that gig might be. He couldn't be more pleased. "Afraid not. It's got nothing to do with blackjack, craps, roulette, baccarat or any other table game."

Reid looked confounded. "What then? There ain't nothing else in casinos besides slots and table games."

"You never heard of keno?"

"*Keno*?" Reid grimaced. "That's a bingo game. What did you do, figure out a numerical system to predict which numbers come up?"

"Well, not quite, but at least you're on the right track."

Reid listened in amazement as Ron told him how months earlier, in his capacity as a NGCB lab technician, he'd gone to the agency's Las Vegas office and reviewed a new computer program written by programmers at Imagineering Systems, the main supplier of the software that operated keno machines in Nevada and Atlantic City. In the process, he'd secretly discovered a glitch before the software was distributed to casinos. Ron's position with the Control Board gave him access to the highly confidential source code and therefore access to the programming in keno machines' random number generators. With that, Ron had realized that he could use his own computer to duplicate the calculations of random number generators and determine the outcome of Keno games ahead of time.

"I know it sounds complicated," Ron said after he'd explained the inner workings of his scam, "but all you need to do is collect the jackpot. Let me worry about how you're going to win it."

Reid rolled his eyes in a mock gesture, as if to say he could hardly care how the hell the gaff would work. "How much is that jackpot going to be?"

"A hundred grand."

"A hundred grand! That's no small potatoes. How many times can we do it?"

"Let's start with once. If it works out, we'll go from there."

A cloud came over Reid's face. "Whaddaya mean, if it works out?"

"That neither one of us fucks up. You're gonna have to be real cool when your keno ticket wins. They've never paid a hundred-grand ticket before. Nothing even close to it in cash."

"Who's never paid?"

"Bally's Park Place casino in Atlantic City. That's the casino we're going to hit."

Ron chose January 14, 1995, for their historic date with destiny, mainly because it would be a busy Saturday afternoon. His choice worked out fine for Reid since he had some personal business to attend to first. It was the Tuesday before the upcoming weekend that they solidified their plans. Reid had to travel to Los Angeles. He would fly to Philadelphia from there and meet Ron at Bally's in Atlantic City Friday night. Ron would take a flight from Vegas and arrive around the same time.

Ron ended up arriving at Bally's first. He made the incredibly dumb mistake of not waiting for Reid and checking into a hotel room under his real name. Reid showed up shortly afterward. They went to dinner at a local restaurant off the boardwalk that Ron had overheard a fellow NGCB technician say served the best food in the entire town, casinos included. It turned out that the food was delicious, and over dessert they discussed the big scam that would go down the following afternoon.

"Are you okay with it?" Ron asked between spoonfuls of succulent chocolate cake.

"No sweat," Reid answered with confidence. "If I can collect slot jackpots, I can sure as hell collect keno jackpots."

"Albeit, this one is going to be for a lot more money."

"Just the same to me," Reid said with soft-spoken bravado. "It's only money."

Ron couldn't poke any holes in his old buddy's confidence. Besides, he'd liked working with him much more than he had with his wife or Lynda Doane. There was no bitching and Reid didn't demand more than half the profits.

They returned to the room, where Reid lounged on his bed and watched TV while Ron descended into the casino to have a walk around.

"Everything cool down there?" Reid asked when his confederate returned an hour later.

Ron nodded emphatically. "I spied on their keno operation. Running smooth as silk. There's no heat. The girls writing the tickets are all smiles." Ron grabbed the remote from the night table between the two beds."

"Hey, I'm watching that!" Reid screeched, indicating the basketball game on the screen.

"Just a minute," Ron retorted. "Just want to check something."

The screen switched to a keno board. A female voice called out the number of each ball as the box corresponding to that number lighted up on the board.

"Is that a real keno game?" Reid asked naively.

"Going on this very moment."

"No kidding!"

"That's the key to the whole thing, Reid. When you're down there playing tomorrow, I'll be up here watching. You're going to have a tiny cellphone receiver in your ear. I will call you on it and give you the winning keno numbers in plenty of time for the upcoming game. You will then write the voucher, approach the counter and have the ticket punched. Then you'll just watch the balls get sucked through the vacuum tube and present your winning ticket when it's over. But just make sure you don't get closed out of the game."

"How many numbers will I be playing?"

"Eight. We're going for an eight-spot. Eight for eight pays the hundred grand aggregate jackpot."

"Right on."

"And don't forget, insist on being paid in cash. They will try to give you a check."

"Got it," Reid said cockily. "C-O-D."

After a light lunch of Nathan's hot dogs in the food court of the neighboring Sands, Reid McNeal found himself in the main keno pit inside Bally's Park Place casino. He'd purposely taken a light lunch as his stomach had been a little queasy from nervousness. Despite his outward coolness, he was still about to stealthily rob the casino of a hundred grand, a monster task. When he belched and tasted the hot dogs rising up with his bile, he berated himself for having eaten them.

He sat down in one of the comfortable padded chairs in the back row of the pit. Up front were the two big keno boards, the red game and the blue game. They looked like giant tic-tac-toe boards, the upper halves containing the numbers 1 to 40 in four rows, the lower halves the numbers 41 to 80. On the counter was the large globular glass bowl sprouting rabbit ear tubes into which the keno balls got sucked and aligned themselves in order. This process of drawing the numbered balls was identical to the one used in state lotteries.

Reid had been told to focus on the red game to his left.

A woman's voice through a speaker announced, "Game 14 closed."

Reid looked up and watched the red board. He concentrated for a moment on the earpiece in his right ear, as if trying to feel it there. Then as if by magic, he heard Ron's voice come through. "All right, Reid, it will be the next red game after this one, game number 15. Have your pencil ready. I will give you the eight numbers twice."

Reid looked down at the mini-desktop built over the chair's arm. Lying on the surface were his eleven keno vouchers. On the first voucher he would mark the eight winning numbers Ron gave him. On the second he'd mark those same numbers, using the voucher as a double-check. On the remaining nine vouchers he would mark random numbers, mixing in some of Ron's. These vouchers were cosmetic in nature, to lessen suspicion by not having Reid win with the purchase of a single ticket. Hitting an 8 for 8 ticket cold was unbelievable enough. Possessing that ticket with no losing tickets would strain an already strained credibility.

There came a hissing sound as the keno machine revved up to start the game. The eighty balls began flying haphazardly in the giant bowl, as though caught in the path of a monster hurricane. There was a whizzing sound accompanying the swirl. Then one by one, twenty keno balls were sucked upward through the vacuum hose into the rabbit ears, ten into each ear. The woman's voice called out the number of each one as it settled in its position in the ear: "The number 3…17…46…" On the red board affixed to the wall on the left, Reid saw the corresponding number boxes light up.

Upstairs in their hotel room, Ron sat at the small round coffee table in front of the TV. The table he had moved from its position by the window. The TV was tuned to the same keno game Reid was watching live in the keno pit. He watched the numbers light up on the red board and heard the woman's voice call them out. He felt the sensation of being there. Casinos supplied this viewing so that patrons could play keno by using the TV remote to choose their betting options on the screen.

Ron concentrated thoroughly, his vision tunnelled to the board on TV and then to the opened screen of his laptop, which sat directly in front of him on the coffee table. As he saw and heard each number, he keyed it into the computer program he'd installed on the laptop's hard drive. His eyes carefully double-checked that the numbers on his computer screen matched those on the TV screen: 3...17...46...There would be no interruptions. He'd called the hotel operator and advised her not to put calls through to his room for the next two hours. He was taking a nap.

In the casino, Reid sat in front of the board and watched as calmly as he could. There was no need for him to record the numbers; he knew Ron was doing that upstairs. Out of nervousness, he kept track of how many numbers had been called. He heard "59." That was the eighteenth number he'd counted. Or was it the nineteenth? Then he heard "The number 7." Then: "Last number, 79." His count had been accurate. At least he wasn't losing his mind.

Suddenly the remaining balls stopped colliding in the glass bowl and the whizzing silenced. The twenty numbers corresponding to the balls in the rabbit ears were lit up on the red board above.

Reid knew that approximately fifteen minutes would pass before the next red game started. Ron had said it would take just a few minutes for his computer program to calculate the winning numbers. As soon as it did, Reid would hear those numbers through the earpiece, slowly and repeated a second time.

In the interim, the blue game to the right was played. Reid watched it aimlessly. The sounds of the whizzing balls were deadened by both his disinterest and his concentration on his right ear. He was desperately afraid that somehow he'd fail to receive Ron's numbers. He hadn't thought of it before, but now he wondered whether Ron would be able to do it again if something went wrong and they didn't win the jackpot that first game.

Upstairs, Ron double- and triple-checked the numbers on his laptop screen against those on the TV screen. Then he quadruple-checked. His eyes took in each number individually, made the comparison, then took in each number as a member of increasing groups, starting with two, then four, and finally four groups of five. He repeated the process twice. He checked his watch; he'd taken two full minutes. He exhaled deeply as he pressed ENTER on his keyboard. He leaned back in the chair while the computer worked. On the screen were the words "please wait."

The wait lasted ninety seconds. Then the screen flashed a set of eight numbers: 2, 4, 16, 17, 31, 65, 68, and 80. Ron felt a surge of adrenaline the likes of which he'd never felt before, not even when he'd rigged a $25,000 slot jackpot. He grabbed the cellphone lying next to the keyboard on the table. He dialed, waited anxiously for the automatic connection, then spoke very deliberately, the way a counter-intelligence expert might deliver a secret code that could save the world from nuclear holocaust.

"The numbers are 2, 4, 16, 17, 31, 65, 68, and 80. I repeat, 2…4…"

Sitting in the keno pit, Reid was suddenly jerked away from his thoughts by the sound of Ron's voice through the earpiece. As he listened to Ron's recital of the numbers, he marked each on his first keno voucher. Then along Ron's repetition, he marked each on his second voucher. He listened to Ron's voice say "Over and out." He then compared the two vouchers to make sure they contained the same eight numbers. They did. He pushed one to the side and stuffed the other in his back trousers pocket.

Reid hurriedly filled out the nine remaining vouchers on the desktop. He randomly chose numbers, using some he'd memorized from Ron's voice and some from those still lit up on the board from the previous game. As soon as he finished, he jumped up and approached the counter. Two people were on line in front of him, but he did not panic. There was plenty of time before the betting on the next red game would close.

The woman keno writer greeted him with a lukewarm smile. "Good afternoon, sir."

"Hi," Reid replied cordially. "I'd like to play ten eight-spots for ten dollars each." He laid the vouchers on the countertop. He'd mixed them up so that the third one from the top would be the winner, as per instructions from Ron. The woman slid them into the reader; the machine produced the tickets. Reid laid a crisp $100 bill on the counter. The woman placed the ten keno tickets with Reid's vouchers on the counter. Reid scooped them up and rushed back to his chair in the last row. He immediately took the third ticket and compared it to the third voucher, carefully examining each to verify that all eight numbers matched up. They did. There had been no mistakes.

The ensuing minutes passed like hours, if not days. The wait was interminable. It seemed as though red game number 15 would never be played. Reid tried to stay calm despite his jitters. Ron had told him not to look around or appear nervous. Just sit in the chair and wait for the announcement that the game was closed.

Ron may have instructed his confederate to remain calm, but upstairs in front of the television, he was a nervous wreck. Not that he doubted his computer program would successfully predetermine eight of the twenty winning numbers. It was his buddy downstairs who'd be collecting the money that worried him. Reid was the human element to this incredible scam, its weakest link that could always backfire. He prayed Reid would handle everything exactly as he'd told him. The only way they could be caught was if Reid fucked up.

Ron's eyes focused on the TV screen. He heard the woman's voice announce, "Game 15 closed." He tensed up and waited.

Downstairs, Reid's eyes focused on the red keno board on the right side of the wall beyond the counter. The keno machine started whirring; the balls whizzed around the glass bowl. The first one was sucked into the hose and then popped into the left rabbit ear protruding from the bowl.

"Number 9," the woman's voice said over the mike.

Reid's eyes darted to his top ticket containing Ron's eight numbers; 9 was not one of them.

"32," called the female voice.

Reid's eyes stayed focused on the board. He knew 32 was not one of the numbers. He watched the corresponding box light up in the fourth row of the display.

When the third number called was 54, Reid instantly remembered that they'd had no numbers in the fifties, and then he began to wonder if something in Ron's program had malfunctioned.

The fourth and fifth numbers called also did not match Reid's primary ticket. Now he felt certain that something had gone amiss. He concentrated on his right ear, hoping that Ron's voice would come through with an explanation of what had gone wrong. But there was nothing. Reid could not know that Ron still harbored no doubts about his program, that when the twenty chosen keno balls were aligned in the rabbit ears, their eight would be among them.

He breathed a sigh of relief when the sixth number called finally matched a number on his ticket: 17. And then another when the seventh ball popping into the rabbit ear was 65. The eighth number missed, but the ninth ball into the chute was number 2. The tenth was 31.

Half the twenty numbers had been called, and four of their balls were among the ten in the left rabbit ear. Reid didn't know much about probability, and figured correctly that it didn't make a difference. Either their remaining four balls would end up in the right rabbit ear or they wouldn't. No use trying to figure it all out with his limited mathematical abilities.

The eleventh and twelfth balls sucked through the chute were duds. So was the thirteenth. Whatever the odds were, thought Reid, they were getting worse by the ball. When the fourteenth number called was yet another miss, Reid felt the pit of his stomach drop the way it did when riding an elevator car. He knew six numbers remained to be called, and four of theirs had still not been. Hitting four of the last six was quite a tall order.

That order got taller when the next number called was 69, missing their number 68 by one, which of course meant nothing. Reid actually thought of the old idiom "Close only counts in horseshoes" as he saw 69 light up on the keno board. Now they had to hit four of five. Was that really possible?

"Number 4," the woman's voice called.

Reid knew instantly that 4 was a good number. He'd been a baseball fan his whole life. Lou Gehrig had worn number 4 with the Yankees.

"16."

"Yes!" Reid exclaimed under his breath. 16 was another good number and had once been worn by his favorite NFL quarterback, Joe Montana.

Three numbers to go. Three more balls to be sucked into the right-side rabbit ear. They had to hit two of them.

"68," came the call.

Now it seemed like magic. Suddenly Reid felt a surge of power, as if he were controlling the numbers by sheer will. There were two balls to go. They needed just one of them: number 80. Two shots at it. One more number and the jackpot would be theirs.

Reid squeezed his eyes shut and thought hard of number 80. He saw the figures 8 and 0 flashing brightly in the dark chambers of his brain, as if suspended above a dark desert highway whose yellow speed-limit lights flashed "80." He squeezed harder, willing the highest number on the board to light up.

"Number 1," announced the woman.

Reid felt the wind gush from his sails. But there was still one more chance. His mind vacillated between the high of winning and the despair of having to go through this again should they not.

"Last number…"

His body tensed; he closed his eyes again and listened.

"…80."

They won!

He snatched his ticket off the desktop and one by one verified that each of the eight printed numbers was lit on the red keno board affixed to the wall. They all were! He checked them again; they still were. Eight for eight. A hundred grand!

The next voice Reid heard was Ron's coming through his ear. "Go collect the money."

Reid swallowed hard, took a deep breath and approached the woman at the counter who'd punched his tickets. She gave him the same perfunctory smile she had before.

"I won," Reid said without animation. The euphoria he'd felt had been tempered by the reality that he was still in the commission of a crime and had not yet gotten the money. He laid the winning ticket on the countertop. The nine others he'd played were stuffed in his trouser pocket.

When the woman swept up the ticket, she treated it like any ordinary winner, but then when she put it through the reader, her jaw collapsed. "You sure did!" she said. "Let me get my supervisor right away." She walked off through a door behind the counter.

Reid stood there with his eyes glued on the red keno board. The winning numbers were still lit and a reminder he was about to collect a small fortune in cash. He was mesmerized. He couldn't believe that Ron had actually pulled it off. He knew his friend was a genius, but this was unreal.

His reverie was interrupted by the woman returning with a man who introduced himself as William Tanner.

"I'm Reid McNeal." They shook hands, Reid's winning ticket clutched in Tanner's left hand.

"Congratulations," Tanner said. "You're our first hundred-thousand-dollar keno winner."

"Must be my lucky day," Reid said without much fanfare. He'd planned to say that. "I just decided to try my luck at keno. I played ten tickets at ten bucks a pop, and whaddaya know?"

"Well, you've just won a hundred thousand dollars. If you'll wait here a few minutes, we just have to prepare some paperwork. Then I'll escort you to the cashier and they'll issue you a check."

"Uh...Mr. Tanner, I would like to be paid in cash."

Tanner's eyes narrowed. "Cash? You want to take a hundred thousand dollars in cash?"

"Yes." Reid's jaw tightened with resolve.

But Tanner frowned with skepticism. "You do know that we are required to notify the IRS and that you're responsible to pay taxes on that money."

"I know that."

"You're sure you want cash?"

"Yes."

"All right, then. I'm going to need two forms of personal identification."

Reid began a skit of feeling through his pockets and then realizing he'd forgotten something. "Uh…I'm sorry. I don't have any ID. I must have left my wallet home."

Now Tanner looked at Reid as though he were a whacko. "You want us to pay you a hundred thousand in cash and you don't have any ID?"

"I do have the winning ticket, don't I?" Reid said smugly, looking at it in Tanner's hand.

Tanner gave him a hard stare. "Would you wait here, please?" Without waiting for acknowledgment, Tanner turned on his heel and left through the door in rear, taking the winning ticket with him. The woman, who'd been witnessing the exchange, now busied herself punching players' tickets for the next game.

Needless to say, Tanner was suspicious. Firstly, the odds of winning an eight-spot keno ticket were in excess of 230,000-to-1. Secondly, just days before, Bally's keno computer system had been upgraded by its manufacturer, Imagineering Systems, Inc. For someone to hit the jackpot so soon afterwards was uncanny. Thirdly, not only was McNeal unemotional about his big win, he also had no identification and demanded to be paid in cash. Tanner remarked to his supervisor in the keno office, "This doesn't pass the smell test."

New Jersey gaming law required that any jackpot of $35,000 or more be verified by state gaming division officials. When they arrived at Bally's, they were accompanied by a pair of detectives from the New Jersey Casino Control Commission. This all happened quite rapidly, and the detectives questioned Reid right there in the keno pit while Tanner and his superior looked on. Reid did not say or do anything to diffuse anyone's suspicions. The detectives were hard pressed to believe he carried no ID in a casino.

"Are you sure you don't have any identification documents in your room?" one detective pressed him.

"You are staying here, aren't you?" asked the other.

"Yes and yes."

"I take that to mean you're staying here but don't have any ID."

Reid nodded.

"Then how did you check into your room? The front desk had to verify ID before giving you a keycard."

At that instant, Reid knew his goose was cooked.

"Did someone else register you into the room?"

Reid half-nodded.

"I take that to mean yes."

"Stay here with Detective Del Rossi," the lead detective ordered, then with Tanner and two Bally's security officers swiftly departed the keno pit.

Upstairs in the room, Ron Harris lay dreamily on the bed with the TV on. Although he wasn't watching, it was still tuned to the casino's keno games. He was thinking of a warm vacation somewhere in the tropics, waiting for Reid to come back with the cash. They would divide it up then immediately split town.

There was a knock on the door. It was a little harsher than pleasant, but Ron only thought that Reid, in all the excitement, had forgotten his keycard and was knocking heavily due to his exhilaration. They would toss the cash about the room and have it rain back down on them. A little celebration before leaving.

Ron didn't even bother asking who was at the door. When he opened it, he got the surprise of his life: two uniforms and two suits. Four pair of hostile eyes.

"I'm Detective Peterson with the New Jersey Casino Control Commission," said the lead suit, flashing a gold shield in a sheath. "What's your name, sir?"

Ron was too shocked to say anything but "Ron Harris."

"Do you have any identification?"

"Sure." Ron made his next mistake of inadvertently leading the security detail into his room. He could have told them to wait in the corridor. Instead, they followed him inside and were treated to lots of incriminating evidence. First was the TV airing the latest keno game. Then on the coffee table incongruously set in front of it were Ron's open laptop, two cell phones, a calculator and a police scanner. The scanner alone showed intent to commit a crime.

Ron handed Peterson his driver's license. Peterson looked at it, saw it was issued by the state of Nevada, and handed it back.

"What's this about?" Ron finally asked, emerging from his daze.

"Do you know Reid McNeal?"

"He's my friend. Has something happened to him?"

Tanner suddenly spoke in a highly sarcastic tone: "Yes, he got very lucky."

At this point, Peterson was only conducting an investigation into the oddness of the situation. They could not detain Ron as he had not purchased the suspicious winning keno ticket. So they simply left him in the room and went back downstairs to further interrogate Reid.

While Reid was meekly denying a barrage of accusations in Bally's security office, Ron hastily packed his bags, stuffing all the equipment inside, descended the elevator to the lobby, and without checking out of the hotel jumped in a cab to the Philadelphia airport. He boarded the next flight to Vegas.

While he was airborne, the detectives discovered that Ron was an employee of the Nevada Gaming Control Board. This information sealed their certainty that the jackpot had been rigged and that Ron was behind it. Then, under intense pressure, Reid spilled his guts, even offering that he'd been involved in cheating slot machines in Nevada with his old high school buddy. After signing his confession, he accompanied the detectives back to the room, where a thorough search was conducted.

In Ron's haste to get out of town, he'd left behind more incriminating evidence. Combing through drawers and underneath the beds, detectives found CD-ROMs, computer chips, notes describing changes in Bally's keno machines and a small personal address book that contained phone numbers of people who the detectives assumed would be able to shed more light on the recent activities of Ron Harris.

Before Ron's plane landed in Las Vegas, Reid McNeal was arrested at Bally's and charged with theft by deception and cheating at gambling. When Ron's plane did land, he was met by agents of the very Nevada Gaming Control Board he worked for. They promptly took him into custody on the same charges, and added a new one from Atlantic City: computer fraud. They also let him know that he was both fired from the Control Board and a disgrace to the integrity of the entire gaming industry.

A massive NGCB investigation was launched. Control Board regulators inspected Universal slot machines across the state. Ron's first gaffed computer chip was found inside a machine in Reno. Then another one at a Lake Tahoe casino. Within weeks, more than a dozen were found inside slot machines. Investigators were horrified at the magnitude of this compromise. A subsequent check of the sugar cube-size chips discovered that the coding on some of them matched a similar numerical string found on a CD-ROM confiscated from Ron's Atlantic City hotel room.

Ron Harris had upset not only the gaming industry itself but also Nevada's highest-ranking politicians. Word came down from the top to prosecute him to the hilt; make an example of him. Enormous hauls of dirt on Ron's life were unearthed for evidence. Reid McNeal was persuaded to testify against Ron in court. In exchange for his faithful testimony, all charges against him would be dropped.

Ron eventually pleaded guilty to racketeering for rigging twenty-two slot machines in Las Vegas, Reno and Lake Tahoe, then to attempted theft by deception for the keno scam in Atlantic City. In all, he was sentenced to seven years in prison, but was paroled after serving two. Today, Ron works quietly for a publishing company and still messes around with computers in his shop.

What Ron Harris accomplished boggled by mind. But his stupidity boggled it even more. Imagine how much money he could have scammed had Reid McNeal carried identification when claiming the $100,000 keno jackpot. He probably could have done the same scam numerous times using different people, let alone what he could have siphoned from the slot-machine industry rigging jackpots. How could he have been so dumb to register for that Bally's hotel room under his own name? I wondered. How could he have not double-checked to be sure Reid McNeal had his ID with him? Could such a genius lack such basic intelligence?

I guess the only person capable of answering these questions is Ron Harris.

CHAPTER 9

THE BRITISH/–AMERICAN CRAPS INVASION

Just like a lot of British rock stars invaded America to join American bands in the 1960s, there were those scheming Brits who invaded Vegas in the 1980s to join up with a few renowned American casino scammers. One of those Brits was named Chris Jones. The American with whom he joined forces to scam the world's craps tables was named Richard Marcus. That's right, yours truly.

You won't be surprised that I first met Chris at the Dunes Denny's in the fall of 1989. My own casino-cheating operation had been in a lull. The pastposting team I had been working with for twelve years had disbanded, primarily because of the retirement of my mentor, Joe Classon. I hadn't been doing much besides playing poker on the square and eating late-night breakfasts at Denny's.

One night while alone in one of its coveted booths, I overheard an Englishman by the entrance trying to calm an attractive young woman who was on the verge of hysteria. She was certainly livid enough to take a few swings at him with her pocketbook. Finally, she screeched at him, "Why don't you go back to England!" as she crashed through the door on her way outside. The Brit yelled to her back, "Because I like it here!" Then he came inside the restaurant and sat in the booth next to mine. I noted immediately that he was very handsome, and figured he was a real charmer with the babes, especially American babes who had to fall for his accent if nothing else.

He glanced at the menu, then at me. "Some of 'em are real bitches," he said with a cocky smile.

I knew very well what he meant. As a matter of fact, I'd gone through a similar scene with a soon-to-be ex-girlfriend a few days before, thought it didn't happen at the Denny's. "Yeah, I hear you," I said in a tone of camaraderie.

"What's good here?" he asked.

"Try the French toast," I offered. I had just finished my second order of it.

"What about pancakes?" he asked, laying down the menu.

"Save those for IHOP."

"IHOP?"

"International House of Pancakes."

"Shit yeah," he laughed. "I was there last night, mate. Them bloody pancakes were delicious."

The crowd in the restaurant was lighter than usual. It was four o'clock in the morning. I didn't notice any familiar scammers gathered in the booths. Didn't hear any war stories being exchanged. So I shot the shit across tables with the Brit. We hit it off right away. At one point I asked him, "So when *are* you going back to England?"

He smiled at my subtle reference to the remark his upset companion had made while dumping him. "When I get bored, I guess. I've been here three weeks and've already missed my return flight to London. Dunno, maybe I'll stay a while."

Chris Jones stayed for two years. He became my casino-cheating partner and dear friend. In all my years scamming, I never enjoyed myself as much as I did with him. He was a regular riot. The trips we took together around the world always turned into wild parties and excitement.

Our partnership began forming the next night when we met at the Brewery, a spicy Las Vegas nightclub that rocked on Paradise Road. After a few drinks, Chris let on how he was paying for his good times in Vegas. "Travellers' checks, mate," he said cheerily. "I just report 'em stolen to the issuing bank in the UK. They replace 'em through their US agency here in Vegas, then I just cash 'em at the casino."

"How can that work more than once?"

"Because I cash 'em only with female tellers at the cage." He grinned. "I flirt with them and make 'em forget to ask for my ID. Doesn't work all the time, but it does enough."

"What about the surveillance cameras at the cage?"

"They don't worry me worth a damn, mate. I just wear a ball cap and sunglasses and look like everyone else in this bloody town."

My admiration for Chris grew rapidly by the minute. I could see he was a real natural scammer with all the know-how. I certainly thought his talents were worthy of more than a rinky-dink travellers'-check scam. I told him so.

"What about you mate?" By this time, Chris knew I was into *something*.

"Let me ask you something, Chris. Now that you've been in Vegas for so long, and apparently like it, do you gamble?"

He shook his head emphatically. "I like to make money, mate, not burn it."

"Come on, let's get outta here," I said with a jerk of my head. "I've got a gambling proposition for you."

"I just told you I don't like to lose, mate."

"Don't worry, you won't."

I drove Chris to my apartment. Inside, he chuckled at seeing my living room contained not a sofa and coffee table but a roulette wheel and blackjack table. I would have had a craps table as well but it was simply too big too fit.

"You must be a casino scammer," Chris observed.

"You catch on quick, mate." It sounded odd calling him mate, but every so often I would. "You'd be perfect ripping off casinos with me."

"Ripping off casinos! I'd love to rip off the bloody casinos. But how do you it?"

"You start by listening to me."

"Okay, mate, I'm all ears."

A dozen years before that, I'd stood in the apartment of my mentor, the great Joe Classon, and learned the same pastposting move I was about to teach Chris. Since Joe had packed in his casino-cheating career a few months earlier, I'd been starved to find a new partner to work with, which wasn't easy. You couldn't just put an ad in the help-wanted classifieds that read "Casino-cheating partner wanted to rip off casinos." You might find yourself interviewing some very curious agents from the Nevada Gaming Control Board's Enforcement Division. So I'd kind of drifted around those last few months, coming to grips that my notorious career might be coming to an end. But it was the good old Dunes Denny's that resuscitated me time and again. Had Chris not walked in that night, I might have been done in the casinos eleven years before I actually retired in 2000.

As I began teaching Chris the trade, my mind flashed back to that day in 1977 when Joe began his tutelage of me. As I spoke, I recalled Joe's words. "Did you ever hear the term 'pastposting?'"

Chris laughed as though it were a ridiculous question. "Of course, mate. That's betting the ponies after you know which one already won the race. But that's extinct now."

I cracked up, thinking of dinosaurs, not horses, being labelled as extinct. "I'm not talking about horses; I'm talking about casinos."

"Pastposting *casinos*?"

"Exactly. It's making your bets after you already know the outcome of the game, whether it be a hand of blackjack, spin of roulette or throw of the dice at craps. Do you know how to play craps?" Craps was my preferred game to cheat with a two-man pastposting team.

"I played it once and went broke before I got the chance to touch the bloody dice."

"Then you know what the pass line is and what odds bets are."

"The pass line is betting against the house, ain't it?"

"Yes."

"I'm not so sure about the odds bets, though."

"Come on, let's sit down. I'll explain the whole game to you."

I grabbed two beers from the fridge, poured them into mugs and gave one to Chris. We sat on stools at the blackjack table. In the table rack were tubes of discontinued casino chips I'd bought from a casino supply store. A loaded card shoe sat in the middle of the layout. I pushed it back to the inside edge of the table, where it sat when in use. We made a toast and clinked mugs. Then I got down to teaching my new student the business of pastposting craps.

First I explained the general rules of the game. A craps shooter's first roll of the dice was called the "come-out roll." If he rolled a 7 or an 11, he won. If he rolled a 2, 3 or 12, he lost. Any other number rolled was called a "point" and had to be rolled a second time *before* a 7 in order for a pass-line bet to win. If the 7 came out before the point, the pass-line bets lost.

Odds bets came into play once a point was established. You then had the option of taking odds for an amount equalling your original pass-line bet. The reason this bet was so popular among craps players was that the odds offered were "true odds." There was no built-in house advantage on the bets. Let's say, for example, you bet $10 on the come-out roll and the shooter rolls a 4, establishing 4 as the point. You then have the option of placing $10 behind your original $10 bet. Since the true odds of the shooter rolling another 4 before rolling a 7 are 2-to-1 against, the casino pays you $20 for your $10 odds bet on the 4 when it wins. So if the shooter does indeed roll the second 4, you would be paid a total of $30, ten dollars for your original bet and twenty for your odds bet. True odds for a point of 10 were also 2-to-1. For the points 5 and 9, they were 3-to-2, and for the points 6 and 8, they were 6-to-5. If the shooter rolls a 7 before the point, you lose both your original and odds bets.

Four casino employees worked a craps table. There were two standing dealers who worked their respective halves of the table. Between them sat the boxman, the table supervisor who verified the dealers' payoffs and watched over the game. Busy tables often sat two boxmen, each charged with his half of the table. Then there was the stickman standing directly across the table from the boxman. His job was to announce each roll of the dice and push them back to the shooter with his stick after gathering them from either end of the table.

I tapped the felt on the blackjack table. "Make believe this is the pass line on a craps table," I said. I reached into the rack and grabbed a stack of red $5 chips and another of purple $500 chips.

"Are those real chips?" Chris asked excitedly, noting that they came from the Tropicana casino.

"Yes."

Sizing up the filled tubes in the rack, he beamed, "You've got a fortune in there, mate!"

I laughed. "They're real, but they're not worth anything. Every five years or so, casinos change their chips. These are discontinued chips that are no longer redeemable."

"Kinda works like currency, right, mate?"

I thought for a second. "Yeah, something like that." I placed three $5 chips on the imaginary pass line. "This is the original pass-line bet," I said. "Now let's say it wins. The dealer is going to pay it like this." I cut into the three red chips with three identical red chips, just like a craps dealer would on a real game. The result was a $15 payoff next to a $15 winning bet. Chris looked on as though waiting for something to happen.

"Then the move goes down." I picked up the three $5 chips that represented the original bet with my left hand and with my right replaced them with two purple $500 chips and a $5 chip on top, totalling $1,005. "It's done *after* the dealer pays the bet and moves on to the next player around the table. Then you grab the dealer's hand and yell, 'Hey! You paid me wrong. I just bet a thousand dollars here and you paid me fifteen!' They realize their mistake and pay you the thousand bucks."

Chris looked up at me with an expression that said he wanted to get off that stool, out of my apartment and never see me again. "Are you trying to hustle me, mate? That little trick wouldn't fool a pigeon in Trafalgar Square."

"Maybe not," I said, "but it's fooled casinos in Vegas for thirty years."

Chris looked at the configuration of red and purple chips on the layout.

"I guess you'd like me to tell you how," I said with bravado.

"If you can convince me that little chip-switch'll work, I'll eat those chips."

I got off the stool, went into the kitchen and returned with a cereal bowl and a container of milk. I scooped the chips off the felt and tossed them into the cereal bowl, then generously poured in the milk. "*Bon appétit!*"

After we got done laughing, Chris said, "You're really serious about this stuff, aren't you, mate?"

"Serious?" I said in mock exaggeration. "Someday there's going to be a book about it."

"Well, if you want me to be one of the chapters, you'd better start making me a believer."

"I will. It works like this..." I launched into a detailed explanation of why this particular form of pastposting worked, in exactly the same manner Joe Classon had explained it to me. The move was called a "ten-o-five," its name derived from the value of the chips switched in, $1,005. It was an extremely effective craps pastpost that combined simple ingenuity and pragmatic psychology. The premise of the move was to switch in chips of a larger denomination *after* the outcome of the gambling decision. The inherent beauty of it was that a player's hands were supposed to be on the layout at that moment; he would be collecting his chips or restacking them for the next bet. Nearly all pastposters, I had learned over the years, tried to switch or increase their bets after they knew the outcome but *before* they got paid, when their hands were not permitted on the layout. That fashion led to a much higher chance of getting caught.

"But once the dealer pays your bet, he's done with you," Chris said with his palms spread to emphasize what he thought was an obvious point, one prohibiting the type of pastpost I'd explained. His skepticism was well founded, and virtually all gamblers, even the most intelligent, would have thought along the same lines. But what none of them knew was how the psychological element negated that logic.

"Just bear with me, Chris," I said. "You will understand all that, but first I want to explain the basics of a craps pastposting operation." He nodded to convey his willingness to be patient.

I went on with a step-by-step exposition of the move. The procedure entailed a two-man "mechanic-claimer operation," the mechanic being the bet-placer and switcher, the claimer the person collecting the money paid on the pastposted bet.

The claimer stood behind the mechanic on either end of a busy craps table. The mechanic bet $15, three red $5 chips, on the pass line where players betting with the shooter placed their chips. If the pass-line bet lost, the mechanic simply made the same bet for the next roll after the dealer removed his losing chips. When it won, the mechanic reached down to the layout as soon as the dealer paid his bet and made the switch, taking out the three original red chips and replacing them with two $500 purples and a red – a ten-o-five. This was done by picking up the three reds with one hand while laying down the move-chips with the other, all in a split second. The move done, the mechanic yielded his place to the claimer, who laid a stack of purple "backup" chips in the players' rack built into the table rail and began claiming that the dealer had paid his bet wrong, that he had bet purple chips and had only been paid with reds. The purpose of those backup chips was to convince the dealer and the boxman that the claimer was a legitimate high roller who would only be playing $500 chips. They would ask themselves why a guy with ten grand of purple chips in his rack would be making lowly $15 bets. This was part of the psychological manipulation that my mentor had taught me years before.

The beauty of the mechanic-claimer procedure was that the dealer, stickman and boxman never saw the claimer until he was already claiming. This was important because if the same person betting $15 on the pass line for several losing rolls all of a sudden shows up a winner on a $1,000 bet nobody had seen him make, the pit would become much more suspicious than if it were evident that a *new* player's $1,000 bet was his *first* bet. It was with that philosophy that a good two-man craps pastposting team divided the roles of a move between the mechanic and claimer. Also, when dividing responsibilities, the pressure on each person was kept at a minimum. The mechanic was responsible only for the mechanics of the move. The claimer's responsibility was limited to claiming the money. Nobody had to bite off more than he could chew.

I explained to Chris that he would be the claimer and I'd be the mechanic. Performing the actual moves took practice and timing, whereas claiming them only required balls and common sense. As Chris had no prior experience, it was only possible for him to be the claimer.

At a craps table, I would be strategically positioned next to the dealer, or as close to the dealer as I could get. It was best to get the move in as soon as possible, and when you were right next to the dealer, he not only paid you first but also blocked the view of both the stickman and boxman with his arms as he did so. Another advantage of being first was that there were always several winning bets to be paid after yours. This meant that the dealer's motion would continue right through your bet. He'd pay you, then continue moving forward with chips in both hands ready to pay the following bets. In essence, once he paid you, he forgot you. But when the claimer came over the top to claim, the dealer was suddenly pulled back to a bet he had paid and forgotten about. Optimally, my $15 bet would be the first to be paid on a winner.

"You stand behind me to the inside," I said, "on the side closest to the dealer. You relax and you wait, always keeping your eye on me until the last instant before I do the move. When I do, I will then back off the table and slip around to the other side of it. As soon as I've vacated the space, you rush up against the rail, stick the stack of purple backup chips in the rack with one hand and slap the dealer's hand with the other." I suddenly slapped the back of Chris's hand, startling him, even though it was a gentle slap.

"See how that startled you?" I asked. "Imagine how it feels to a craps dealer. They never get touched, so when you gently hit their hands, it's the equivalent of smashing them over the head with a hammer. And by doing that, you own them. You've shocked them so much that they can't remember what bet had been there prior to the move."

"Even if they know they hadn't seen any purple chips on the layout?"

"Doesn't matter," I said, appreciating Chris's intelligent question. "It's what they see when you're claiming. You've already shocked them, and now you're claiming a flagrant mistake on their part, all the while with your backup chips in the rack in plain view. You see? It's all a massive psychological con."

"I'm starting to like this, mate."

"I thought you might."

"When do we do the first move?"

"This coming weekend. But there's more you have to know, starting with the claim. When you claim that the dealer paid you wrong, be aggressive. Be a tiger. Repeat after me – 'Hey! You paid me wrong! I'm betting purples and you paid me five-dollar chips. What is this crap!?'"

Chris repeated it word for word with the same intensity. I made him repeat it three more times.

"And be careful with the language you use," I said. "Don't use terms like 'nickels' for five-dollar chips. That's too slick. You don't want to come off like a wise-ass. You only want to sound like a legitimate high roller insulted by the dealer. And most important of all, do *not* hesitate. Jump in there immediately. If you're a fraction of a second late, the whole thing is blown. Make sure that your purple backup chips are correctly placed in your rack while claiming. You put them there as soon as you hit the table. While you're claiming, you keep glancing at me. I'll be at the opposite end of the table where you can easily spot me. Unless I grab my nose, you continue claiming. If I do touch my nose, you abandon the claim, pick up the move off the layout, take the backup chips out of the rack, and get out of there. When you leave, you leave aggressively, not like a wimp. You want to give the impression that you're coming back, not hurrying out of the casino.

"Walking away from the table, you maintain a steady pace. You walk rapidly but you don't run. I'll be following you. If the situation deteriorates and I want you to quicken the pace, you'll hear me shout 'Chester.' That's just a name we use to indicate serious heat in the casino and you really have to get out of there fast. If you here me shout 'Gallo,' you *run* out of the casino, and I mean as fast as your Queen- of- England's ass can because you're in their sights and they're coming after you. Once you get out of the casino, you go to the emergency meeting place, which will never be in a casino. If ever grabbed up, you say nothing, not one word – *absolutely* nothing. You don't try to talk your way out of it; you don't lie. You just keep your mouth *shut*. If they call Gaming and have you arrested, then you're arrested. Opening your mouth can only make the situation worse." I paused for a second to let all that sink in. "Any questions so far?"

"When do we do the first move?" he asked again with a ruddy smile.

"I guess you think you can handle this."

"Nothing to it, mate."

Lots of prospective claimers had boasted similar confidence only to shit in their pants once they stood at a live craps table. "We'll see," I said even-keeled, not threatening his confidence. "There's one more phase to the move that's very important. It's called the 'bet-back.' After you get paid, you bet back two hundred five dollars, two black chips with a red on top. Win or lose, you leave the table and head for the meeting place outside the casino."

"We can't stay at the table and do the move again?"

It was a rookie question. I explained to Chris that you could pull the wool over the casino's eyes one time at any given table, but not twice. "That bet-back will make them digest easier what has just happened. They'll think it weird that you'd bet a red chip on top of two purples, but doing it a second time on top of two blacks will make them think you're just the kind of high roller who likes to cap his big bets with a red chip, like a superstitious quirk. On every bet-back you use the same capper that was used on the move. If we do a 10-25, which is two purple chips capped with a green $25 chip, your bet-back would be two-hundred-and-twenty-five dollars, two blacks capped by a green."

"How come you don't just switch in three purple $500 chips for the three red $5 chips? That way we'd make five hundred more."

It was another rookie question. "Because the move would never get paid. The capper is what makes it all possible. You can't convince a dealer that he missed three purple chips on the pass line, but you can two purples with the red on top. The red-chip capper makes him think that he *could have* missed the two purples underneath. You see, it's all part of the psychology we use to beat the casinos."

"And what happens if they refuse to pay?"

"That will happen, but less than percent10 percent of the time if everything is done right. When it does, you just say, 'Thank you very much,' and you leave. Remember never to get nasty with casino personnel in any situation. Always be polite. I suspect that with your charming English accent, you'll get off pretty good in Vegas casinos."

Chris nodded and smiled. "Especially with women dealers." He raised his beer mug. "To Helen," he said in a toast.

"Who's Helen?"

"The babe I was fighting with at Denny's. If it weren't for her, you and I never would have met."

I shrugged. "To Helen."

The first craps attack that launched the British–American invasion took place at the Desert Inn on October 17, 1989, which just happened to be the day of the second largest San Francisco earthquake of the twentieth century. No real tremors were felt along the Las Vegas Strip from the quake, but one was felt at a particular craps table that night at the Desert Inn.

Chris was handsomely dressed in a blue pinstriped suit he'd purchased with his "replacement" travellers' checks. He wore a gold watch and pinky ring that had come his way along the same route. I was attired casually in jeans and a pullover. As I was not the claimer, there was no need for me to look the part of a high roller.

We sat in the casino's keno pit. I handed Chris ten $500 purple chips that I'd obtained in the baccarat salon while showing some action just to exchange black chips for purples. He would use them for backup. "Don't forget to put them in the rack as soon as you start claiming," I reminded him, then gave him two $100 black chips and one $5 red for the bet-back. "Make a single $205 bet after they pay you the grand. Win or lose, you leave the table."

Chris nodded. "I got it."

"One thing I forgot to tell you. Sometimes the heat comes down *after* they pay the move. You might be in the middle of the bet-back roll when it happens. If I give you the 'nose,' just get out of there immediately. Leave your bet on the table. Don't worry about it; we'll take the loss."

In craps, unlike any other casino game, it could take a long period of time, often several minutes or more, before the outcome of a bet was decided. In the case of a pass-line bet, which our move would be, the shooter might establish a point and then throw the dice more than a dozen times before either making his point or "sevening-out," upon which all the pass-line bets were declared losers and swept away. If a claimer had his bet-back on the pass line when heat suddenly came down on him, he had to leave the casino but could not grab up his bet before its fate was determined. Doing that would be a flagrant violation of gaming regulations and could lead to prosecution in itself. So the only course of action was to abandon that bet and leave the casino.

After digesting that, Chris said exuberantly, "Could get hairy, mate."

"It rarely happens."

"I'll be ready if it does."

"Then let's go."

We got up, and Chris trailed me loosely through the busy casino to the craps pit. The tables were hopping; because of the heavy action on both ends two boxmen sat next to each other at most of them. Sometimes you had to go up against this situation, but you always tried to find a good table with a single box. The advantage was that the lone boxman had to constantly turn his head from side to side to watch all the payoffs. With double-box, where each boxman watched only the action on his side of the table, neither had to turn his head. The ideal situation at craps was a table that had only one boxman with heavy action at only one end of the table. That left the other end of the table more or less unsupervised. With such conditions the dealer was in effect isolated to face the claimer. The boxman couldn't back him up and say that our pastposted bet wasn't there before it had won, simply because he hadn't been watching that side of the table.

The table I selected for Chris's first claim had only one boxman with good action on either side – heavy green-chip betting with a few blacks scattered along the perimeter. There were also plenty of red-chip bets along the layout with which our original bet would blend in perfectly. We waited until the dice "sevened out," then took our positions at the table. I squeezed in first between the two players closest to the dealer. Chris stood behind me. The dealer was a young Latino with a soft face. I didn't want to put Chris up against a macho type for his first move. In fact, I would have preferred a woman dealer, but conditions at this particular table were otherwise ideal. I didn't want to pass on the opportunity.

The new dice shooter was three players away from me, around the horn of the table. He jiggled the dice in his hand and let them go. The glittering red cubes skittered toward the other end of the whale-shaped table, crashed into the wall, and tumbled to a halt near the center of the green felt layout, flashing their white dots. One came up 6, the other 1 – a pass-line winner 7. People around the table cheered.

The stickman at the middle of the table opposite the boxman called out, "Winner – seven!" The dealer grabbed a stack of red chips and a stack of greens, then his hands shot forward along the pass line to pay the winning bets. My $15 bet of three red chips was second in line. As soon as the dealer paid it, my body jerked forward to make the switch. My left hand snatched up the three reds while my right laid in two purple chips with a red capper, $1,005. The speed of the move was lightning quick. I pulled back and vacated my spot at the table. Barely two steps away, I heard Chris shout "Hey!"

He had bolted forward, grabbed the Latino dealer's arm with a force strong enough to knock the red chips in his hand all over the layout. Now watching from behind the stickman, I realized that Chris had been much too violent in his claim, had practically attacked the guy. His overreaction was the result of bottled-up energy that had come gushing out of him like agitated seltzer. "Hey!" he barked again, loud enough that the eyes of the stickman and boxman jumped on him. "I just bet one thousand dollars here and you're paying me with five-dollar chips. What is this crap?"

The dealer was shocked at the sight of the two purple chips sitting underneath the red. He turned to look at the boxman, who just shrugged, then picked the three red chips he had paid Chris off the layout, grabbed his stack of black $100 chips, cut out ten of them, and placed them with a lone red chip on the pass line next to the chips I had switched in. There was not a single utterance between the dealer and boxman. The dealer then proceeded to pay the rest of the winning bets on the pass line while Chris looked across the table, stealing a glance at me. I nodded subtly to let him know he'd done fine.

Chris picked up the chips the dealer had paid along with the move-chips and placed them in the table rack, realizing in the same instant as I that he'd forgotten to put his backup chips there before claiming. Then he placed two black chips on the pass line with a red on top, $205. At least he'd remembered the all-important bet-back.

The shooter shook up the dice and rolled a 6. For Chris's bet-back to win he needed to roll another 6 before the fatal 7. The guy turned out to be very lucky and held the dice twenty minutes before rolling the 7, great for players around the table buying all the numbers. But he never rolled that second 6, and for us that could have been dangerous because Chris had been obliged to stay at the table, literally stuck there until the shooter either made his point or sevened out. Had heat come down off the move on the previous winner, I would have signalled Chris to abandon the $205 on the layout before its fate was determined.

Fortunately, the move was clean, so when the shooter finally did seven out, Chris casually walked away from the table, through the casino to the exit on the far side and across the street to the Frontier, where I found him waiting anxiously in the keno pit, the same way I had waited for Joe Classon after claiming my first move a dozen years before.

"How'd I do, mate?" he asked, jumping out of his chair to shake my hand.

"You were great, Chris!" I enthused. "Except for one thing."

"I know," he rushed to say. "I forgot to put my backup chips in the rack."

"Rookie mistake. Try to remember next time. Every little detail is important. But the main thing is, you've got both the balls and the smarts to do this." I didn't make a big deal out of his error. My goal was only to encourage him and instill confidence. All in all, he'd been great.

"No heat came down on the move?" he asked.

"Nothing."

"Man, you put that move in so quick I didn't see it!"

I smiled and patted his shoulder. "I've been doing this for a long time."

"Then let's go do another one. I'm ready."

"Okay, but one more thing: You were a little rough on that poor dealer. It was good that you got right in his face like a tiger, but you never have to assault a dealer like that. You scared the living daylights out of him. Just tap his hand softly. Believe me, that'll do the trick. That and a good, strong claim."

"You're right. I guess I really clobbered the bloody guy."

"Yeah, if you grabbed a woman dealer like that, you might be sitting in jail right now instead of a thousand bucks richer."

I collected Chris's chips and told him to wait there in the Frontier keno pit while I ran back to the Desert Inn to cash out. An hour later we were on a craps table at the Dunes. Everything was planned the same except for one change. If the shooter didn't hit a 7 or 11 winner on the come-out roll of the dice, I would do a double-decker move. Not only switch the chips on the pass line but the odds chips behind them as well.

Our craps table at the Dunes also sat a single boxman. This time we were on the other side of the table but in the same positions. The dealer was a guy in his forties, with a bit more experience than the Latino from the Desert Inn. But that was of no concern to me. The move was rock solid and all dealers were beatable. Even the sharpest ones were no match for the power of the move.

The table had been cold a while, shooters rolling a lot of craps dice (2, 3 or 12), then sevening out quickly after establishing points. We found ourselves in a situation where we couldn't move because there wasn't enough action on the table. When craps tables go cold, they empty fast. When that happened we had to be patient and wait for the table to regain its momentum. During a lull such as this, we stayed at the table protecting our positions. I bet red chips and Chris hung behind me.

When the table warmed up, the stickman pushed the dice across the felt to me. But I declined with a brushing-off movement of my hand, not making eye contact with him. Since I would be the mechanic for the upcoming move, I could not roll the dice. Doing so would bring attention to me and might later cause a problem for Chris while claiming from my vacated position.

So the dice passed to the man beside me. He picked up two of the five white-dotted red cubes offered by the stickman, rattled them up in his hand and tossed them against the mirrored wall at the other end of the table. They came up 4, so he'd need to roll another 4 before a 7 to win.

I placed three red chips behind the three I'd originally bet on the pass line, paying special attention to their placement so that the dealer would not have to touch them. Odds chips placed too close or too far behind the pass line risked readjustment by the dealer. The more times he noticed my bet, the better chance he'd have of remembering it later.

The shooter did not make the 4, so the dice passed along to the player on his right. Chris and I prepared again for a winner and a move; if the shooter won on the come-out roll with 7 or 11, I would make the switch. We'd have to wait for another occasion to do the big odds move. My philosophy was always to move when you had the chance, not to wait for a shot at more money.

The new shooter crapped out snake eyes (two 1s), then established 8 as the point on the following roll. I again meticulously placed the three red odds chips. The player next to me took odds as well. His taking odds was advantageous to our cause. Since his bet was next to mine, which would later become Chris's, the dealer would most likely be in the process of paying that player when Chris touched his arm and went into his claim. By taking odds, the player was in effect forcing the dealer to spend more time paying off his bets. That would keep the dealer's hands as close as possible to the chips I would have just switched in. So when Chris claimed, the dealer would not have passed him by too far. If, on the other hand, the dealer had already paid two or three people after Chris by the time he claimed, there would be that much more room for suspicion on the casino's part, even though the time lapse would have been the same. This because the dealer's hands would have been farther away from his chips, perhaps pushing the thought into his head that Chris had had enough time to slip in a late bet. Again, it was all psychological.

The shooter rolled three different numbers, and then – boom! – a pair of 4s for a winner 8, the hard way.

I needed just an instant longer to do the double switch. I had already cut the move-chips in my right hand into two layers which facilitated laying them in. I had the three chips (ten-o-five) for the pass-line move angled off the three chips (another ten-o-five) for the odds move. What the dealer would see when Chris claimed was two sets of two purple chips underneath a red, two separate bets of $1,005.

The dealer's chip-filled hands passed in front of my waiting hands and dropped off three red chips to pay my pass-line bet, then three red chips behind to pay the even-money portion of my odds bet. Since the odds on the 8 paid 6-to-5, the dealer capped the odds payoff with three blue $1 chips, bringing the total amount of the odds payoff to $18 for the $15 bet. In effect, the dealer had "bridged" that odds payoff, placing the three blue chips evenly across the top of my set of three red chips and the identical set he had just dropped off next to it, forming the bottom of the bridge.

That bridge complicated the move, but I was well prepared for it; experience had taught me that many craps dealers paid in that fashion. What I had to do was gingerly slide the bridge to the left by pushing it with the move-chips in my right hand until those chips had taken the position vacated by the right side of the bridge, which was the three original red chips I had placed as the odds bet. Then with my left hand I had to pick up the left side of the original bridge, which was the three red chips the dealer had paid, while my right hand slid the three blue chips back toward the right until they were evenly across the top of the newly formed bridge. The final result was that my original three-red-chip odds bet was now the left side of the new bridge and the two-purple-chip-one-red-chip move the right. The three blue chips still evenly on top locked it all perfectly in place. Seeing the new concoction, the dealer was made to believe that he never saw the two purple chips now "buried" underneath the bridge. The effect of that construction, compounded by the two purples also sitting at the bottom of the pass-line bet in front and the claimer's backup purples in the table chip rack, was staggering.

Click...click...clack, and I got the move in cleanly. Chris claimed as soon as possible, remembering this time to put the backup chips in the rack.

"Hey! Hey! Hey!" he hollered. "What is this crap! I'm betting thousands here and you gave me red chips!"

When the dealer saw the double whammy and lifted the blue chips off the top of the odds payoff to see the purples underneath, it blew his mind. Chris's was blown as well. The two ten-o-five sets were laid in perfectly, the changed odds-set locked in under the bridge made by the three blue chips. As he claimed, Chris was thinking that the dealer and boxman had to be reasoning that it was impossible for someone to make a move like that – if that thought had ever occurred to them at all.

The dealer and boxman exchanged a look that confirmed their minds were blown. Whether or not they were suspicious of the sudden appearance of all those purple chips, the boxman immediately instructed the dealer to pay the bet. The dealer's face flushed red, from embarrassment, not anger. He quickly apologized to Chris and gathered the chips he'd just "errantly" paid. Then the boxman passed him a stack of purple chips from the table's reserve on the layout in front of him. The dealer paid Chris $1,005 for the line bet and $1,206 for the odds, $2,211 in all. Chris thanked him for "correcting the mistake," then bet $205 on the pass line for the next come-out roll. The shooter established a point, then sevened out. The dealer scooped Chris's losing chips while Chris sauntered off with the purples.

I stood behind the stickman and observed. There was no heat, although I got a big kick out of something the dealer had said to the boxman. His words were "Impossible it was a move; it was too fast." What the dealer was saying, at least subconsciously, was that it had to be a move but so fast they had to pay it.

Afterwards, we were kicking back at the Denny's next door, eating a late-night breakfast.

"So whaddaya think?" I asked Chris. "This beats your travellers'-checks scam, doesn't it, mate?"

"Can't think of anything else I'd rather be doing," he said.

"In that case, let's give it a go." We clinked glasses, enjoying the thought that the world's craps tables held our illicit fortune.

The next night we were in position on a craps table at Caesars Palace. Now we'd get to see how Chris fared against a female dealer, who he was sure was susceptible to his charms. I had no reason to doubt him as he'd done just fine against those two male dealers I'd moved on.

The shooter rolled an 11 on the come-out roll and I popped in the move, a lone ten-o-five on the pass line. I withdrew my place and Chris stepped up to the rail, placing his backup purples in the rack. He smiled at the woman dealer as he gently touched her hand and said in his British accent, pointing at the move-chips, "Excuse me, honey, you made a little mistake there. I bet purple chips and you paid me reds."

Not only did Chris receive the shock of his life, but I got a pretty good one as well when the woman, a pretty brunette, bitched, "Don't touch me, asshole! And that bet wasn't there!"

Chris feigned immediate indignation. "What do you mean, it wasn't there?" He kept his cool and his charming accent.

"There were just three red chips. If there had been purples, I would have seen them."

"I beg your pardon," Chris carried on, "but I am certain of what I'd bet. Now please just pay me correctly."

The cute brunette evidently had enough. "Listen, you British jerkoff," she snapped, "take your accent and your chips and get the hell off my table!"

Chris looked wide-eyed at the boxman. "What *is* this crap?" he said in a voice that he'd inadvertently made funny, then looked at me briefly. I did not touch my nose; I wanted Chris to fight for the payoff, at least see what the boxman's reaction would be.

"The dealer said the purples weren't there," the boxman said aggressively, "which means they weren't."

Chris got pissed off. "I heard what the dealer said," he yelled back at him, then took a shot by saying "If she paid attention to her layout instead of all the men walking past the table, maybe she would notice what color chips were on the pass line."

Whatever Chris thought his remark would accomplish, it only succeeded in offending the woman. She turned up the volume of her bitching, calling him an insensitive cad. "You'd be better off taking your action back across the pond!" she shrieked at him. "And I hope you drown along the way!"

The argument became heated and the name-calling increased, to the point that she called him a faggot and he retorted by calling her a witch. The boxman strongly advised Chris to pick his chips off the layout before he called security and had him arrested. There was no way he was paying the bet. Chris refused to leave and continued battling both of them. The game had stopped; the stickman brought the dice to the middle of the table.

Finally the pit boss arrived to see what the ruckus was.

"Chris's mean countenance melted into a graceful smile. "I'm sorry for the commotion he said calmly, but there has been a mistake made at the table." He indicated the ten $500 chips in his player rack. "I bet purples and your dealer paid me off in reds."

I watched the scene from the opposite side of the table. I'd been ready to flash Chris the sign to pack it in, a rub of my nose, but I held back. Suddenly I saw that he was making headway with his claim. The reason why was that the pit boss was a woman. An alluring one at that.

And she was enamored by Chris and his accent!

She barked at the dealer, "Pay this gentleman's bet immediately." The dealer protested, but the lady pit boss overruled her like an irate judge in court. The dealer grunted, then grudgingly paid Chris $1,005.

Later that night, Chris met up with the foxy lady pit boss. The next morning she woke up in my bed with Chris. I had given him the keys to my apartment and slept in a cheap motel.

"You really are a wonder," I said to him after she'd left. We were sitting at my blackjack table, fiddling with chips and drinking orange juice.

"I told you, mate. No woman can refuse me. Either with sex or with craps – what did you call these moves again?"

"Pastposts."

"That's right. Either with sex or with pastposts. I'll get the money and the honey every time."

He didn't get the money every time, but he did *almost* every time. For the next two years, my casino-cheating career was spent exclusively beating the craps tables with Chris Jones. He became one of the best claimers I'd ever worked with. Not only did he charm the chips off the women dealers and pit bosses, he proved equally effective with the men. He knew just how to ingratiate himself to all casino personnel and disarm their suspicions. When he did have a miss, he handled it just as well. He learned how to maintain his calm regardless of what angered dealers and boxmen said to him. Never again did he get into a verbal shoving match with casino personnel like he'd had with the woman dealer and boxman at Caesars.

For a year, we beat up on Vegas's craps tables, bombarding them with straight pass-line moves and odds moves whenever the opportunity arose. When the Mirage opened its doors in November 1989, I started switching in bets on craps tables using yellow $1,000 chips. We were making original bets of $75, three $25 green chips, and taking odds behind for the same amount. When the bet won, I switched in $2,025, two $1,000 chips with a $25 green capper, for both bets. With a winning point of 4 or 10, the payoff was $2,025 for the pass-line bet, $4,050 for the odds bet. The total profit for those monster moves was $6,075, at the time a record-setter.

When we finally had so much heat that we were chased out of town, we took our travelling British–American craps invasion up to Reno and Lake Tahoe, then east to Atlantic City. Although the gambling resort on the boardwalk had grown up to the ripe old age of eleven, it was still an incredible candy store for us. We set all kinds of records on its craps tables. Perhaps not in the value of the payoffs, but certainly in the amount of chips used in the switches.

Since chips of a higher denomination than $500 were larger in size than those lesser valued, we could not work with $1,000 chips in any of Atlantic City's casinos. The problem was that the bottoms of the chips would stick out and make it obvious that dealers could not be failing to sight them on the layout before they paid winning bets. Even though our psychology overcame what they remembered having seen before a move, it could not mitigate the effect of a dealer, boxman and pit boss all looking down at a bet with yellow $1,000 chips sticking out underneath green chips. Their conclusion would be, no way a dealer could miss that.

So in order to recoup some of the lost earnings due to larger $1,000 chips, we upgraded from a three-chip switch to a four-chip switch using $500 purples. The first of these new configurations, christened a "fifteen-o-five," was done at Resorts International, where I bet four red $5 chips on the pass line. When the shooter rolled a 10, I took the odds and placed four more red chips behind. A few rolls later, when the shooter made the 10 and won the bet, I switched in the double four-chip bomber – three purples with a red capper in the front and three purples with a red capper in the back. The payoff was $1,505 for the pass-line move and $3,010 for the odds move – a $4,515 monster. Our only problem ended up being the confusion in the pit among the casino's personnel. It took them ten minutes to sort it all out and get Chris paid.

We ended up renting a house near the beach in Brigantine and stayed there for four months, working nothing but Atlantic City's craps tables. The beating we gave them during that period stretched the boundaries of imagination, but it was very real. We hit on more than 95 percent of Chris's claims and earned half a million dollars.

And then, following that angry Caesars dealer's advice, we took the show across the pond to Chris's hometown, London, where he hadn't been for a while. Few of the classy British casinos had craps tables, but those which did got a taste of the British–American European invasion. Chris even suggested that we switch roles. Standing outside the Victoria Casino on Edgware Road, he said, "How 'bout I do the chip-switching and you do the claiming?"

"Are you serious?" I asked seriously.

"I sure as hell am bloody serious, mate," Chris blurted.

"Why do that?"

"Because you'll surely charm the pants off the lady crap dealers with your New York accent!"

"Get off it!"

But he persisted.

"Do you really think you can put in a move?"

"I don't know about one with the odds, but I'm willing to give it the old whirl with a straight pass-line move."

I was very reluctant, but he finally convinced me. I guess I really wasn't surprised when Chris laid a beauty on one of the Victoria's two craps tables. He switched in two £500 chips with a red capper. When I claimed it, the woman dealer smiled at me and paid. And she did like my accent; she even complimented me on it!

We made modest profits in London, then flew to Monte Carlo and beat two of their American-style casinos, Café du Paris and Loews International, out of as much as they could take. But we had much more fun chasing the topless beauties spread all over the French Riviera's beaches. One thing I could say for sure: I got laid more hanging around with Chris than ever before!

Our bottom line together: two million bucks and two hundred babes.

Chapter 10

Savannah – the Best of 'em All!

When it first hit me that I had probably discovered the best cheating move in the history of casino gambling, one that appeared absolutely flawless, with minimal risk – even when getting caught red-handed – I experienced a feeling of euphoria that would have been complete had it not been for the sliver of doubt that naturally crept into my brain. During two decades of cheating the world's legally operating gambling casinos at their own games, using a variety of sleight-of-hand moves, some rank, others good, still others *really* good, that so called dream move had eluded me until a hot August night in 1995.

I was sitting at the bottom of a shabby roulette table inside the dingy Silver Spur casino at the intersection of Main and Fremont in downtown Las Vegas. Diagonally across the worn, coffee-stained layout sat my partner in crime, Pat, who'd been working the casinos with me for the past sixteen months. We were both casual in jeans and cotton shirts, perhaps overdressed for the usual assortment of downtown degenerates.

Pat and I often went downtown to test new cheating moves before going for the real money on the Las Vegas Strip. The trick here was to place a red $5 chip atop a green twenty $25 chip on the roulette layout in such a way that the dealer would not see the bottom chip's greenness and therefore assume both chips were red. Knowing that dealers in the bust-out joints downtown were required to announce green chips on the layout, we'd know right away if the little Korean girl named Sun saw the one I was presently trying to hide underneath the red. We hoped she didn't, but as I delicately placed the two round chips in the first of the three 2-to-1 column boxes at the bottom of the layout, carefully measuring the angle and distance I let the top red chip protrude off the green, I had serious doubts about the whole damned scheme, but Sun never called out, "Green action on the layout," and I was absolutely sure she'd looked at my bet – at least three times. Seeing it now, the green chip stuck out at me from the back like a sore thumb.

Pat and I shot each other surprised looks. I furrowed my brows at him as if to say, "Maybe she actually didn't see it." But I was thinking she *had* to see it, that perhaps she was just too lazy to call it out to the supervising floorman, or she had indeed called it out but had one of those ultra-soft oriental voices that didn't carry well amid the constant din and blipping noises in the casino.

Sun spun the ball and we waited. If the bet lost, we'd place it again; if it won, we'd have our answer. Would she correctly pay me twice the $30 in chips sitting in the betting box, or mistakenly pay $20 – 2-to-1 for the two red chips we hoped she *thought* were there?

The ball dropped into the black number 10 slot on the spinning wheel, a first column number that made my bet a winner. I tensed and watched the dealer. Both her hands swept piles of losing chips off the layout, then one reached for a stack of $5 reds in her multicolored chip well along the base of the wooden wheel. She cut swiftly into my two chips twice, paying me only $20 instead of the $60 she should have paid.

Which meant she hadn't seen the green chip underneath. She'd taken it for a red. Sun made the mistake we'd wanted.

I looked down on the layout at the perfect linear formation of three sets of two chips, specially admiring the set containing the green. I didn't bother interrupting Sun to claim the $40 she still owed me. Instead, I glanced over at Pat and met his large smile with one of my own. We both knew at that instant we were on to something big – we were going to be rich.

A week earlier, we had been relaxing in Pat's apartment, our habitual Las Vegas meeting place, having just returned from a casino-cheating road trip up in Reno and Lake Tahoe. Pat popped open a beer, stretched out on the sofa. I was supinely installed in the recliner, munching from a bag of Doritos.

"You know what, Richard," Pat said, "I've been going over something in my head. Did you ever think about putting the big-valued chip under the red *before* the dealer deals the cards...and then do a switch when the bet loses?"

I knew exactly what he was thinking. At the time, all our cheating moves were based on switching chips only *after* winning bets. We'd bet $5 reds, switch in chips of much higher denominations once having knowledge of the winning outcome. The casino term for that move was "pastposting."

What Pat was visualizing was doing just the opposite: make the big bet up front legitimately, then pull it off once you knew it lost. The casino term for that was "dragging." Sure, I'd thought of it. It would be nice to bet a couple of grand and leave it there if it won, rake it off when it lost. But the only way such a maneuver was feasible was to somehow hide the fact you were betting big at the outset, very difficult to do, and then you'd have to rake off your big bet when it lost, leaving the casino in the dark.

"You want to bet a five-*thousand*-dollar chip underneath a $5 red and yank it off when it loses?" I whistled at such audacity.

At the time, in certain casinos, we'd already been working with $5,000 chips, provided they were the same size as the smaller denomination chips, which was the case in about a third of Vegas's casinos. Since we'd been working mostly on blackjack tables, I envisioned his pinching scenario on a blackjack layout. There were seven betting spots on it, never more than seven bets. American blackjack tables were not like the ones in Europe or on some of the islands where one gambler was permitted to place his bet behind another's inside the betting circle. But even if multiple betting were permitted in American casinos, I could never imagine a dealer, even the most inattentive one, failing to see a big-valued chip underneath, no matter how many bets were jammed-up on a blackjack table. The dealer was just too close to the chips, practically right on top of them.

I told Pat my thoughts, and he let the idea go, but then my casino-cheating brain began churning. Pat noticed and said, "What's rolling around in that head of yours, Richard?"

"You know something, Pat? Your idea has possibilities. But not blackjack...roulette."

Pat wasn't as sharp as I when it came to creating and designing casino moves. His real talent was taking off the money, playing the part. He would've been a great actor. With his stout body and pleasant features he had the presence of a Jackie Gleason.

"That trick hiding a $5,000 chip underneath a red just might work on a roulette table, at the bottom. With all the action on a crowded roulette layout, a dealer never has the time to really case all the bets. And if we built camouflage bets around it, it's possible the dealer won't see it, especially in casinos where the dim lighting creates good shadows."

Pat instantly caught on, so we got to work designing the prospective move. All our casino material was kept in Pat's spare bedroom. We had table layouts, cards, dealing shoes, chips, dice, even a regulation blackjack table that I'd inherited from my old casino mentor. A roulette wheel and table would have been welcome but were just too big to fit.

I brought out a green-felt roulette layout and spread it snugly over the dining room table. Lying on a coffee table facing the sofa were two stacks of red chips we hadn't bothered cashing out. I grabbed both and sat them on the bottom edge of the layout, then told Pat to get into his little hiding place and extract a big chip. We never practiced with fake or minimum-value chips. When we worked with $500 purple chips, we practiced with purples. The same went for $1,000 yellows and $5,000 chocolates.

Pat sprang off the couch, scurried into the kitchen and opened a box of cornfakes. From underneath the half-empty paper bag of cereal, he pulled out a creamy chocolate gaming chip from Caesars Palace. He smiled as he let it drop into my hand. I couldn't think of anything so small and round besides diamonds and rare coins that valuable.

I placed the chocolate chip in the first column box on the layout, then capped it with three reds, cracking them slightly off the chocolate toward the imaginary dealer. I moved up to the dealer's spot to determine whether I could see the chocolate beneath the reds. At first glance I saw it easily. Discouraged, I reached back down the layout and adjusted the chips, trying to find the precise angle where the obtruding wedge formed by the three reds hid the chocolate. I was not seeking to defy the chocolate chip's being there, only prevent its color from being seen from where I stood, which meant that the dealer would know about the bottom chip's presence but not know its denomination. The crucial idea was to make him assume it was also a red. Roulette dealers seldom peeled chips off a bet to peek at the bottom one.

Pat resumed my position at the top of the layout while I tinkered with the bet at the bottom.

"There!" he cried out suddenly. "I can't see the chocolate underneath."

I broke out laughing. "Are you shittin' me?" I wasn't sure I really wanted to believe him. I didn't want to be a victim of false hope.

"Richard," he said with deliberate emphasis, "I just told you I don't see that chocolate chip." He bent down, craning his neck from side to side, examining the vertical set of chips from different angles. "I still don't see that chocolate chip."

I was delirious with both pleasure and excitement. I went over to him, gently shoved him out of the way and looked down at the bet. What I *didn't* see amazed me. Not only was the chocolate completely out of view, I had to strain to determine that four chips, not three, were set there. The chocolate chip seemed to vanish underneath, sink into the felt below. To finally see it I had to meander around the layout and put myself where the dealer would never be. I went back to the dealer's position and admired the little stack in the first column box for several seconds. Then I peeled off one of the red chips, which didn't change anything. I peeled off another and still the chocolate underneath remained hidden. I could barely tell there was a chip under there at all. It was impossible to hide the slight difference in elevation between one and two chips, but that was not our objective.

Now we knew only a single chip, if angled correctly atop, concealed the bottom chip's denomination, and that the first column box, being the farthest betting point on the layout from the dealer, was ideal for hiding chips.

"Pat, I don't fucking believe it," I said, looking up at the bright chandelier above the dining room table. "Look at this...We're standing under this bright light. Can you imagine what this'd be like inside a casino with all those shadows?"

We stood silent for a few moments, each contemplating what this little discovery could mean for the future of our cheating-the-casinos business. If not a hell of a lot more money, at least a hell of a lot more adventures. We broke out a bottle of champagne, toasted the new findings optimistically, polished off the bottle, then got to serious work on the layout.

Six hours later at dawn, the move in its basic form was designed. One of us would place three slightly protruding red chips atop a chocolate in the first column box at the bottom of the layout. The other would stand by the spinning roulette wheel to signal the outcome of the bet. As in any other business, legitimate or thievery, things kept simple were the most efficient. The idea we came up with to communicate this information was deliciously simple. If the ball fell into a losing number, the person watching it, whom we called the "caller," would yell loudly, "Damn it!" at the soonest possible instant, in some cases even before the dealer could read the number. That would signal the person at the bottom, whom we called the "raker," that he had to immediately rake off the chips, stick the chocolate safely into his pocket and replace four red chips in the first column box, apologizing to the dealer for not having realized that the ball dropped when caught. Since people got excited and cursed all the time in casinos as their bets won and lost, the caller's shout would be nothing out of the ordinary.

When the bet won, all the caller had to do was remain silent. The raker would simply leave the winning bet there on the layout and just claim it, saying excitedly something like, "By golly, I hit a big one!" and then just collect the payoff as one expected to do when winning a bet in a casino.

It was that simple. The most ingenious casino-cheating move in history entailed nothing more than making a big bet that you raked off the layout when it lost and collected the money when it won.

Two days after our successful Silver Spur experiment, we flew back up to Reno to test the move with a $500 purple chip. Before venturing chocolates on the Vegas Strip the kinks had to be ironed out. I would be the caller and Pat the raker, mainly because of his tremendous gift for ingratiating himself with people. He knew how to take the edge off tense situations, which this new move certainly risked provoking. Grabbing a losing bet off a gaming table before the dealer could sweep it was as flagrant as you could get. Dealers might freak out and scream. We had to be prepared for anything.

The third week of August is always the busiest time of year in Reno. It's when the Hot August Nights Festival comes to town, a four-day bash that brings to Reno thousands of vintage automobiles mostly from the 1950s and sixties'60s. During the day the precious cars parade down Virginia Street and at night the parties from the street spill over into the casinos, mobbing them up real good for us. We preferred working inside crowded casinos where we meshed with everyone else. And we dressed that way too. On the day shift, we were casual in shorts, T-shirts and ball caps. At night, we'd put on jeans and neat polo shirts, sometimes sports jackets if it wasn't too hot outside. But never leather because that was too slick and stood out. Nobody ever took special note of us and we took precautions to hide the fact we were together.

The first afternoon, in between the motorcar parades, we went out and picked up a couple of grand pastposting blackjack tables. We wanted to be assured of making our money for the trip before adventuring into the unknown with the new roulette move, which we christened Savannah, because before going back out to work on the evening swing shift, we'd taken a little detour into a "titty bar" where one of the nude dancers who successfully hustled us for a lap dance went by the obvious fake name Savannah.

We chose the Eldorado casino for the first Savannah-move experiment. By the time we got inside around midnight, the place was really hopping and filled with a chorus of slot machine tunes. You could barely walk behind the tables, let alone find one with a vacant spot to get down a bet. We waited forty minutes before Pat was able to squeeze through the noisy crowd and stand at the bottom of a roulette table with a cute blond dealer. I managed to twist my body forward enough near the spinning wheel so I could follow the ball's revolutions with my eyes. From where I stood there was a little revolving blind spot on the inner disk, which would delay my call by a fraction of a second if the ball dropped into a number slot passing momentarily out of view. But that small risk we were willing to take.

Pat cautiously placed his four chips in the first column box as early as possible, the moment the dealer removed her marker from the previous winning number. Like everything else intrinsic to the move, the timing of his bet placement was crucial. When doing a move like this, you want to avoid eye contact with the dealer. You want to pass by unnoticed. It was second nature for dealers to glimpse at a player's face when seeing him place chips on the layout, and that glimpse lengthened when a player put his bet down late. By placing his bet early, while the dealer was busied restacking the chips swept from the previous spin, Pat avoided spooking her. When she finished stacking and cased the layout for the upcoming spin, Pat's bet was one of a hundred already out there, blended in perfectly, the three reds jutting off the purple. There was no need to camouflage it with stacks of chips as we'd discussed in the planning stages. Several other players at the table did that for us with their bets.

Pat looked at me and nodded subtly, his signal that everything was a "go."

I nodded back to let him know I was ready.

The cute blond spun the ball, then began recasing the bets on the layout. She still did not notice Pat's purple chip hidden underneath the reds.

I concentrated deeply as the ball whizzed around the wheel

several times, each revolution a little slower than the last. When it finally fell into number 16, in the first column, I let out a sigh of relief. But then it bounced out, ricocheted around the bowl and dribbled along a few more numbers before dropping dead into the black number 8 slot – a loser. I hesitated a half second to be sure the ball didn't bounce out again before yelling, "Damn it!" maybe a bit too loud. I felt all pent-up and equally pissed off that the ball had jumped out of a winner.

By the time I got my eyes off the wheel and down to the first column box, there were no chips in it. Pat had scooped them up, and there hadn't been the slightest peep from the dealer. She'd seen absolutely nothing. There was no need even to replace the chips.

Pat flashed his gleaming eyes at me. He was clearly impressed by what he'd seen. So was I. Neither of us had expected the rake-off to go unnoticed.

He gave me a soft nod, then eased away from the table toward the darkened lounge off the casino floor. I stayed behind for fifteen minutes to see if any steam came down afterwards. Though that purple chip had been invisible to the dealer, it nonetheless could have been seen by any number of gamblers or spectators around the table – who might decide to rat for whatever reason. Though most people didn't alert casinos when they witnessed cheating, we always had to be prepared for those who did.

When I joined Pat at the packed bar and ordered a coke, he was already hopping in step with the jazz combo and on his second beer. A true Irishman.

"Richard, that dealer was dead standing!" he said in a flourish, without breaking stride from the music. "If they're all like her, we'll never have to give these casinos back a chip."

We clinked glasses, then I said, "All we need to know now is how dealers react when they catch you raking the chips, and how the pit handles our winners."

"We'll find out soon enough," Pat said, and gulped down the rest of his beer.

Anytime you had a large-denomination winning chip showing up on a casino layout without being announced beforehand by the dealer, you had steam. Even in the classiest casinos in Vegas. Dealers everywhere were required to announce "black action" once a black chip was spotted on the layout, or "purple action" if a player laid down a purple. Approval had to come from the floorman before the dealer spun the ball or dealt the cards. The first thing casino employees often thought on learning of the presence of an unannounced large winning chip was that it had probably been pastposted and the casino was getting taken for the wager.

The beauty of our little gig was that if there was any question as to whether our roulette bet was legitimate, and not a pastpost or late bet, all the casino had to do was call up their surveillance eye in the sky and have the operator on duty run back the tape. By the late 1980s, just about all the casinos in America – in the world, for that matter – had twenty-fourtwenty-four-hour video surveillance on all their tables. So in theory, we were actually protected by the casino's own security system, the very fact that so juiced us up about this new move. In the past, the cameras had been a constant threat to our operation because we'd always slipped in the big bets late. When pit bosses had threatened to review tapes in challenge to the legitimacy of our bets, we had to back off claims and get the hell out of Dodge. But now, we actually wanted their surveillance systems in perfect working order.

At three o'clock in the morning we were back in position at another Eldorado roulette table as the ball spun around the shallow bowl. The casino was still crowded but this time we didn't have to wait to get our bet down. Pat was readying himself to either pick up the chips or claim; I was up at the front by the wheel, getting ready to signal the outcome. The ball landed on a losing number. I yelled, "damn it!" and Pat raked off the four chips.

He got caught red-handed.

"Hey!" another little oriental female dealer screamed. And this one's voice *did* carry amid the casino din. "What are you doing, sir! Put those chips back down! Your bet lost!"

Pat went into his drunken routine. "Oh, I'm so sorry," he blurted out, as he swayed unsteadily with an empty glass I hadn't even noticed in his hand. "I guess the ball already landed. I didn't realize it." He reached back down with calculated clumsiness and placed three red chips on the layout. I noticed right away he didn't put back four, the same number of chips that had originally been there.

So did the dealer. This little girl was sharp. "Sir, you had *four* red chips out there, twenty dollars!" she said just as sharply.

OUpon hearing that I smiled inwardly. She affirmed never having seen the purple chip underneath.

"Oh…I had four of them red…red…redbirds out there," Pat said, slurring his words perfectly, the consummate actor.

"Put the fourth one back down!" she barked, like a little oriental dictator.

Pat did as he was told.

The floorman, who'd noticed the ruckus, came up to the table from behind the dealer. "What's the matter?" he asked her.

"No big deal," she said, toning it down. She indicated Pat with a slight head movement. "The gentleman didn't realize the ball dropped, so he tried to pick up his bet."

Pat kept playing the part, knowing it wasn't curtains down until the situation was totally diffused. He offered the floorman his wavering handshake. "Yeah, she's right," he said with a slur. "I tried to pick up my bet like a real slob."

The floorman laughed easily and said, "No big deal, sir. Enjoy yourself at the Eldorado." Then he walked back into the pit and forgot about it. I said to myself, If you only knew how big a deal this was eventually going to be!

Pat hung around five minutes, made a few foolhardy $5 bets before leaving the table for our predetermined meeting place outside the casino. We had chosen the keno pit at the Circus Circus casino down the road. Whenever there was steam, even if the situation was smoothed out like Pat had done at that table, we met outside the casino. You never knew what could happen afterwards – the rats, or the dealer could get steamed up again on her own, suddenly remembering something that could alert her to the reality of what had happened.

I stayed at the table ten minutes, concluded everything was clean, then went off to join my partner at Circus Circus.

"Pat, this is big!" I said with a grin. "Nobody said another word."

We'd experienced two losers without any communication problems; my two "damn-its" had been well received by Pat, and he'd managed to get the purple chip off the layout both times without incident. The fact that the dealer had caught him the second time was of no concern. The key was that she had never seen his purple chip. We had worried about the possibility of the chip becoming visible as the dealer's eyes were drawn to the action of the rake-off, but now that appeared like another potential obstacle we could put to bed. The farther we progressed into the experiment, the more potential obstacles dropped like dominos, and I was becoming more and more convinced that our new dream move was turning into reality – even before seeing a payoff. It had already dawned on me how easy it was. Its simplicity was astounding.

A half hour later we were again in position at a roulette table inside Harrah's Casino. The dealer on the game was a tall Nevadan named Randy with a seemingly carefree attitude. The table was full, the atmosphere seductive. Half the people seated and standing around the table were clad in their Hot August Nights T-shirts and ball caps; almost everybody had a drink or cigarette in hand. The casino was still humming with noise.

Pat laid down the bet, again paying special attention to crack the three red chips slightly off the purple, creating a perfectly angled wedge. I noticed briefly that a girl next to him did a double take at his chips. She probably saw the purple underneath, but I had no intention of calling off the move because she was now a potential snitch. In ripping off casinos you lived with that lurking possibility.

Randy took a cursory glance at the layout and spun the ball. In sync with his size, his spin was powerful. The ball made several revolutions before the hissing sound of its speed cadenced into a plunk-plunk rattle as it began careening back and forth, landing in one slot, popping out, then landing again. The ball's course tested my patience. When finally all the sounds from the ball were gone, and there was just the steady hum of the revolving wheel, a sudden burst emanated from the bottom of the table.

Pat had exploded. He'd seen the ball land and stay put in the red number 1 slot as soon as I had.

We had a winner!

"That's me!" Pat cried, clapping his hands loudly, pointing to his winning chips, clenching his fist as he jerked his arm outward and pulled it back, a gesture reminiscent of a hockey player's reaction after scoring a goal. Had Pat had his stick, I'm sure he would've raised it above his head, too. "That's my five hundred bucks in the first column box!" He pointed again at the chips. "That's my purple chip sitting under there."

The exact words in Pat's claim were also rehearsed. Following the script was essential. Knowing that the dealer hadn't seen the purple chip before spinning the ball, we knew as well he didn't see it now, either. It was of the utmost importance to make him see that purple chip as soon as possible because now it was a winner. Had Pat started claiming a winner without actually saying he had bet a purple chip, the dealer would not have realized its presence, so well it was hidden underneath the three reds. He most certainly would have figured Pat was just gassed up about winning a $20 bet. We knew we couldn't allow such a scenario to take place. The more time that elapsed before the dealer realized the purple chip was there, the more dangerous the situation became. If too much time passed, the dealer, and then the floorman or pit boss arriving on the scene later, might think the bet was late or even pastposted, and hold up the payoff to check with the eye in the sky. Of course the legitimacy of our bet would be protected by the camera, but we wanted a quick payoff without steam, so Pat kept repeating, "Five-hundred dollars on the column, five-hundred dollars on the column," as he pointed at his chips, not letting up until he was certain the dealer saw the purple.

Randy at first looked down confusedly at the smaller Pat. I interpreted his bizarre facial expression as the unspoken words, What is this ranting and raving lunatic at the bottom of my table talking about?

But Randy's facial muscles contorted quickly to produce an expression of concern when he picked up Pat's bet and the purple chip on the bottom jumped up at him. He knew he was going to catch flak for not having called out the purple to his supervisor.

I backed off the wheel to watch from the background as the scene developed. People around the table began laughing and cheering for Pat as if he'd just hit a home run. It never hurt having support from other gamblers. It was a heck of a lot better than the rats. In negative situations people at the table often helped us unintentionally. Sometimes a suspicious pit boss, wanting to hold up and delay a game because of a questionable bet, refrained from doing so because he didn't want to aggravate the impatience of players and give the impression the casino was fretting over having to pay a big bet.

Randy immediately called over the floorman, who'd been leaning against an adjacent blackjack table that facilitated his flirting with a pretty girl playing the end seat. The floorman would've preferred that Randy find someone else to bother, but duty called.

"The man standing at the bottom bet a purple on the column," Randy told him, with a demeanor not at all as calm and carefree as it had been before he got bit by Pat's purple chip. "It won."

The floorman shrugged. "Why didn't you call it out before you spun the ball?"

"I never saw it."

The floorman got a little interested. "Was it there before you spun it?"

The only thing Randy could tell him was that he was sure there were four chips in the first column box before he spun the ball. That was his subconscious memory talking – an element we always counted on when our bets won.

The floorman pressed him on it. "You're certain?"

"I always case my bets," Randy answered quickly.

"Then pay him," the floorman instructed, returning to the blackjack table to resume his conversation with the pretty girl on the end seat.

Randy plucked two purple chips from the purple stack in his chip well, grabbed a stack of reds with his other hand, dropped the two purples next to Pat's purple, which he'd removed from the bottom of the bet to show the floorman, and cut into Pat's three red chips with his own red stack twice.

Well, there it was! We had out first payoff on the new Savannah move – $1,030. The two bets we lost cost us a total of twenty bucks. Had Pat replaced the chips both times, we would have lost forty. In any case, who wouldn't like those odds?

We met back up at the Circus Circus keno pit. Pat gave me all the chips. I went back to Harrah's to cash out. Before doing so, I took a final evaluating look at the wheel where we'd just taken off the money. Randy was still dealing, and the floorman was still flirting with the girl. Everything was spotless.

It was past four o'clock in the morning and we were both feeling pretty beat, so we called it a night. Before going back to our hotel room we stopped back at the titty bar. Surprisingly, Savannah was still there wagging her butt. Pat was really in a jolly mood so he splurged for back-to-back titty dances. After the lovely Savannah finished her little number of waving her tits and ass in our faces, Pat laid a $100 bill on her. Usually he gave the dancers twenties, but his high spirits warranted the hundred.

"That's a big number you gave her," I said after Savannah flashed us her pretty, phony smile and was gone.

Pat reached across the table and rubbed my shoulder. "Don't worry, Richard," he said merrily, "Savannah made that little dance well worth it. And I'm not talking about the girl." He paused for effect. "Did you get that, Richard?"

I got it.

Later, lying awake in my bed, too pumped up by the day's activities for sleep, I thought about how unbelievable this move would be. It really was as close to perfection as possible. I thought of the worst case scenario. That would be getting caught raking the losing bet and having the purple chip exposed, in which case the casino would put the whole thing together and comprehend we were taking free shots at them.

But what could they do about it? What real evidence would they have? What would a prosecutor claim in court? That the defendant bet four chips, three reds on top of a purple, which he premeditatedly concealed, with the intent to switch out the purple and replace it with another red if the outcome of the bet was not favorable to him? Sure, that makes a pretty good argument, and any jury would understand it. But one key piece of evidence would be missing. How could the casino prove there had ever been a purple chip under the three reds in the first place? The answer was they couldn't.

All the fantastic things you hear about casino surveillance systems, such as that famous cliché about surveillance cameras reading the date off a dime, are only partially true. Yes, they can read the date off a dime, but only if the lens is zoomed in for that particular purpose. Casino cameras are only zoomed in when surveillance personnel are already suspicious about certain activities and are trying to get a closer look at a suspected cheating move and film close-ups of faces and fingers to use later as evidence in court. But against us, that was zero. We were hit and run cheaters. Their cameras never had the chance to zoom in on us. Even if by some miraculous chance a camera above a roulette wheel was zoomed in on our bet, it could never see that bottom chip well enough to positively identify it. Zoomed images are grainy.

Aside from video evidence, what other tangibles could the casino have on us? The next morning at breakfast I painted a scenario for Pat: "Say I get caught snatching up the bet and drop the purple chip. Then it rolls right to the dealer, and she grabs it and puts it in her chip well, insisting I had bet it and lost and was then trying to grab it off the layout before she could sweep it. That's about the worst scenario, right?"

Pat nodded his agreement.

"Okay, so now they could prove the purple chip was in my possession, but that doesn't prove I'd bet it. Because if I'd actually bet it, then why didn't the dealer call it out to the pit, in accordance with casino dealing policy? See what I'm saying? The casino's own policy protects us. Any black, purple, $1,000 or $5,000 chip on the layout must be announced to the floorman before the dealer spins the ball. If not, then technically it's not there. No bet with a big chip had ever been made. So how can a prosecutor say, 'The defendant bet a purple chip under three reds,' if casino policy itself dictates that no purple chip had ever been bet? Not only is that the policy in all the casinos, it's also a Nevada Gaming Control Board regulation."

"Richard, the more you talk, the more I like it," Pat said, grinning.

I continued: "Even if they got lucky and had two different tapes of me – one showing me getting paid, another showing me grabbing up losing chips on a different table, they couldn't use the tape from the payoff to support the tape from the rake-off because no crime was committed by simply getting paid, nor could they use the tape of the rake-off to say I *would have* swiped off the chips on the tape where I got paid if *that* bet had lost. It's like double jeopardy in murder cases.

That's right," Pat said excitedly. "They can't use evidence from one crime as evidence for another."

I laughed. "I think we got the *nuts* with this move."

During the next three days and nights, Pat laid $515 down in the first column box on thirty-three different roulette tables in all the major casinos in Reno. Our luck ran good. The bet won fourteen times, better than one in three. Of the nineteen times it lost, Pat got the purple chip off smoothly eighteen of them, more than half the time without the dealer even noticing. Each time he got caught, he went into the drunken "I didn't know the ball had dropped" routine, successfully avoiding major confrontations with irritated dealers.

The one time Pat didn't get the purple off the layout was nobody's fault. The rolling ball hit the little blind spot just as it fell into a number slot and my call was too late. The dealer swept away Pat's chips, including the purple, and stacked them in his chip well. He had actually stacked the purple chip with all the reds, never noticing it had been on the layout, not even when he had it in his hand.

Of the fourteen winning bets that weekend, twelve passed without incident and Pat got paid quickly by the floormen. Every time, of course, the dealer went through the initial shock at seeing the purple chip buried underneath, but none questioned the legitimacy of the bet.

At the Reno Hilton, after a floorman instructed his dealer to pay Pat the $1,030, he went deep into the pit to tell the pit boss what had happened. The pit boss approached the wheel to see who their purple-chip player was. By the time he was at the table, Pat was already gone and heading to our meeting place outside the casino. His sudden disappearance bugged the pit boss, who immediately scanned the casino with one of those patented pit boss eye-tours in search of Pat, which was funny because he had no idea what the person he was looking for looked like. Shaking his head, he went back to the podium and picked up the phone, probably to call the eye in the sky, or maybe alert the shift boss about the incident.

Like always, I stayed behind to gauge the casino's reaction. When the pit boss hung up the phone and swiftly strode out of the pit, I followed him loosely across the casino. He went into the main craps pit, where an older, obviously higher ranking pit boss – maybe even the shift boss or casino manager – was standing behind a busy craps table with a lot of heavy black-chip action. They conversed a minute or so, but the big boss didn't seem too concerned about hearing somebody won a grand off a purple chip nobody had seen on a roulette game before the dealer spun the ball. He was more intent on watching the big craps players. The roulette pit boss shook his head and returned to his pit.

We ran into another sticky situation at the Silver Legacy, Reno's newest and largest gaming establishment. It boasted a giant mining rig in the middle of the casino that every so often swung into action and created the movements and sounds of digging up silver deposits. We'd put in many hours there as the opportunities were endless. Pat had already both picked up losers and gotten paid four times when we found ourselves on what turned out to be the last wheel for the trip.

The dealer called for the floorman as soon as Pat made him aware of the winning purple chip. I could tell immediately that the floorman was a wise-ass type and was going to be a problem. He had an annoying strut with a chip on his shoulder. Like in all walks of life, you had your share of assholes working in casinos.

The guy visually measured Pat, who was dressed casually in jeans and a light designer windbreaker, and just decided for whatever reason to challenge him. Pointing disdainfully at Pat's bet, he said derisively, "You know something, I've been in this business twenty years, and I've never seen anyone make a bet like that."

This punk of a floorman didn't know the person he was up against. Pat took his turn to size up the guy with his eyes, then said starkly, "You know something, I've also been in this business twenty years...and I don't give a fuck."

Wasn't much room for a riposte there.

It was never our intention to get fresh with casino personnel. We were always a class act, but sometimes we got provoked by assholes and had to hold our ground. Earlier that same day in the same casino, a floorman had asked Pat in a suspicious but not impolite tone why he'd put three red chips atop a purple. Though his bet structure was indeed a bit odd because legitimate purple-chip players didn't normally mix purples with reds, it was none of the casino's business how Pat placed his chips.

But since the floorman had asked courteously, Pat didn't need to come off rude like he'd been with the wise-ass floorman getting in his face. As always, he found the perfect response, one that even served to dissipate the steam. He said simply, "The three red chips I bet for the dealer." The floorman had smiled his acknowledgment and told Pat that players wanting to bet for the dealer usually placed those chips directly in front of their own bets, not on top, so the dealer would understand the bet was for him. Pat played dumb and laughed with the floorman at his feigned ignorance. Before the incident was over, the floorman ended up giving Pat a comp for two in the hotel's best restaurant. Pat had lobster, I had steak.

The next morning, flooded with excitement about the weekend's results for the promising new Savannah move, we caught a flight back to Vegas. For the four-day trip we cleared seventeen grand after expenses, including the $100 bill Pat laid on the lovely Savannah herself. We couldn't wait to get back to Vegas and try Savannah with $5,000 chips in the big Strip casinos. The thought of taking free $10,000 shots at casinos was just too much: Bet a chocolate chip on a 2-to-1 shot, get paid ten grand if it won, lose twenty bucks if it lost. Who would ever believe it!

For me, this anticipation was even greater because Pat and I had decided to switch roles. He would be calling "damn it" at the top of the table by the wheel while I got paid or raked off the huge bet at the bottom of the layout.

I chose my favorite casino in the world to drop the first chocolate-chip bomb on a roulette table: Caesars Palace. I had always made the most money there and it was on their tables where Pat and I had done the first chocolate-chip blackjack past-posts.

It was a busy Saturday night during Labor Day weekend. I put on a lightweight summer suit for the occasion. After all, we were dealing with $5,000 chips. I had to not only act the part of a legitimate high roller, I had to dress it as well. Though I could never assume the presence of my great partner Pat, I needed to have my own chocolate-chip appearance at Caesars. He was casual with a Caesars T-shirt, which made his beer belly stick out a little, swimming trunks, and a matching Caesars ball cap. In view of our contrasting appearances, nobody would think we were together.

I strolled through a blackjack pit that had two roulette tables at the end. Pat followed me in the same direction across the double-rowed pit. I stopped in front of a jammed-up roulette game with a short Japanese dealer named Soko. She was wearing glasses with lenses as thick as coke bottles. Watching her was comical. She was so small she had to reach way over to grasp the chips at the bottom of the table. When she looked up at me, I got sprayed by the light reflecting off her glasses. Thinking she could neither see the chips clearly nor reach out far enough to grab them effectively, I couldn't resist. To break the ice on this move I needed every advantage possible, no matter how unfair.

I signalled Pat that I'd found the table I wanted. He moved in and took his position by the wheel as I squeezed in between two Chinese men sitting at the bottom of the table. Soko was finishing paying the winning bets from the last spin. I looked up by the wheel, saw Pat ensconced in position. He gave me a soft nod that let me know he was ready. However, *I* was nervous. I was doing something new for the first time and for a considerable amount of money. If the bet lost and I froze up, five grand would be down the drain.

Soko removed the number-marker from the layout, and the Chinese and other gamblers around the table began placing their bets. The difference between the tables here and those up in Reno was not the volume of action but the amount of money the roulette chips spread over the layout represented. In Reno, roulette chips usually represented dollars. At Caesars their preferred value was often $5 and $10, and it was not uncommon for a high roller to plaster the layout with $25 chips, even $100 blacks.

My hands had become sweaty, and I had some difficulty cutting the three red chips off the chocolate. I wanted to get the bet down cleanly the first shot, because in the event of a surveillance situation later, I didn't want to be seen on camera manipulating the chips as though they had to be laid down in some precise fashion. A sharp surveillance guy might get wise to the move if he saw me on tape. All he had to do was realize I'd intended to hide the chocolate and from there figure out the rest.

I put the chips back in my suit jacket pocket and rubbed my hands along the sides of my trousers, trying to dry my hands the best I could. When I removed the chips again, I managed to get them down in the first column box but wasn't too satisfied with the placement. I had cut the reds off the chocolate a bit too far. Looking down at them, the effect was like the jaws of a shark. Suddenly, the Chinese guy on my left leaned back in his chair and looked up at me with a furrowing eyebrow. I thought I detected a slight smile outlining his lips. I was certain he saw my chocolate chip and appreciated its value. But did he sense I planned on swiping it off if it lost? At first, that thought unnerved me, but then I chided myself for being ridiculous.

I looked again at Pat, who glanced at my bet and indicated it was placed well enough from his point of view, which was similar to the dealer's. From where he stood he could not see the chocolate chip.

I still had second thoughts and might have reached out to fix up the chips, but it was too late. Soko had spun the ball. I felt my neck muscles tightening as the ball revolved around the cylinder. And it was rolling slowly; it was going to drop terribly soon. I had forgotten to ready myself for a slow spin. When sizing up the little Japanese dealer, I didn't think about the corresponding small lapse of time there'd be from the beginning of her spin until the moment the ball dropped into one of the number slots on the wheel.

I barely had time to swallow the bile rising up in my throat before the click-clack of the dropping ball reverberated in my head. Then Pat was shouting loudly, "Damn it!" as Soko's eyes were coming back from the spinning cylinder, the marker wrapped up in her hand as she reached toward the layout to place it. She put it on number 00, then her two hands began working their way in unison toward my bet. She had an easy sweep to make because there were no winning bets on the layout. All she had to do was sweep off all the chips, not having to worry about inadvertently removing winners off the layout, which slowed a dealer's progress.

I hesitated a fraction of a second before my left hand shot out and grabbed the chips. There was no doubt about my tardiness. When timing is everything, a fraction of a second can be an eternity. Thinking I was caught red-handed, I fumbled putting the four chips in my left jacket pocket, worried about dropping the chocolate on the floor. In that instant of my own ineptitude, I completely disregarded what I'd considered to be my advantage in Soko's nearsightedness, and even feared that she might have seen the chocolate chip. My eyes jumped directly to hers as soon as the chips were finally in my pocket. She was still sweeping losing chips off the layout. She didn't look up at me, didn't react at all – nothing! I couldn't believe it. As late as I'd been, she hadn't seen me snatch up the chips.

My head turned to Pat. He nodded to reassure me that Soko hadn't seen anything. I took in a deep breath, blew out the air and settled down. The two Chinamen began rattling away in Chinese. I was sure they were talking about me and what they'd just seen, but neither one turned his head to look up at me. I kept my eyes glued on Soko for ten seconds. She was busy restacking the chips in her working bay, putting the fresh stacks in her chip well. She wasn't giving me the time of day. Satisfied I had indeed snatched that chocolate chip cleanly off the layout, I backed away from the table and walked off.

Ten minutes later Pat showed up where I was waiting in the sports book at the Barbary Coast casino.

"Richard, you were a little late over there," he said, smiling. "It looked like you were playing chicken with the dealer. I wasn't sure who was gonna pick the chips up first."

"I was a little nervous," I admitted. "I got taken by her slow spin."

"Don't worry about it," he reassured me. "It was clean."

"I think those Chinamen saw me."

"*Saw* you?" Pat laughed from the gut. "Richard, if they had tickets to the show at Caesars tonight, they probably already ripped them up."

We shared a laugh and went over to the bar next to the sports book. The Barbary Coast was hopping like all the other Vegas Strip casinos on Saturday night. We had to wait a couple of minutes to get drinks, so we talked a little strategy. We agreed that if everything appeared clean after a pick up, it would no longer be necessary to leave Caesars. We'd arrange an internal meeting spot off the casino floor where I would wait for Pat. If any steam came down after I left the table, he'd come over immediately and flash the signal to get out. Should I win the bet and get paid, I'd automatically come back over to the Barbary Coast sports book.

We gulped down our drinks and headed back across Las Vegas Boulevard to Caesars. We both were eager to get back in there. The cocktail had done me good. I was now exuding confidence, all the jitters gone. I would find another table, put the bet right down, pick it right back up if it lost, get paid the ten grand if it won. Nothing was stopping me now.

Cruising the pit, I passed by Soko's table. The two Chinamen were still there, and when one saw me he nudged the other almost childishly, and they both looked at me and laughed. Pat had been right. I must have given them all the entertainment they'd needed for the night. I would've loved to take another shot on Soko's table but simply couldn't because of general security principles. If I did and my bet won, and a pit boss decided to go to the video to check its legitimacy, I'd be running the risk that they'd rewind the tape back far enough to catch the sequence where I raked off the chips earlier on the same table. That would be a real stupid way to give up our newly discovered move.

I found another beauty of a dealer on a roulette game in the main pit near the front entrance. I joked to myself that if I had to get out quick, I couldn't have been in a more advantageous location. The dealer was an older guy named Ray whom you would've sworn was an ex-boxer. He had one of those punched-in noses and was kind of ugly, but in spite of all that gave the impression of being a "sweetheart" dealer. He was helping people place their bets, explaining corresponding payoffs, smiling continually.

This time I got the bet down without my hands sweating, and the three red chips were cut perfectly off the chocolate. One thing about cutting the chips like that: when they were cut right, I knew it. A sudden click went off in my head, like a safecracker feeling the tumblers give way just before the vault popped open.

Ray spun the ball, and it was one of those spins where the ball goes around and around, then gets stuck along the rim and refuses to drop into the bowl. That can be really exasperating when you're trying to break the ice with something like this. Ray was forced to retrieve the ball and spin it again. This time it dropped into the number 4 slot, a winning outcome, but then bounced out, ricocheted around the wheel and finally found a loser where it stayed put. Pat had stayed focused on the wild ball and was now yelling, "Damn it!" at the soonest possible instant. I was equal to the task. My hand shot out and grabbed the chips long before Ray had even turned his head from the wheel. The rest of the people at the table had no reaction, though I hardly looked at them.

Mumbling an expletive, I turned away, not looking back at anything. I was pleased with my performance and had complete confidence in Pat to report back the details. The only negative there was not winning the bet. But that would come with a little patience.

Pat was just a couple of minutes behind me in the Caesars keno pit. He gave me a nod, then a head-jerk, urging me to come back into the pit and find another table. Obviously, the last pickup had gone so well it wasn't necessary to discuss anything. Once back on the prowl through the pits, I gave Pat a glance and a shift of my eyes, indicating I wanted him to follow me through the long corridor toward the far end of the casino.

I pulled up to the bottom of another roulette table in the back pit of Caesars by the sports book. I placed the bet, lost and raked off. The dealer caught me, scolded me, and I put back four reds in the first column box, killing the steam. At another wheel, as the ball was spinning, the shift and pit bosses arrived to carry out their shift-changeover chip-count, and I was forced to pull off the bet at the last instant.

We found ourselves back in the keno pit, tired, the whizzing sound of eighty keno balls flying haphazardly inside their giant bowl on the counter guarding our silence. When the last of twenty winning balls was finally sucked through the vacuum tube, Pat said, "Maybe we ought to pack it in. We can come back tomorrow on the day shift." I agreed.

Sunday afternoon we drove directly to the Barbary Coast, parked the car in its garage and walked across the boulevard to Caesars. It was a real scorcher outside. We were both dressed in shorts and Polo shirts. I wore the ball cap; Pat left his at home.

Inside, the casino wasn't crowded. Many guests were either out cooling off in the pool or watching sporting events in the race and sports books. Sparsely populated casinos were not ideal, but I was anxious to get a bet down and a payoff. In spite of the lack of big action, there were a few good wheels in the main pit up front, and all the pit bosses seemed relaxed as they usually were on Sunday afternoons.

I found a tall, chubby Latino named Guillermo dealing to a group of Europeans on a lively roulette table with a few legitimate black-chip players. One guy was betting blacks straight up on the numbers while one of his two decked-out female companions was stacking green casino chips on odd. The rest of the layout was sufficiently covered by an assortment of roulette chips. The only problem was that there were too many people – women – packed around the table. I had the impression that each of the European gamblers had not only a wife or girlfriend with him, but a mistress, too. I tried to twist and turn into my position at the bottom of the table, but one of the black-chip gambler's girlfriends was standing against it, impeding my approach. Here, I had to be careful because I didn't want to make a scene with the girl and the gambler. I had to somehow gently nudge her just enough to open up a space from where I could maneuver without rubbing her the wrong way – or the right way, which might make the guy think I was trying to bird-dog his girlfriend. Creating an uneasy atmosphere around the table could cause the gambler or one of the girlfriends, or somebody else at the table, to rat me out if I ended up grabbing the bet off the layout.

I tried the best I could to squeeze into position, but it was in vain. The threesome was having too much fun, and now they were holding hands and touching each other as they spoke French and sipped their cocktails. The worrisome thought of accidentally knocking over their drinks when they rested on the edge of the layout entered my mind.

With all these negatives, it seemed the best course of action was to find another table, or just simply wait until the French at the bottom left. But then I made a rash decision. I took a few steps to my right, skirting the threesome, and positioned myself against the inside corner of the table, at the last allowable spot next to the dealer. I then placed my $5,015 inside the third column box, which was located on the bottom right of the layout. I made the tiniest adjustment when cutting the three red chips off the chocolate to compensate for the angle change between the dealer and the chips now sitting in the third column box instead of the first column box.

Pat had a surprised expression on his face, but he understood. I furrowed my brows, silently asking him, "Is this okay with you?"

It was not automatic. Identifying into which column a winning number fell was not nearly as simple as red or black, or odd or even. Red or black was simply visual. Odd or even required a first grade education, but with columns you had to invoke your brain's memory, or actually make the match with your eyes, which took longer. The first column we had both already memorized since we'd been working exclusively on it from the inception of the move. But I could not expect Pat to have the third column memorized any more than I had myself. There was, however, a built-in simplifying factor for the third column: all its numbers were divisible by 3. I had no idea about Pat's mathematical skills, or if he even recognized that simple math was applicable to our situation, but nevertheless, he was nodding with a shrug that said, "Why not."

I left the chips in the box and steeled myself in concentration as Guillermo spun the ball. It made several revolutions around the wheel, then fell dead in the number 3 slot. Everything was perfect. The ball didn't bounce out, and Pat had the easiest of calls because number 3 was in the top row, the first number in the third column. It was also, of course, divisible by 3.

He remained silent.

I exploded. All that pent-up energy came rushing out of my body. I let out a thundering "Yes!" and followed it up with a monster claim. "I hit the big one!" I shouted, clapping my hands with an assortment of exaggerated gestures. It wasn't all an act, however. I was genuinely both thrilled to death and immensely relieved. Our number had finally come in. The tension had been building up in me that whole weekend. "I just love Caesars Palace," I carried on. "That's ten grand in the *third* column for me, Guillermo...ten thousand dollars!"

Guillermo looked down at my bet, casually lifted off the three red chips, flinched momentarily when he saw the chocolate underneath, put the reds back down next to it, then reached into his chip well and delicately peeled off two Caesars $5,000 chips from the handsome chocolate stack sitting behind the red, green, black, purple, and yellow chip-stacks in the well. He put the chocolates on the layout in front of him and announced, "Chocolate going out," to let the pit personnel know he was paying out chocolate chips. Finally, he placed the two chocolates next to mine in the third column box.

"Are these yours also?" he asked me, indicating the three red chips sitting in the box next to the chocolates.

I was in seventh heaven. A clean $10,000 payoff! "No, Guillermo," I responded loftily. "They're yours."

"Thank you, sir."

He paid himself $30, pocketed that plus the three red chips I had bet, picking up a $45 tip for the spin.

We cleared ten grand. I picked up the three chocolate chips and admired them in my hand, appreciating them as a jeweler did precious stones.

The floorman came over to take a look at me. There was no misgiving in his eyes whatsoever. He just wanted to catch a glimpse of Caesars' newest chocolate-chip roulette player.

Before leaving the table, I placed two of the chocolates in the middle of the layout and asked Guillermo to change them into ten yellow $1,000 chips. This would facilitate our cash-out procedure later. Working Savannah with the chocolates, we'd have to take cash-out precautions to avoid both the IRS and Caesars surveillance discovering our move.

I think the best feeling I ever had in my life was leaving that roulette table with a fistful of yellow chips from Caesars Palace. I let them jiggle in my hand, delighted in their sweet rattling music as I crossed through the main casino, down the passageway toward the back entrance and out the door. I had purposely taken the long route out of the casino because I didn't want the floorman, or any other personnel who'd been in that roulette pit, seeing me walk right out of the casino after having made the winning $5,000 bet.

I kept listening to the chips rattle in my hand as I crossed Las Vegas Boulevard, thinking the sounds made by the expensive chips were actually more elegant than those made by $5 reds when you jiggled them in the same fashion. Maybe I was nuts, but the high I felt was immense.

Pat was all smiles when he entered the Barbary Coast to give me the details. "You were fabulous, Richard!" He gave me a big handshake.

"Nothing came down after I left?"

Pat shook his head. "The floorman came up to the dealer right after you were gone and asked him if he'd ever seen you before. Then he looked at the stacks of chips in the dealer's well and wrote something down on his pad."

"Oh, that's nothing," I said knowingly. "He was just taking note of the ten yellow chips I walked with."

Whatever doubts I'd had about Savannah were all rubbed out now. The move was perfection, undoubtedly the best cheating move involving casino chips ever conceived. It was the culmination of a gifted cheating-casinos career. And it was so deliciously simple. Sure, there were scams out there I didn't know about; someone somewhere probably had something better that didn't involve the manipulation of gaming chips. But one thing I was absolutely sure about was that Savannah had the best payoff to risk ratio in the business.

During the fall of 1995, we blitzkrieged Vegas with the chocolate-chip Savannah move. One weekend we got paid ten times in ten different casinos, walking away with a hundred grand. When during another we went cold and couldn't hit a winning bet on any of the columns (we'd begun working all three columns), we made a procedural change. We began placing our chocolate chips in the even-money 19 thru 36 box at the bottom left side of the layout. The distance from the dealer was a tad shorter, but frankly it didn't matter. Our bet placements were just so good that dealers never saw the chocolate chip underneath the reds.

Arriving at that decision was not cut and dry. Mathematically, in the long-run, we'd be giving up 25 percent of the money. However, the long dry spells we dreaded would be reduced since the 19 thru 36 bet had almost a 50 percent chance of winning. And if for some reason Savannah ended up having a short lifetime, that betting change might prove more profitable overall.

Pat had a brazen idea to maximize the number *and* the amount of the payoffs. One night over a beer while we were barbecuing lobster tails, he suggested the previously unthinkable. "Why not put *two* $5,000-dollar chips underneath the reds in the casinos that take $10,000 on the even-money bets?"

I couldn't help but laugh. It was so ridiculous it would probably fly. I pulled Pat's glass out of his hand and kiddingly smelled its contents. "What have you got in this glass, Pat?"

He shrugged playfully and said, "I don't know, Richard, I'm just trying to improve the move."

"Stick to cooking those lobsters."

At that moment, I obviously didn't know that in the coming months we would not only be hiding two big chips under the reds – but even three. In Atlantic City and elsewhere in the country where casinos didn't have $5,000 chips, we ventured the use of double and triple-chip hiding. In Las Vegas, we eventually graduated to the double-chocolate Savannah and had success with $10,000 payoffs on the 19 thru 36 box. In order to accomplish that, it was necessary to constantly distract the dealer from the time we placed the bet until the roulette ball dropped into a number slot. The caller at the front of the wheel had the additional responsibility to keep the dealer engaged in conversation, so he wouldn't have a chance to look down and case our bet. With the double-chocolate underneath, we couldn't depend on chip camouflage alone.

The highest posted outside-payoff limit I'd ever seen in Las Vegas was at the Desert Inn, where you were allowed to bet $10,000 on all the 2-to-1 propositions. We went for the $20,000 prize by hiding two chocolates on the columns several times but never had the luck to win a bet.

Meanwhile, we did just fine with the 19 thru 36 bets at five grand a pop. Pat would call; I would rake and claim one weekend, then the next we switched roles. We'd gotten another sixty Savannahs paid during the rest of that fall, 1995. Then the steam started coming. More and more often, pit bosses began going to the eye in the sky before paying us. Word was bouncing around Vegas that a "wheel team" was hitting the roulette games hard with chocolate chips.

I already knew that everyone connected to casino surveillance had identified me and my unknown partner in their videotapes. Each time pit bosses went to the sky to verify our bets, we got filmed while waiting. It was impossible to avoid that. By that time, I was already known by the Nevada Gaming Control Board and dozens of other casino regulatory bodies around the world as one of the most innovating international casino cheaters in the business. But that in itself didn't matter. What made the difference was the length of time before they put the whole thing together. Constantly seeing the same two guys on the tape had to tell them something was going down, despite the video evidence that legitimized the bets. Even if my name *wasn't* connected to the tapes, they'd still have to be awfully suspicious.

Knowing that Savannah's life might be reaching the end of the line, I decided to implement Pat's crazy suggestion of hiding two chocolate chips underneath – but with a twist. Instead of putting another chocolate underneath, we'd put it on a second bet. In addition to the bet on the first column, we'd make another on the 19 thru 36 box. If they both won, we'd pick up fifteen grand. If only the column bet won, we'd pick up five grand – ten for the win in the column minus the five lost on the 19 thru 36. If the 19 thru 36 won and the column lost, we'd break even.

"We don't pick up the loser and leave the winner?" Pat asked.

"It's not worth the risk. If the dealer sees us pick up the loser, we can't claim the winner. Then we're caught with our pants down when they spot the chocolate lying on the bottom of the winner while we tried to pick up the loser. No, the only time we pick up is when they *both* lose."

Pat whistled at the sheer boldness of such a move.

"We might as well milk it to the end," I said with a coy smile. "Nothing lasts forever."

We decided to give Vegas a rest until New Year's Eve, let the town cool a while. During that break we discussed strategy for the two-bet scenario and ultimately decided to stay with the same m.o. – the caller at the top by the wheel and the raker, who'd rake off both bets himself, at the bottom. The only change we made to the bet itself was that two red chips would be placed on top of the chocolate instead of three, to facilitate the double rake-off, in that the total number of chips handled would be less.

We practiced picking up the two bets. There wasn't much difference. After experimenting with both one and two hands, I felt more comfortable doing it with only one. Although there'd be two bets to pick up, by placing each in the neighboring extremities of their respective boxes, the actual distance between them was less than two inches, therefore, I could scoop them both up in practically the same amount of time as I'd been scooping up the single bets all along. It would just be a tad more complicated getting the six chips back in my pocket and replacing them on the layout with the six reds. We were confident that the dealers would continue missing the chocolates on the layout while casing the bets, despite the second one's presence.

We arrived at the Las Vegas Hilton at ten-thirty New Year's Eve. The casino was already going strong; we had our choice of three or four good wheels, each invitingly flashing their red, black and green numbers like a rainbow.

An old-timer named Benny was dealing a roulette game with another female old-timer working behind him as a helper. With Savannah, the presence of helpers created no additional problems. They never saw the chocolate chips underneath, nor had a helper ever caught us raking off chips. In fact, their presence behind the dealer was a positive. In situations where a pit boss was suspicious about our winning $5,000 bet, he had to wonder, How could they have beaten *two* dealers on a wheel? From time to time such pit boss reasoning may have saved us an eye-in-the-sky inquiry. To what extent the helper's presence actually did favor us was immeasurable.

The casino was extremely noisy, exacerbated by a brass band playing in the elevated bar lounge just off the casino floor. I cleared my throat as I approached the roulette table. I knew I'd have to strain my vocal cords in order to be heard when it was time to claim.

I wedged myself between two couples of rowdy college kids wearing UNLV football jackets and ball caps. I thought I must have looked funny among them in my suit as I reached inside the jacket pocket to ready the chips. Just as I placed down the two bets, the band gave a flourish to start a new number, as if to signal the beginning of our show.

Benny spun the ball on cue, really letting her rip. The guy was no slouch despite many years in the casino. It was one of the longest spins I'd ever witnessed, and as the ball went around and around, Benny cased and re-cased the layout, never giving either of my bets more than a passing glance. I had the comical thought that ten – even twenty – identical bets could have been placed out there without a single chocolate chip exposed to the dealer. The whole damned table could be filled with an army of rakers ready to swipe off the losing bets in unison at the caller's command.

"No more bets," Benny announced deliberately, waving his long arm across the layout to halt the betting. One of those dumb college kids who'd been drinking too much and letting his cigarette ashes sprinkle the bottom of the layout was still ignorantly betting his chips; he received a sharp rebuke from the old dealer. I reflected that if I ended up getting caught raking off my bets, there'd be a real scene, judging by Benny's countenance.

But we had a stroke of luck. Our first attempt at the double-Savannah (as we christened it later) was a double-winner. Number 31 came in, a 19 thru 36 *and* first column winner. I went through my song and dance, claiming at the top of my lungs over the music that I had just won $15,000. Benny looked down at my bets, nodded and smiled coolly at me. I was convinced he saw the chocolate chip on the bottom of each bet. He swept off the losers, and the helper passed him a stack of $5 chips. He took the red stack and cut it into my two bets, paying me $30 for the first column bet, $15 for the 19 thru 36 bet. He hadn't seen *either* of the chocolate chips, and that was a disaster because now I had to change the claim.

"Whoa!" I hollered belligerently. "Benny, I'm betting $5,000 chips and you paid me off in reds. What's going on here!"

Benny looked down at my bets and at the chips he'd paid me, then looked back up at me and said curtly, "Don't be an asshole, sonny."

I couldn't believe my ears. I wondered if he now saw the chocolates and figured I'd taken a shot and slipped them in there after he paid me, or if he still didn't see them at all and just mistook me for a wisecracking asshole. The $5,000 chips at the Hilton were actually shaded more gray than chocolate and blended in so perfectly with their $5 reds you really could miss one underneath, even when being told it was there.

"Benny, you don't seem to understand," I said sharply, pointing to both sets of chips on the layout, bringing my index finger as close as possible without touching them. "I bet five thousand dollars on each box. Don't you see my $5,000 chips there?" I asked with genuine incredulity.

Benny looked down at my bets again, then back at me as if I donned a cape and mask and was telling him the earth was flat. "What are you trying to pull here? There are no $5,000 chips on the layout."

"Look again," I said, practically pleading.

"I *am* looking. You have two bets of fifteen dollars."

At that point I had to take another glance at my bets. Was it possible that somehow I'd fucked up and never got the chocolate chips down on the layout? Could that wonderful color combination have fooled me also?

Suddenly the helper, who hadn't said a word during the entire confrontation, came to my rescue. "Benny," she said timidly, "I think there's a chocolate underneath" – she poked her head down the layout with squinting eyes – "both his bets."

Benny finally lifted off the two red chips on the 19 thru 36 bet. When he saw the chocolate, he went into shock. His body literally swayed as he stared blankly at the chocolate chip. For a moment, I thought the poor guy was going to tumble or have a stroke or something. The helper had to tell him to lift the reds off my first column bet. When he saw the second chocolate, he went stiff and started to look terrible. The color drained from his face and his mouth sagged. I began feeling nervous looking at him. I was hoping the floorman would arrive quickly, almost like a reticent corner man praying for the referee to step in and save his fighter from a further shellacking. Finally, the helper called over the floorman, perhaps saving Benny's life.

The floorman was a young guy not yet out of his twenties. Benny still couldn't talk, so the helper explained the situation for him. The floorman didn't ask any questions. He went immediately down the pit to get the ranking pit boss. They returned to the table together. By that time, Benny had regained a little of his composure. At least now he could talk, and I was relieved to notice the color returning to his face.

The pit boss was in his mid-fifties and had one of those hawk faces with a hooked nose and small beady eyes. I got the impression he was the type of guy who wouldn't trust the pope. He looked suspiciously at me, then at my chips on the layout.

What he saw with those beady eyes were my two original bets of $5,010, a chocolate with two reds on top, and the three sets of three red chips Benny had paid me.

"How could you not have seen those chocolates?" the pit boss asked Benny rather crudely, without much respect for his age.

"I thought the bottom chips were also red," Benny answered weakly.

The pit boss turned his hawk face on the helper. "Did *you* see those chocolate chips before he spun the ball?"

"No."

The pit boss turned into a ball of steam. "All right, hold this up a minute." Without looking at me, he turned on his heels and started back through the pit. At that point I had to get assertive. Any other approach would have been to show weakness.

"What's the problem?" I called out loudly to the pit boss's back.

He turned smartly back toward me. "I'm sorry, sir," he said with cold politeness. "I'm going to have to verify that your bets were there before the dealer spun the ball."

I feigned being insulted. "What do you mean, verify that my bets were there?"

"That's casino policy, sir. All winning bets of a hundred dollars or more not called out by the dealer must be verified by surveillance before they can be paid." He went to the podium, picked up the telephone and called surveillance. Then he began talking heatedly with another pit boss having the air of being one of the higher-ups. From the intensity of their conversation, I guessed they'd already heard about the unseen winning chocolate chips showing up on roulette layouts. And now there were *two* of them less than two inches apart on the same layout.

I gritted my teeth and took a deep breath. I knew I was in for a battle. Getting them to pay me the fifteen grand when they knew they had got beat risked being a drudgery.

Pat receded into the background and watched the situation develop from another pit across the casino. I understood. We both knew this was one of those times where surveillance started filming close-ups of everyone around the wheel as soon as they got the call from the floor. There was no need for Pat to pull the same exposure as me.

The atmosphere around the table grew quiet, except for the college group who continued bantering away. They seemed amused by the situation. Benny and the helper stood stiffly, Benny nervously fiddling the number marker while the helper repeatedly steepled a small stack of roulette chips in her working bay. Neither one dared looking at me.

Five minutes went by, then ten, then fifteen. Usually surveillance verification didn't take longer than ten minutes. Surveillance systems worked just like your old VCRs. All the operators had to do was rewind the tape and playback the action in question. They might look at it several times, examining everybody at the table to see if they could put something together, but I knew in this case there was nothing to see on the tape besides my legitimate bets.

After twenty minutes, there were four pit bosses huddled in very animated conversation in the middle of the pit, each one alternatively shooting glances in my direction. I began to understand what was happening. They were stalling. The surveillance operator upstairs had notified them that the camera above the table did not record the events. That happened frequently for various reasons. They could have been filming something else with that camera, its tilted lens panning to catch action on or around a nearby table, as well as inside the pit. Without surveillance verification, somebody in the pit would have to make a decision on his own.

Finally, after a half hour had gone by, the casino shift boss approached me from behind. He was not one of the bosses who'd been engaged in that conversation inside the pit. He introduced himself without offering his hand. "Sir, excuse us for the delay, but matters like this take a little time."

He was full of shit. They'd decided that without video tape to indicate otherwise, I had no doubt taken advantage of their two old-time dealers and popped in two chocolate chips after the ball dropped into the number 31 slot. They figured they would make me sweat a while, make me crack under the pressure. I noticed two uniformed security guards milling behind the table, part of their little bluff. What the Hilton bosses didn't know was that I was prepared to stay there till next Christmas. My bet was legit; I had committed no crime whatsoever. That was the strength of Savannah.

The shift boss let two hours go by. I now stood alone with the two dealers. Because of the ongoing holdup of the game, neither Benny nor the helper could be relieved and were required to stay there until it resumed. The other players had all cashed out their chips and left the table. No doubt I was feeling the heat, but I had to stay there under the gun. If I backed off and left, there was a chance they'd bust me trying to leave the casino. When midnight struck and people all around the casino began raising their glasses to toast the new year, our table remained eerily silent. Benny and the helper were also feeling the heat. Their jobs were on the line.

When the shift boss finally did reappear, he came up from behind the dealers inside the pit and was accompanied by the young floorman. He then surprisingly shook my hand and ordered Benny to pay me $15,000. He said that he couldn't pay my $5 chips because they'd pushed my bets over the $5,000 limit. I claimed that I'd bet them for the dealers; he said he was sorry but the limit was the limit. I had the feeling because of the little smirk he gave me that he already knew that line about betting the reds for the dealer.

Benny obediently placed three chocolate chips next to my bets. I saw that his fingers were trembling. The shift boss and floorman stood behind him and watched hawkishly. I could feel both the shift boss's contempt and the floorman's embarrassment. I certainly realized that we were done in the Hilton for a while, so I pushed the three chocolates toward Benny and asked for a chip-change. That seemed to annoy the shift boss even more, and I knew the reason why. He'd been hoping that I would go over to the casino cage and cash out the three chocolates. If I did that, the casino could hassle me with all those IRS reports concerning cash transactions of $10,000 or more. Obviously he didn't think someone smart enough to be beating the casinos at their own game was also cool enough not to walk into federal heat.

Benny cut me out fifteen yellow $1,000 chips. Before I left the table, I noticed his forehead was dripping with rivulets of sweat. I felt a little sorry for the old guy, but business was business. To both compensate Benny and celebrate the first double-whammy Savannah, I tossed him a black chip. Then I went to the cage and placed nine yellows on the counter. The remaining six we'd cash out another time.

The female teller smiled and asked where I'd been playing.

"You must be the only person in the whole casino who doesn't know," I said with a chuckle. She didn't appear to understand my wry humor, so I told her I'd been playing roulette. She picked up the phone and called the pit. "I have nine yellows," she said into the phone.

I turned around to face the roulette pit where I'd spent the last two hours. From where I was standing I could see the hawk-faced pit boss nodding with the phone to his ear. I imagined he was really teed off having to verify my action, and even more so on hearing that I was only cashing out nine of the yellow chips.

The teller hung up, took two $5,000 packets of $100 bills from her drawer, removed ten bills from one, and finally counted out the nine grand and pushed it across the counter. I crammed the wad of cash into my pocket and left the casino, thoroughly enjoying the thought that I had spitefully cashed out only nine yellow chips under their noses. There was nothing they could do except watch me walk out the doors with a triumphant smile on my face.

Outside, I jumped into a cab and headed immediately to meet Pat at the Gingermill, a lounge on the Strip we used for emergency situations. The $15,000 may have been paid but the steam inside the Hilton was awesome. I just wanted to get out of there quickly.

Pat was seated on one of the plushy couches bordering a little circular fire-island that sprouted a low flame. I let myself sink into the cushion next to him.

"Richard, that was a long one," he said.

"You might say our hourly rate's going down a bit, but I never doubted for a minute I was getting paid. They were trying to bluff me out the door."

A sexily clad waitress came over to take our drink order. Pat ordered me a Perrier water and a beer for himself. When she was gone, he said, "Do you think we're done with Savannah in Vegas?"

I nodded. "For a while. But don't worry about Savannah. She's got at least nine lives."

We then took Savannah on the road. We showed her off in Atlantic City, Connecticut, Mississippi, Louisiana, in the Caribbean, and on the Midwestern riverboats. Because $5,000 chips couldn't be used outside of Las Vegas, we began hiding two and sometimes even three $500 or $1,000 chips underneath the reds. The caller at the top of the wheel had to keep the dealer distracted during the whole time the bet rested on the layout so that the purples or yellows wouldn't be discovered. In that regard we couldn't be perfect. About 5 percent of the time, dealers saw the big chips underneath before spinning the ball. When that happened, the raker just lifted them off, saying he didn't intend to bet the big chips. We seldom took steam for that. Another 5 percent of the time with the use of multiple big chips, dealers saw them while the ball was spinning. In that case, we were forced to take the legitimate gamble, which didn't hurt us at all. In fact, we were lucky sons of a bitch when forced to gamble legitimately. I would say that we actually won more than we lost.

Savannah just seemed to be one helluva lucky lady. And my ex-associates are still out there showing her off.

Overall, it's been a $12 million gig – and counting.

EPILOGUE

One of the TV episodes based on my book *American Roulette* was filmed in New York in the fall of 2004. I spent two enjoyable days with the production crew in Manhattan, where I was interviewed and got to show off my classic Savannah move, among others in my arsenal. The crew members were so enthralled by my demonstrations that they wanted to skip off the set and hop down to Atlantic City so we could do it for real.

A year later, in the fall of 2005, I met up with a British production crew in Atlantic City to film several similar episodes for British television. Then I flew out with them to Vegas for more filming and interviews. We really had a great time, and I got to meet up again with Chris Jones and several other ex-casino-scamming partners I had not seen in a long time. It was there that I also got acquainted with John Roy, the main character from the Bet and Run scam who'd flashed by like a comet that day I sat inside the Dunes Denny's more than two decades earlier. John was perhaps the most energetic guy I'd ever met. One night over beers with the entire production crew, he recounted the story of what had happened that day. It still remains the greatest story I've ever heard.

It turned out that the two dozen Dunes security officers who'd flooded the Denny's rooftop on their hands and knees were searching for a 7.44-karat diamond ring. It was selling for two hundred grand and had just been stolen from a posh jewelry store inside the Dunes hotel. John was the thief, and those security officers pursuing him believed he had flung the diamond onto the roof during the chase.

We all sat around the cozy Peppermill Lounge and laughed as John recounted the story. "It was unbelievable," he said. "Gunther and I had been casing that jewelry store for a month. We weren't stickup artists, so we had to figure out a way to get that ring. We finally decided it was best to do it the same way we ran out of the casinos with the cash.

"So I get all dressed up in a suit and walk into the jewelry store. I'm wearing sneakers, but my long pants cover them and the saleswoman doesn't notice the oddity. I'm posing as a high roller who just made a big score in the casino, and I want to buy my wife a big present to show how much I love her. What better gift than a big diamond ring? Meanwhile, Gunther's sitting on the Harley on the other side of Denny's, a few hundred yards away. The plan is, once I get the woman to put that ring in my hand, I'm out the door, just like we did in the casinos. Then I jump on the back of the bike and we're gone. It was great because the jewelry store was right inside the hotel's south entrance, just twenty feet or so. There was only one security guard sitting on a podium between the store and the exit doors. I knew I could run right by him and be out the door in a few seconds.

"She puts the ring in my hand, I admire it, make some comments about how much my wife's gonna love it, then – boom! I hit the doors. The woman screams, the security guard jumps off the podium, but I'm already outside running across the Dunes parking lot toward Denny's. But halfway there I trip over my goddamn sneaker laces and fall flat on my face. I get up, but now there's a whole platoon chasing me and I'm banged up and running out of gas. Just before they catch up with me, I make a motion like I'm flinging the ring, like I wanted to get rid of the evidence. I don't know why I did that, but the ring never left my hand. I had it tucked in my palm.

"The guards cuff me, drag me back to the Dunes property and throw me in the back of a four-door Oldsmobile, their unmarked security rover. Meanwhile, the ring is still palmed in my hand. As the guy's driving me to their security office on the other side of the Dunes, I shove the ring in the crease of the seat. I wasn't really thinking about somehow getting it back later, only that I didn't want them to find it on me.

"So now the chief of Dunes security is interrogating me in his office. His men had told him they couldn't find the ring anywhere around Denny's, so now he demands to know what the hell I did with it. I just tell him I don't know what he's talking about. Then they bring in the woman from the jewelry store to ID me. She points at me and goes, 'Yeah, that's him.' But I still deny I stole the ring. The security chief keeps pressing me, so finally I say as a joke, 'Whaddaya want me to tell you, that I swallowed it?' Next thing I know, I'm at Valley Hospital strapped to a gurney getting fucking x-rayed. The dick believed me and convinced himself I'd had enough time to pop the diamond out of the setting and swallow it. Now two Vegas police detectives are with me. One of "em says, 'If that stone shows up on the x-ray, we'll just sit and wait until you shit it out.' Little do the idiots know that the stone is stuck in the crease of the backseat of that Oldsmobile. When the tech comes in and tells the cops that the x-ray's negative, they get all pissed off and take me to jail. My bail's set at three grand.

"Well, Gunther comes down to the jail and bails me out. Since they don't know I'd had a biker on a Harley waiting for me, they can't connect him to the crime, so it's safe. It was two o'clock in the morning, and I knew that as soon as the sun came up, I had to start looking for a lawyer. When I told Gunther what I'd withdone with the ring and what the cops thought I'd done with it, he cracked up…"

"It was about the funniest thing I'd ever heard in my life," Gunther chimed in, his shiny pate as bald as it had been that last day he sat on the Harley waiting for John to jump on. "The first thing I asked John was how we could get the ring back. I assumed it was still in the seat, unless, of course, they cleaned out the car, but that was unlikely. I knew a fence in town who would gladly pay 20 percent on it, which was forty grand. I figured there had to be some way to get into that Oldsmobile and steal the ring again. But when John said it was their roving security vehicle, I knew immediately that getting inside it was going to be a big problem. So we were standing there outside the jail, straining our brains for a plan to get the ring. Hopefully one that wouldn't land us back inside the jail. After a while it seemed hopeless, so we split.

"Then we're driving uptown along the Strip and an idea his me like a thunderbolt. 'Jumper cables!' I scream, all gassed up. 'I figured out a way to get back into that Olds.' As soon as I explained it to John, he knew it could work."

The two ex-partners in crime shared a delicious smile of remembrance.

Gunther continued: "Since we knew that the rover never stopped making its rounds of the Dunes, except during a change of shift or when the officer driving it had to take a piss, there was no chance for us to break into it. But maybe we could get in it while the guy was driving. What if we parked our car in the Dunes' north parking lot, then walked around the hotel to the south end of the lot and flagged down the Olds and told the officer that we couldn't get our car started because the battery was dead. Surely he'd have cables and could give us a jump. All we had to do was get him to let us in the Olds, which we assumed he would since it was a half mile to where our car was parked.

He could just drive us there and then jump start the car."

"The only problem,", John said, "was we had no car. Gunther had his motorcycles and I had just arrived back in Vegas and was getting around by cab. Plus we needed another guy to help us out. Two guys had to approach the guard driving the Olds, so that one of us could get in the back. If one guy alone tried to get in the back, the guard might get spooked and think he was about to get robbed or something. But I couldn't be there since the guard might recognize me as the guy who'd ripped off the jewelry store. Imagine that! Twelve hours after they bust the thief who stole the ring, the security guard sees him back on the property trying to get a car jumped. Wouldn't that be great! He'd probably think I was there to pull a heist of the casino cage and that our stalled car was the escape vehicle..."

Everybody cracked up at John's theatrics with this. He'd also been quite entertaining in his TV segment.

"So I called Rene and Raul Lopez," Gunther said, "the twins who'd helped us run the cash out of casinos. Rene was down in Mexico doing dope deals, but Raul still had their old Plymouth Duster in Vegas. He agreed to use it for our recovery operation, and the Duster was great because it looked like the kind of beat-up old car that wouldn't start every other day.

"So with John waiting at a booth inside Denny's, I drove Raul's Duster with Raul in the passenger seat into the Dunes parking lot. I parked at the extreme north end of the lot. We got out of the car, entered the casino from the north entrance and walked all the way through to the south exit, passing the jewelry store, which was open twenty-four hours. Once outside, we waited for the roving Oldsmobile to turn the corner. Three minutes later it did. I waved my arms above my head and stepped into its path. The Olds stopped promptly, and I asked the officer behind the wheel to help us. I acted all stressed out, and think I said something like 'Sorry to bother you, but my car won't start.

I need a jump. Do you have cables?' The guy told us to hop right in. So Raul got in the front seat; I got in the back.

"I figured I had about thirty seconds to find the ring, the time it would take to traverse the property to where we'd parked the Duster. But on the first swipe I felt the hardness of the ring in the lining, and it wasn't planted in there very deep. And let me tell you – man did I get a high when I felt it! It was like touching a brand-new Harley in the showroom. I eased the ring into my pocket, thinking how lucky we were that nobody else had found it first.

"The security officer attached the cables, and I started the Olds right up. Then he disconnected them and threw them back in his trunk. I made a big fuss like he saved our lives and gave him a $10 bill, thanking him profusely. He wished us luck and left." Gunther shrugged gleefully. "A week later we had our forty grand for the ring."

"What happened with the legal case?" I asked John.

"At first, nothing," he said. "I skipped bail and moved to Florida. Then five years later, in 1988, I'm driving on the Interstate and get pulled over for speeding. There was a warrant out for my arrest. I got busted, extradited to Las Vegas and thrown in the Clark County jail. I ended up pleading out to grand theft and spent a year in prison."

"What have you been doing ever since?" I asked.

John laughed. "I went back to my old job in New York, the one I had before coming out to Vegas twenty-five years ago."

"Which was what?"

"Panhandling."

"Panhandling?"

John nodded and laughed again.

And so the most daring of the world's greatest gambling scammers can still be found hustling handouts in the streets of Manhattan. I knew then that if I ever wrote this book, John would be the first character portrayed on its pages.